LIFE AND LABOUR

OF THE

PEOPLE IN LONDON

I V

THE TRADES OF EAST LONDON
CONNECTED WITH POVERTY

LIFE AND LABOUR

OF THE

PEOPLE IN LONDON

BY

CHARLES BOOTH

FIRST SERIES: POVERTY

IV

THE TRADES OF EAST LONDON
CONNECTED WITH POVERTY

REVISED EDITION
[1902]

REPRINTS OF ECONOMIC CLASSICS

Augustus M. Kelley · Publishers
NEW YORK 1969

First Published 1889 & 1891

(London: Williams & Norgate, *14 Henrietta Street, Covent Garden*; *20 South Frederick Street, Edinburgh*, 1891)

Revised Edition 1902

(London: Macmillan & Company; The Macmillan Company, *New York*, 1902)

Reprinted 1969 by

AUGUSTUS M. KELLEY · PUBLISHERS

New York   New York   10010

LIBRARY OF CONGRESS CATALOGUE CARD NUMBER

68-55487

PRINTED IN THE UNITED STATES OF AMERICA
by SENTRY PRESS, NEW YORK, N. Y. 10019

LIFE AND LABOUR

OF THE

PEOPLE IN LONDON

LIFE AND LABOUR

OF THE

PEOPLE IN LONDON

BY

CHARLES BOOTH

ASSISTED BY

JESSE ARGYLE,   GEO. E. ARKELL,   ERNEST AVES
DAVID F. SCHLOSS.   STEPHEN N. FOX
CLARA E. COLLET, BEATRICE POTTER

First Series: Poverty

THE TRADES OF EAST LONDON
CONNECTED WITH POVERTY

London
MACMILLAN AND CO., Limited
NEW YORK : THE MACMILLAN CO.
1902

[*Published first in 1889*]

Table of Contents

THE TRADES OF EAST LONDON.

NOTICE.

In dealing with East London we have found some of the local employments to be so characteristic of the life of that part of London, and a knowledge of their conditions so necessary to the consideration of the evils called " sweating," that we have devoted separate articles to them, forming in this edition a separate volume. The employments dealt with thus are Dock Labour, Tailoring, Bootmaking, Cabinet-making, Tobacco manufacture, Silk weaving, and women's work generally.

No such case exists for dividing other districts of London industrially from the Metropolis as a whole, but by way of comparison a chapter is added to this volume describing tailoring and bootmaking in Central London

The accounts of the East London trades here given refer to the year 1888—that is, to the period immediately preceding the strikes of 1889-90, and the changes then brought about.

THE TRADES OF EAST LONDON.

CHAPTER I.

INTRODUCTION.

THE following table shows the industrial position of East London and Hackney, as compared (1) to the rest of London, (2) to the whole of London, (3) to the whole of England, stated in a very simple and general way by percentages of the employed population in 1881.

	East London and Hackney.	Rest of London.	All London.	All England.
Agriculture and Breeding	·76	1·39	1·25	11·5
Fishing and Mining	·16	·25	·24	5·1
Building	6·15	8·44	7·93	6·8
Manufacture	39·95	25·25	28·38	30·7
Transport..................................	11·77	8·06	8·87	5·6
Dealing.....................................	11·29	11·12	11·24	7·8
Industrial Service (or labour not allotted to any particular industry)	8·84	8•10	8·26	6·7
Public and Professional Service	5·34	9·15	8·30	5·6
Domestic Service	12·62	23·99	21·53	15·7
Indefinitely employed or Independent	3·12	4·25	4·00	4·5
	100·	100·	100·	100·

NOTE.

IF we add to each class by occupation the numbers of those who may be supposed to be dependent thereon, and so include the whole population, we get the following figures for East London and Hackney. The difference between this statement and that in the text, lies chiefly in Domestic Service, which (rightly) assumes a less important position, as those so employed consist largely of women and young people who support themselves only :—

Agriculture and Breeding	·97
Fishing and Mining.........	·21
Building	7·97
Manufacture	37·95
Transport	14·01
Dealing	12·65
Industrial Service............	10·62
Public and Professional Service	5·33
Domestic Service	6·91
Indefinitely employed and Independent	3·38
East London and Hackney ...	100·

From this table it will be seen that, as compared with the figures for the whole country, East London is strong in manufacture, transport, dealing, and industrial service; whilst, compared to the rest of London, the preponderance of those engaged in manufacture is still more marked. In public and professional service the remainder of London has nearly double the proportion of the East End, and this is the case also with domestic servants.

Industrial service includes clerks and such labourers as do not claim the status of any particular trade : of both of these large numbers are to be found in East London. Similarly, dealing, *i.e.*, buying to sell again, is largely represented, but it is when we come to transport and manufacture that we touch the industries special to the locality.

Subdividing these general headings (Table C, pages 8 and 9), we find that navigation and docks account for the surplus under transport ; and tailoring, bootmaking, and cabinet-making for that under manufacture. In the chapters that follow, each of these subjects is separately treated, as well as tobacco-working and silk-weaving, which, though not either of them involving such large numbers, are no less characteristic of East London.

Looking at the subject in another way : comparing East London in 1881 with East London in 1861, we get the table on the next page, prepared from the census returns, in which the approximate numbers as well as percentages are given.

It will be seen by this table that the whole population of the district increased in the 20 years from 654,000 to 879,000. Every class by occupation increased numerically more or less, but several of them decreased in proportion to the rest, notably manufacture, which in 1861 absorbed nearly 42 per cent., but in 1881 had fallen to 38 per cent., while on the other hand dealing had increased from 11·73 per cent. to 12·65 per cent., and industrial service from 8·25 per cent.

A.—East London and Hackney.

Table showing approximate numbers supported by each class.

	1861						1881					
	Occupied or Self-supporting.		Dependent wives, children, &c. (estimated).		Total.	Per Cent.	Occupied or Self-supporting.		Dependent wives, children, &c. (estimated).		Total.	Per Cent.
	Males.	Females.	Males.	Females.			Males.	Females.	Males.	Females.		
Agriculture	2932	218	1761	3710	8621	1·30	2864	116	1790	3759	8529	·97
Fishing and Mining	561	3	336	708	1608	·25	630	13	386	809	1838	·21
Building	16,594	44	10,034	21,138	47,810	7·30	24,045	71	14,848	31,183	70,147	7·97
Manufacture	81,761	49,311	45,904	96,691	273,667	41·82	98,078	58,555	57,051	119,814	333,498	37·95
Transport	34,628	219	19,053	40,133	94,033	14·37	45,872	287	24,834	52,155	123,148	14·01
Dealing	25,236	5626	14,757	31,085	76,704	11·73	36,011	8265	21,574	45,308	111,158	12·65
Industrial service	19,179	156	11,142	23,471	53,948	8·25	34,181	472	18,958	39,815	93,426	10·62
Public and Professional do.	10,784	3479	6392	13,465	34,120	5·21	14,097	6834	8392	17,624	46,947	5·33
Domestic do.	3972	35,977	1909	4021	45,879	7·02	6753	42,738	3634	7632	60,757	6·91
Indefinitely employed and Independent … }	4680	3468	3192	6723	18,063	2·75	8145	4100	5647	11,860	29,752	3·38
Total population	200,327	98,501	114,480	241,145	654,463	100·	270,676	121,451	157,114	329,959	879,200	100·

to 10·62 per cent. These changes were part of a general movement, the change over all England in the same period being from 29·6 to 28·2 for manufacture, from 8·4 to 9·0 for dealing, and from 5·3 to 8·5 for industrial service.

The next table (B) shows us the number of persons who were actually occupied (or self-supporting) in each class in 1861 and 1881, and this is followed by a third table (C) in which the composition of the three great classes, manufacture, transport, and industrial service—which between them include more than 60 per cent. of the population—is analyzed. These tables also are prepared from the Census returns.*

In constructing the longer table care has been taken to give in greater detail the sub-divisions of those employments which are more largely followed in East London than in other parts of the metropolis or in the country generally. The figures tell the story of waning as well as prospering trades. We notice that the numbers of those occupied in shipbuilding decreased from 4877 to 3684, the percentage these bear to the whole employed population falling from 1·63 to ·94. Here we have a brief record of an unsuccessful strike, and the bodily removal of an industry to the North. Shirtmakers and seamstresses fell from 8223 to 6929, or from 2·75 to 1·76 per cent., a decrease due, it is said, to Irish competition. Sugar refiners decreased from 1437 to 616, or from ·48 to ·15 per cent., in consequence, it is said, of the importation of bounty-fed sugar; whilst silk and satin workers dropped from 9611 to 3309, or from 3·22 to ·84 per cent.—a result attributed mainly to the Cobden Treaty with France. On the other hand, trimming and artificial flower makers increased from 1510

* Only the totals for all London are published with the Census, and to the courtesy of the Registrar-General we owe the information from which our tables are prepared. It has been unfortunate that the date of the Census is so remote as 1881. The need of a more frequent Census is badly felt. Changes occur so rapidly that before 10 years have passed, the information obtained becomes dangerously stale.

B.—East London and Hackney.

Table showing the actual number of persons occupied or self-supporting in each class.

	1861						1881					
	Males.		Females.		Total.	Per cent.	Males.		Females.		Total.	Per Cent.
	under 20.	over 20.	under 20.	over 20.			under 20	over 20	under 20.	over 20.		
Agriculture	350	2582	11	207	3150	1·06	282	2582	14	102	2980	·76
Fishing and Mining	68	493	3	—	564	·19	74	556	4	9	643	·16
Building	1881	14,713	10	34	16,638	5·56	2631	21,414	13	58	24,116	6·15
Manufacture*	14,459	67,302	11,855	37,456	131,072	43·86	15,799	82,279	16,375	42,180	156,633	39·95
Transport*	6693	27,935	95	124	34,847	11·66	10,056	35,816	126	161	46,159	11·77
Dealing	3599	21,637	1385	4241	30,862	10·33	4897	31,114	1818	6447	44,276	11·29
Industrial service*	2842	16,337	104	52	19,335	6·47	6839	27,342	137	335	34,653	8·84
Public and Professional do.	1412	9372	878	2601	14,263	4·77	1994	12,103	1153	5681	20,931	5·34
Domestic do.	1173	2799	10,329	25,648	39,949	13·37	1512	5241	14,533	28,205	49,491	12·62
Indefinitely employed and Independent ... }	—	4680	—	3468	8148	2·73	—	8145	—	4100	12,245	3·12
Total employed or self-supporting ... }	32,477	167,850	24,670	73,831	298,828	100·	44,084	226,592	34,173	87,278	392,127	100·

* For sub-divisions of these classes see Table C, pages 8 and 9.

C.—*East London and Hackney.*

Occupied or Self-supporting. Division of certain Classes.

Occupation.	1861 Males under 20	1861 Males over 20	1861 Females under 20	1861 Females over 20	1861 Total	1861 Per Cent.	1881 Males under 20	1881 Males over 20	1881 Females under 20	1881 Females over 20	1881 Total	1881 Per Cent.	All England Per Cent.
Manufacture.													
Machinery and tool-makers	596	3421	8	93	4118	1·38	651	4367	11	52	5081	1·30	1·91
Ship-building { Ship and boat-builders, ship-wrights, ship-carpenters	210	3221	1	8	3440	1·15	210	2461	1	—	2672	·68	·40
Mast, oar, and blockmakers, riggers, and sail makers	102	1332	3	—	1437	·48	56	941	4	11	1012	·26	·07
Carriage and harness-makers	283	1348	16	34	1681	·56	308	1871	22	65	2266	·57	·74
Metal-workers	1407	6555	69	110	8141	2·73	1474	7094	93	181	8842	2·25	4·08
Earthenware, &c.	161	740	23	105	1029	·34	170	658	32	46	905	·23	·62
Gas and chemicals { Gas works service	43	723	—	—	766	·25	57	1094	—	—	1141	·29	·16
Match makers	54	—	220	—	274	·09	72	61	289	177	599	·15	·03
Dye, paint and chemicals manf.	82	945	8	—	1035	·35	128	779	10	112	1024	·26	·22
Furs and leather { Furriers and skinners	105	252	240	133	730	·24	157	945	315	667	2084	·53	·07
Others	186	652	38	131	1007	·33	171	985	50	136	1342	·34	·22
Hair, grease, bone, &c. { Brush and broom makers	256	607	204	315	1382	·46	229	890	268	691	2078	·53	·11
Others	197	1158	307	204	1866	·63	154	899	403	444	2000	·51	·14
Cabinet makers & upholsterers	1304	4857	91	368	6620	2·21	1289	7660	120	410	9479	2·42	·51
French polishers	168	505	64	60	797	·27	261	1039	84	164	1548	·40	·08
Wood carvers	102	293	1	—	396	·13	102	741	1	2	846	·21	·03
Carvers and gilders	254	791	4	—	1049	·35	203	1027	6	28	1264	·32	·07
Wood and furniture { Sawyers	137	1005	—	—	1142	·38	127	964	—	—	1091	·28	·21
Wood turners	277	941	340	356	1914	·64	311	1037	447	811	2606	·66	·12
Coopers	241	2117	—	—	2358	·79	156	2045	4	—	2205	·56	·16
Others	270	1971	47	219	2507	·84	183	952	62	253	1450	·37	·15
Paper, floorcloth, and waterproof { Paper and envelope manf.	90	104	212	126	532	·18	102	251	278	363	994	·25	·18
Paper box and bag makers	23	—	481	56	560	·19	90	242	632	1060	2024	·51	·08
Waterproof goods makers	8	—	20	—	28	·01	28	164	26	120	336	·09	·06
Others	205	634	88	64	991	·33	250	690	115	130	1115	·28	·08
Textiles, &c. { Silk and satin manufacture	149	4306	407	4749	9611	3·22	67	1423	233	1586	3309	·84	·50
Trimming makers	75	—	147	433	655	·22	56	207	469	888	1710	·43	·05
Carried forward	6935	38,478	3039	7564	56,666	18·75	7055	41,597	3971	8400	61,023	15·52	11·05

Occupied or Self-supporting. Division of certain Classes.

	1861 Males under 20	1861 Males over 20	1861 Females under 20	1861 Females over 20	1861 Total	1861 Per Cent.	1881 Males under 20	1881 Males over 20	1881 Females under 20	1881 Females over 20	1881 Total	1881 Per Cent.	All England Per Cent.
Brought forward	6985	38,478	3039	7564	56,066	18·75	7055	41,597	3971	8400	61,023	15·52	11·05
Textiles, &c. (continued) — Artificial flower makers	34	—	480	341	855	·29	17	141	288	785	1231	·31	·05
Rope, &c., makers	357	708	38	36	1139	·38	282	577	68	68	995	·25	·10
Others	236	2016	390	1637	4279	1·43	229	1572	418	1239	3458	·88	7·53
Tailors	791	3689	1070	4916	10,466	3·50	719	5528	2344	7083	15,674	4·02	1·37
Milliners and dressmakers	46	—	1088	9046	11,080	3·71	46	358	2952	10,327	13,683	3·51	3·08
Shirt makers and seamstresses	15	—	990	7218	8223	2·75	43	252	1201	5433	6629	1·76	·71
Dress — Boot and shoemakers	2758	8315	1326	3035	15,434	5·18	1970	10,906	1545	2837	17,318	4·46	1·85
Others	324	1650	749	2721	5444	1·82	274	1700	434	1106	3514	·89	1·12
Sugar-refiners	25	1411	1	—	1437	·48	49	560	2	5	616	·15	·03
Bakers and confectioners	452	2901	315	248	3916	1·31	689	3295	414	641	5039	1·28	·83
Food, drink, and smoking — Brewers	27	798	—	2	827	·28	33	783	—	2	818	·21	·21
Tobacco and cigar manf.	276	1342	292	46	1956	·65	442	2054	383	394	3273	·83	·09
Others	184	776	65	3	1028	·34	155	880	85	225	1345	·34	·39
Watch and instrument makers	343	2004	27	50	2424	·81	396	2385	36	88	2905	·74	·34
Fishing-tackle and toy makers	66	318	25	135	544	·18	66	317	33	121	537	·14	·04
Printing & Book-binding — Bookbinders	234	530	519	395	1678	·56	359	1094	681	903	3037	·77	·17
Printers and others	965	2057	66	63	3151	1·06	1949	4031	87	91	6158	1·58	·58
Machinists (undefined)	—	—	177	—	177	·06	76	164	1054	2081	3375	·86	·10
Others	341	309	298	—	948	·32	950	4025	379	351	5705	1·45	1·11
Total of Manufacture	14,459	67,302	11,855	37,456	131072	43·86	15,799	82,279	16,375	42,180	156,633	39·95	30·75
Transport. Navigation and docks	5467	22,126	91	106	27,790	9·30	7767	23,727	120	126	31,740	8·09	2·96
Railways	199	1116	1	2	1318	·44	551	2921	2	14	3488	·89	1·18
Roads	1027	4693	3	16	5739	1·92	1738	9168	4	21	10,931	2·79	1·44
Total of Transport	6693	27,935	95	124	34,847	11·66	10,056	35,816	126	161	46,159	11·77	5·58
Industrial Service. Commercial	1208	5257	84	—	6579	2·20	3928	9795	111	260	14,094	3·59	1·92
General labour	1634	11,050	20	52	12,756	4·27	2911	17,547	26	75	20,559	5·25	4·78
Total of Industrial Service	2842	16,357	104	52	19,335	6·47	6839	27,342	137	335	34,653	8·84	6·70

to 2941, or from ·51 to ·74 per cent.; printing and book-binding from 4829 to 9195, or from 1·62 to 2·35 per cent.; furriers, skinners, and leather workers from 1737 to 3426, or from ·57 to ·87 per cent.; paper box and bag and envelope makers from 1092 to 3018, or from ·37 to ·76 per cent.; tobacco workers from 1956 to 3273, or from ·65 to ·83 per cent.; tailors from 10,466 to 15,674, or from 3·50 to 4·02 per cent.; cabinet makers, &c., from 6620 to 9479, or from 2·21 to 2·42 per cent.; bootmakers show an actual increase from 15,434 to 17,318, but by percentage a decrease from 5·18 to 4·46 per cent.

The schedules of occupations according to census, which we have had for each of the registration districts comprising East London, have been used by us as the first basis of our trade inquiries. In addition we have had the figures yielded by our own inquiry, giving the probable number of adult men engaged in 1887 in each of the trades selected for special study. Our estimate bears out the general impression that from 1881 onwards, the tailoring, boot-making, and cabinet-making industries have been still on the increase, both numerically and by percentage.

Our second basis has been found in the Factory Inspector's books (kindly laid open to us by the authorities) from which, aided by some information from private sources, we have been able to construct a fairly complete directory of the factories and workshops in East London, belonging to each group of occupations.

In studying each trade we have begun by trying to distinguish the different branches of the trade, and to learn the *modus operandi*. We have then communicated with, and have seen and talked to, as many representatives as possible of all classes connected with the industry—from the wholesale dealer to the poorest of the wage-earners, obtaining from them what information they could or would give us, hearing from each his own story. In this way, at some cost of time and trouble, we have been able to form a distinct picture of each trade studied. This picture we trust we may succeed in transferring to the mind of anyone who reads the following chapters.

CHAPTER II.

THE DOCKS.*

THE London Docks are the scapegoat of competitive industry. They may be safely placed in the category of those unfortunate individuals who are always in the wrong; on the one hand they are expected to find work for all the failures of our society; on the other, they are roundly abused for doing so. "Go to the docks" might be used for a nineteenth-century equivalent of a mediæval expression which has become meaningless in these agnostic days. For the popular imagination represents the dock labourer either as an irrecoverable ne'er-do-well, or as a down-fallen angel. It does not recognize that there are "all sorts and conditions" here as elsewhere in the East-end. And the companies that employ this unduly typified being stand, in the public mind, between two fires of contradictory criticism. The economist in his study frowns sternly as he deplores the attractions of low-class labour into London; the philanthropist, fresh from the dock gate, pleads, with more sensational intonation, the guilt of the dock and the waterside employer in refusing to this helpless labour more inducement to remain, more possibility to live decently and multiply freely. The indifferentist alone stands by the side of the existing institution, and talks glibly of the inevitable tendency of inevitable competition in producing an inevitable irregularity of employment, failing to realize that these so-called "inevitables" mean the gradual deterioration of the brain and sinew of fellow-countrymen. But happily the public has a taste for facts, and we may hope a growing sense of proportion. I venture, therefore, to describe the life of the

* Reprinted by the permission of the Editor of the *Nineteenth Century* (date of original publication, September, 1887).

East London Docks, and to distinguish between and characterize the different classes of labour. I am, moreover, enabled, through the courtesy of dock officials, to give the actual numbers of those employed; and to preface this sketch by a short notice of the circumstances which have led to the present state and methods of employment.

The three docks of East London are the London and St. Katherine, the West and East India, and the Millwall. The two former were opened at the end of last and the beginning of this century respectively, and during the first fifty years of their existence possessed the virtual monopoly of the London trade. For in those days of large and easily earned profits, companies were bolstered up by extensive charters, and suicidal competition was as yet an undreamt of end to industrial enterprise. But towards the middle of this century the owners of the riverside woke up to the value of their possession. The small wharf which had sufficed for the unloading of the mediæval craft and the eighteenth-century sailing vessel or barge, but which had been supplanted by the magnificent chartered premises of the inland dock, sprang again into active life. Restrictions were swept away, and in 1850 wharfingers were recognized by the Custom House authorities. From London Bridge to Woolwich, year by year, one by one, new wharves rose up out of the mud of the Thames bank—until the picturesque outline of broken-down building and shore was exchanged for one continuous line of warehouse and quay. In 1868 the Millwall Dock covered the space left over by the West and East India in the Isle of Dogs. The competition of the wharves had at that time become severe, and the Millwall was started with all the newest appliances and methods of saving labour and reducing the cost of operations. The trade of London was meanwhile advancing by leaps and bounds, and until, and for some years after, the opening of the Suez Canal profits increased and labour was freely employed. But even during the good times the two big companies were beginning

to scrutinize their paymaster's sheets; for, with the daily
increasing competition, the lavish and leisurely employment
of unnecessary hands was no longer possible if these companies were to hold their supremacy of the London trade.
In 1865 the directors of the London and St. Katherine
introduced piece-work and the contract system. The good
times, however, did not last. The tide of commerce turned
against the greatest port in the world. The slow increase
in the volume of goods handled was accompanied by shrinking
values and rapidly declining profits; the opening of the
direct route to the European Continent and foreign competition strengthened by foreign protection revolutionized
the transhipment trade. Goods formerly housed in London
were unloaded straight from the oceanic vessel into the
continental boat. The loss of trade to the metropolitan
port consequent on the development of the outports was
intensified, as far as East London is concerned, by the
opening of steam docks further down the river by the
two great companies. Greater economy in the cost of
operations became a life and death necessity to the dock and
waterside employer. And the pressure came from below as
well as from above, for the wages of all classes of employés
had risen during the days of large profits. Corn and timber
porters and stevedores were making £2 to £3 a week. In
1872 the casuals of London and St. Katherine's and of the
West and East India had struck for and gained fivepence an
hour in exchange for two shillings and sixpence a day. The
Millwall, to defeat a combination among their men, had
imported country labour. The masters were powerless to
reduce wages; but they gave the usual alternative answer
—more efficient management, labour-saving machinery
and piece-work; meaning to the manual worker the same
or even higher wages calculated by the hour, but fewer
hands, harder worked, and more irregularly employed.

And the fierce competition for a declining business was
not the only agency at work in producing spasmodic and

strained demands for labour. The substitution of steam for
sailing vessels, while it distributes employment more evenly
throughout the year, increases the day to day and hour to
hour uncertainty. In bygone days at certain seasons of the
year a fleet of sailing vessels would line the dock quay. The
work was spread over weeks and months, and each succeed-
ing day saw the same number of men employed for the same
number of hours. At other periods of the year there was
no work, and the men knew it. Now the scene is changed.
Steamers come and go despite of wind and tide. The
multitudinous London shipowners show no sign of wishing
to organize their business so as to give as regular employment
as is practicable ; the value of a steamer to its owner does
not admit of leisurely discharge : the owner insists that
the steamer shall be out in so many hours ; and a tonnage
which a few years ago would have taken so many weeks to
unload is now discharged in a day and night worked on
end at high pressure. Hence the introduction of steam,
besides the indirect effect of heightening competition, has a
special influence in reducing the number of hands needed,
in increasing the irregularity of the hours, and in rendering
casual labour still more casual and uncertain.

Such, in briefest outline, are the trade events which have
helped to bring about the present state of dock employment
in East London, and which are still at work effecting further
transformation. The futility of the attempt to separate the
labour question from the trade question is becoming every
day more apparent; and unless we understand the courses
of trade we shall fail to draw the correct line between the
preventable and the inevitable in the deep shadows of East
End existence. I think it will add reality to a picture of
life in and about the docks if the reader will follow me in a
short account of the actual work undertaken by the docks,
the different varieties of which have an important bearing
on the classes of men employed and on the methods of
employment.

Dock labour in London is, properly speaking, the employment offered by the import trade. In the export trade the shipowners contract directly with a body of skilled men called stevedores, for whose work the dock company are in no way responsible. These men act under master stevedores, and are the only section of dock or waterside workmen who have formed themselves into a trades union.*

The import work of the docks consists of five operations. In the first instance the sailing vessel or steamer enters the dock waters in charge of the transport gang, and is placed in the proper berth for discharging. In old days there she would have waited until it suited the dock company to pay her some attention. Now, at whatever time of day, and, in the case of steamers, at whatever time of night, the vessel settles into her berth, the ship-gangers with their men swarm on to her deck and into her hold. Then begins the typical dock labour—work that any mortal possessed of will and sinew can undertake. The men run up and down like the inhabitants of an ant-hill burdened with their cocoons, lifting, carrying, balancing on the back, and throwing the goods on the quay. It is true that in the discharging of grain and timber special strength or skill is required. With timber a growth on the back of the neck called a " hummie," the result of long friction, is needful to enable a man to balance a plank with any degree of comfort. But timber and grain are in East London practically confined to the Millwall Docks, and it will be seen that more difficulty in the work means a higher class of men, and in the case of timber porters of a body of men who stand outside the competition of low-class labour. Now, leaving the dock quay, we watch the warehousing gang. Here, again, it is heavy, unskilled work. To tip a cask, sack, or bale on to a truck, and run it into a warehouse or down into a vault, or on to

---

* Since the first publication of this article, a union of labourers has been formed, supported by subscriptions from the general public. It remains to be seen whether it is a *bonâ fide* Trades Union.

the platform of a crane, to be lifted by hydraulic power into an upper chamber, is the rough and ready work of the warehousing gang. Next, under the direction of the warehouse or vault keeper, the goods are stowed away awaiting the last and final operation. For the dock company not only shelter the wares committed to their charge, but prepare them for sale, and in some instances make them "merchantable." A large body of coopers mend the casks and plug them, after Government officials have tested the strength of the contents; the company's foremen sort and sample all articles for the importing merchant, and in some cases operate on the goods under his directions. For instance, sugar is bulked which has been partially "washed"; rum vatted, coloured, and reduced to standard strength. It is in these various operations that the docks prove their capacity for absorbing all kinds and degrees of human faculty. The well-educated failure, that unlucky production of the shallow intellectualism of our Board schools, can earn fivepence an hour as tally-clerk, setting down weights and measures, and copying invoices; aged men and undeveloped boys are equal to the cleaning and the sorting of spices, while "the Wools" and "the Teas" attract the more vigorous class of irregular labour, for the sales of these articles take place at certain fixed periods of the year, and the employment dependent on those sales is heavy, worked under pressure for time, and during long hours.

In truth the work of the docks is typical of the life of a great city. Extremes meet, and contrasts are intense. There is magnificence in the variety and costliness of the multitudinous wares handled by the most decrepit and poverty-stricken worker—a hidden irony in his fate, touching all things and enjoying none. All the necessaries and most of the luxuries of our elaborate civilization pass familiarly through the dock labourer's hands, or under his feet. The fine lady who sips her tea from a dainty cup, and talks sentimentally of the masses, is unaware that she is tangibly connected with them, in that the leaves from which her tea is drawn have been recently trodden into their case by a gang of the great unwashed. And it is in this work of unpacking, preparing, and repacking goods that the numberless opportunities for petty thefts occur, which supplement the income of the less scrupulous, and which necessitate the large body of dock police, with the custom of "rubbing down" each labourer as he passes the dock gates. Sometimes the honesty of the worker is severely tried. Imagine the tantalizing spectacle to a born lover of tobacco of masses of this fragrant weed actually consigned to the flames, as "undeclared" by Custom House officials. To see it burning and not to be able to take so much as a pinch! I know a socialist whose grievances against society are centred in this burning pile of the great comforter, and who enters his paltry protest against this ungainly order of things by lining his coat pockets at the risk of two months' hard labour and dock ostracism.

I herewith give the numbers of those employed by the three East London docks, classed according to regularity or irregularity of employment.

WEST AND EAST INDIA DOCKS.

Outdoor staff:

Foremen, &c.	457	
Police	114	Total . 818 regularly employed
Permanent labourers	247	
Irregularly employed:		
Maximum	2355	Average 1311 irregularly employed
Minimum	600	
Preferred for employment or "Royals"	700	2129

LONDON AND ST. KATHERINE DOCKS

Outdoor staff:

Foremen, &c.	400	
Police	100	Total 1070 regularly employed
Artisans	150	
Permanent labourers	420	

Irregularly employed:

Maximum . . . . 3700 ⎫
Minimum . . . . 1100 ⎬ Average 2200 irregularly employed
Preferred for employment or ⎪ ────
"Ticket men" . . 450 ⎭ 3270

MILLWALL DOCKS.

Outdoor staff:
Contractors' permanent staff of labour . . . 300
Irregularly employed (gaining livelihood here) . 500
────
800

It will be observed that the Millwall Docks employ comparatively few hands. The trade is chiefly corn and timber, the discharging of which needs special skill and sinew. The Millwall Dock hands are therefore superior to the ordinary dock and waterside labourers. And there are other reasons for excluding the majority of workers at these docks from any general description of London labour. They are for the most part countrymen imported some years back to break a combination of corn porters. Cut off by their residence in the interior of the Isle of Dogs from the social influences of the East-end, they have retained many traits of provincial life. As a rule they belong to some religious organization, and are united together in clubs and benefit societies. And the system of employment prevalent at the Millwall Docks appears to be efficient and satisfactory in its results to men and masters. The whole work is let out to large labour contractors. This form of the contract system is not open to the objection rightly advanced against the small working-man contractor. The men who undertake the whole responsibility and liability of the various operations of discharging, warehousing, and overside delivery at the Millwall Docks are naturally, if only from self-interested motives, above the temptations of treating and bribery from candidates for employment. They combine the close personal supervision of the practical man earning profit instead of drawing a fixed salary, with the long-sighted policy of the large employer anxious for the physical and moral well-being of the workman. Moreover, in this case the contractors live near their work and associate freely with their men. Each master has a small permanent staff of labourers, guaranteed £1 a week and averaging 33*s* all the year through. The irregular hands, most of whom in the past times of good trade were on the permanent staff, are well known to the contractors, and shift about from one to another earning a more or less regular livelihood, and rarely leave the Millwall Docks in search of other work. The true casual is seldom employed, for from lack of skill or power of endurance, the loss on his work is excessive.*

The methods of employing the lowest class of labour differ in the West and East India and in the London and St. Katherine Docks, though the work undertaken by these companies is practically the same. The West and East India Company have resisted the pressure in favour of piece-work and the contract system ; and have shown a laudable desire, from the working-man's point of view, to retain a large permanent staff. On the other hand there is no recognized class of "preference" labourers, but the fore-man of each department has on his books a certain number of men called "Royals," who are actually preferred for employment on account of superior power, long service, or more regular application for work. These men and others

---

* Evidence has been given before the House of Lords Committee on the Sweating System proving that dock labourers of the ordinary type are employed in certain operations of an unskilled character at the Millwall Docks ; and the existence of " Sweating " (*i.e.* a systematic deduction from the men's earnings, either by sale, contract, or bribery to secure employment) has, I think, been ascertained. These evils, however, are admitted by the working men witnesses to prevail exclusively in the employment of the unskilled labour, and therefore to affect only a small minority of Millwall Dock hands. But the presence of sub-contracting and bribery under large contractors demonstrates that these evils are not dependent on any peculiar system of employment, but arise out of the character of those employed.

are taken on each morning according to the needs of the
day. They are chosen by the company's foreman and are
paid 5d an hour. As an encouragement to good work, and
supposing the task has been accomplished at a certain rate
of profit to the company, a "plus" is divided in definite
proportions among the different members of the gang.
This "plus" averages a halfpenny an hour to the ordinary
worker. The daily earnings of the irregular hands at the
West India Dock varied last year from 2s 9d to 4s 3¼d,
and averaged about 3s 6d without "plus."

The London and St. Katherine's Company have a smaller
permanent staff in proportion to the work done, and
depend more on casual labour. A considerable number of
men, possessing a preferred right to employment, act as
an intermediate class between the permanent staff and the
"casualty" men. This company has also introduced a
mixed system of employing their casualty men. The
casuals who work directly for the company are paid 5d an
hour; but half the work of these docks is let out to small
contractors, generally their own permanent or preference
labourers. In 1880, the casuals struck against this system.
They declared that they were being "sweated"—that the
hunger for work induced men to accept starvation rates.
The company responded to their appeal. Now the ganger
is bound to pay his hands a minimum of 6d an hour. It
is to be feared, however, that the struggle for work over-
leaps this restriction, and that a recognized form of sweating
has been exchanged for an unrecognized and more demoralizing way of reducing wages—by the bribery and corruption
necessary to secure employment.

It will be seen from the foregoing that the two big dock
companies employ three classes of workers—permanent,
preference, and casual. As this distinction runs through
waterside as well as dock employment, and is built up in
the most important labour formation of East London, I
shall attempt to describe the larger features distinguishing

these social strata; and I shall try to give the more
important economic, social, and moral conditions under
which they are formed and exist.

At least the docks are free from the reproach of other
London industries; they are not overrun with foreigners.
The foreign element is conspicuous by its absence—unless
we are to persuade ourselves that the Irish are foreigners.
For Paddy enjoys more than his proportional share of dock
work with its privileges and its miseries. He is to be
found especially among the irregular hands, disliking as a
rule the "six to six business" for six days of the week.
The cockney-born Irishman, as distinguished from the
immigrant, is not favourably looked upon by the majority
of employers. In a literal and physical sense the sins of
the forefather are visited tenfold upon the children,
intensifying the evil of a growing Irish population.

Unfortunately the presence of the foreigner is the only
unpleasant feature common to East London which is
omitted from the composition of dock and waterside life.
In another general characteristic the life of the docks is
typical of metropolitan existence. There is no union for
trade or other purposes among dock or waterside labourers
—there is even antagonism, or at least utter indifference
and carelessness, between the different classes of dock
employés. The foreman is distinctly the official. Directly
the day's work is over he hurries from a disreputable
neighbourhood back into the odour of respectability which
permeates a middle-class suburb. There, in one of those
irreproachable houses furnished with the inevitable bow
window, and perchance with a garden, or at least with a
back-yard wherein to keep and ride the hobby, he leads
the most estimable life. Doubtless he is surrounded by a
wife and family, perhaps keeps a maid-of-all-work, and has
a few selected friends. He meddles little with the public
business of the district, leaving that to retail tradesmen:
he belongs to no political, and frequently to no religious,

organization, and he disapproves of working men's clubs, which he fails to distinguish from the "public." Bred up from childhood in dock uniform, he has however the interests of his trade at heart. He has watched subsidized foreign vessels stealing the business from English hands; hence the one article of his political creed—the one bond uniting him to all grades of dock labour—faith in protection. Otherwise he lives unto himself. And in this he only follows the example of his superior in social position and culture, the wealthy East-end brewer or dock shareholder. All alike obey the eternal formula of the individualist creed : Am I my brother's keeper ?

It is hardly fair, however, to cite the want of sympathy between the dock foremen and the dock labourers as peculiar to metropolitan dock life. In many trades foremen look at all questions from the employer's point of view, and distrust of the men is proved by a rule which prevails in some trade unions disallowing the membership of foremen. But in the provincial town the foreman and the labourers will inhabit the same street, or at least the same district, and usually there will be some tie, political, religious, or educational, which will bind all classes together. In London it is the exception that proves the rule. Men of the upper and middle class who fulfil their duty towards those of a lower class with whom they are naturally connected by neighbourhood or by business, are forced by the pressure of work to be done to undertake more than their duty. Overtaxed energies, depressed spirits induce the more earnest minds to renounce the interests and amusements of their own station. Grey tones overcast the mind as well as the complexion; and the duty-loving citizen is gradually transformed into the professional philanthropist, viewing all things with the philanthropic bias which distorts judgment and lends an untrue proportion to the fact of existence. His mental vision is focussed on the one huge spot of misery, and in his solicitude to lessen it he forgets, and would sometimes sacrifice, the surrounding area of happiness.

But the universal dislocation of the social life of East London manifests itself in the docks, not only by the absence of all ties between employer, foremen, and men, but in the complete severance of the different grades of labour, and, among the more respectable of the working class, in the isolation of the individual family. The "permanent" man of the docks ranks in the social scale below the skilled mechanic or artisan. With a wage usually from twenty to twenty-five shillings a week and an average family, he exists above the line of poverty, though in times of domestic trouble he frequently sinks below it. He is perforce respectable, and his life must needs be monotonous. His work requires little skill or intelligence—the one absolute condition is regular and constant attendance all the year through. He has even a vested interest in regularity—the dock company acting as a benefit society in sickness and death—an interest which he forfeits if he is discharged for neglect of work. By the irregular hands the permanent man is looked upon as an inferior foreman and disliked as such, or despised as a drudge. He, in his turn, resents the popular characterization of dock labourers as the "scum of the earth."

As a rule the permanent men do not live in the immediate neighbourhood of the docks. They are scattered far and wide, in Forest Gate, Hackney, Upton, and other outlying districts; the regularity of their wage enabling them to live in a small house rented at the same figure as one room in Central London. And if the temptation of cheap food, and employment for the wife and children, induces a permanent man to inhabit St. George's-in-the-East or Limehouse, he will be found in a "Peabody" or some strictly regulated model dwelling. He will tell you: "I make a point of not mixing with anyone," and perhaps he will sorrowfully complain "when the women gets thick together there's always a row." It is the direful result of the wholesale desertion of these districts by the better classes that respectability means social isolation, with its enfeebling and disheartening effect. In common with all other working men with a moderate but regular income, the permanent dock labourer is made by his wife. If she be a tidy woman and a good manager, decently versed in the rare arts of cooking and sewing, the family life is independent, even comfortable, and the children may follow in the father's footsteps or rise to better things. If she be a gossip and a bungler—worse still, a drunkard—the family sink to the low level of the East London street; and the children are probably added to the number of those who gain their livelihood by irregular work and by irregular means.

But the foremen and permanent men are, after all, the upper ten of dock life, and our interest is naturally centred in the large mass of labour struggling for a livelihood, namely, in the irregular hands employed by the docks, warehouses, and wharves of East London. I have not been able to collect complete statistics of waterside employment; but from the evidence I gathered both from masters and men the condition of wharf employment does not materially differ from that of dock labour, and the ratio between the number of applicants for work and the number of hands taken on would be much the same along the waterside as at the dock gates.

Now, we believe, from our general inquiry, that there are 10,000 casual labourers, exclusive of waterside labourers, resident in the Tower Hamlets, employed principally at the docks. The average of irregular hands employed by the three dock companies stands at 3,000*—that is, there is daily work at 3s 6d a day for 3000 men, supposing the business could be spread evenly throughout the year, and

---

* This calculation excludes "ticket men" of L. and St. K.

worked during regular hours. I do not wish to maintain
that these figures represent the exact equation between
those who desire, or are supposed to desire, work and the
number actually employed. But I believe it is an approximately true statement, and that the qualifications on either
side may be fairly balanced against each other. Neither do
I wish to imply that the earnings of an irregular hand can
be calculated by a rule of three sum, working out at
6s 3d a week. On the contrary, the most striking fact
observed by those who live among these people is that
there are definite grades of wage-earning capacity or
wage-earning luck corresponding to a great extent with
distinct strata of moral and physical condition noticeable
in the dock and waterside population of Tower Hamlets.

First, there is the broad distinction of those who are
"preferred" for employment, and those who are not. At
the London and St. Katherine Docks 400 of the irregular
hands have an actual preference right to employment.
These "ticket men" will earn from 15s to £1 a week;
and, as before said, are sometimes transformed into labour
contractors working off their own bat. At the West and
East India, and at most of the wharves and warehouses,
there are a certain number of men who are usually secure
of work if there be any. They are for the most part an
honest, hard-working set, who have established themselves
by their regular attendance and honesty in the confidence
of their employers. These men, together with the more
constant of the casuals, are to my mind the real victims
of irregular trade: if they be employed by small contractors, unprincipled foremen, or corrupt managers, they
are liable to be thrust on one side for others who stand
drink, or pay back a percentage of the rightful wage.
Physically they suffer from the alternation of heavy work
for long hours, and the unfed and uninterested leisure of
slack seasons: and the time during which they are "out
o' work" hangs heavily on their hands. For not only are

they and their families subject to the low moral tone of
the neighbourhood in which they pass their days and
nights, but they habitually associate with the lower class
of casuals, keeping company with them at the gates and
drinking with them at the "public." From my own
observation as a rent collector, and from other evidence,
we know that the professional dock labourer (as distinguished from the drift of other trades, and from the casual
by inclination) earns from 12s to 15s a week, supposing
his earnings were to be spread evenly throughout the year.
But a large wage one week and none the next, or—as in
the case of the wool sales—six months' work and six
months' leisure, are not favourable conditions to thrift,
temperance, and good management. Payment by the
hour, with the uncertainty as to whether a job will last
two or twenty-four hours, and the consequently incalculable nature of even the daily income, encourages the
wasteful habits of expenditure which are characteristic of
this class. The most they can do in their forlorn helpless-
ness is to make the pawnbroker their banker, and the
publican their friend. Many of the professional dock
labourers live in common lodging-houses of the more
reputable kind. If married they must submit to the
dreariness of a one-roomed home which, even in its
insufficiency, costs them from 3s to 4s 6d out of their scanty
earning. More likely than not the wife spends her day
straining, by miserably paid work, to meet the bare
necessities of existence. I say that the work is miserably
paid; but I do not wish to imply that it does not usually
realize its worth : my experience being that the work of
the women of this class, owing to a lack of training and
discipline, is not worth subsistence wage. And the fact
that the wife can and frequently does work weakens the
already disheartened energies of the husband, and with
the inevitable neglect of children and home tends to drag
the whole family down into the lower ranks of casuals.

The earnings of the professional dock labourer are not
only dependent on the vicissitudes of dock trade. The
uncertainty resulting from variation in the demand is
intensified by the day-to-day alteration in the supply of
labour. As far as my experience reaches, dock and waterside employers are the only masters of importance who
neither give nor require characters. A strong man presents himself at the gate. He may be straight from one
of Her Majesty's jails, but if he be remarkable for sinew
he strikes the quick eye of contractor or foreman. The
professional dock labourer is turned away and the new-
comer is taken on. I have heard it argued that the docks
fulfil a special mission towards society in giving men a
chance who have lost their position through one false step.
I answer that for one man taken on, another is pushed on
one side and hundreds are demoralized. The professional
dock labourer retires disgusted; why exert himself to rise
early and apply regularly if he is to be unofficially dismissed, not for any lack of duty or any special failure of
strength, but simply because another has sunk from a
higher plane of physical existence and is superior to
him in brute force? The widely known fact that a man
without a character can live by dock labour becomes the
turning point in many lives : it decides the man trembling
in the balance to choose the evil course—to throw on one
side the irksome shackles of honesty and regularity. And
I altogether deny that the newcomer, if he has sunk from
better things, is "given a chance." If so, it is the same
description of chance yielded by indifferent relatives to
the unfortunate individual with a tendency to drink when
they dispatch him to an outlandish colony, away from the
restraints of public opinion, and far from the influence of
family affection. It is a chance to go quickly and irre-
trievably to the bad. For the casual by misfortune is
subject to exactly the same economic and social conditions
as the casual by profession. Taken on one day, he is

overlooked the next. He may stave off starvation, but he cannot rise to permanent employment. To have worked at the docks is sufficient to damn a man for other work. Indeed his condition is more actively miserable than that of the professional dock labourer. He at least is acclimatized to his surroundings : his mind and body have become by a slow process of deterioration adapted to the low form of life which he is condemned to live. But far more depressing to those who work among these people even than this indifference to their own condition is the sickening cry of the sinking man or woman, dragging the little ones down into a poverty from which there is no arising. Apart from work, and away from the comfortless and crowded home, neither husband, wife, nor children have any alternative or relief except in the low level of monotonous excitement of the East-end street. Respectability and culture have fled; the natural leaders of the working classes have deserted their post; the lowest element sets the tone of East-end existence. Weary of work, and sick with the emptiness of stomach and mind, the man or the woman wanders into the street. The sensual laugh, the coarse joke, the brutal fight, or the mean and petty cheating of the street bargain are the outward sights yielded by society to soothe the inward condition of overstrain or hunger. Alas! for the pitifulness of this ever-recurring drama of low life—this long chain of unknowing iniquity, children linked on to parents, friends to friends, ah, and lovers to lovers—bearing down to that bottomless pit of decaying life.

And decay breeds parasites. The casual by misfortune tends to become the casual by inclination. The victims of irregular trade, and of employment given without reference to character, are slowly but surely transformed into the sinners of East-end society. Like attracts like. The ne'er-do-well of all trades and professions, the haters of the dull monotony of country labour, drift to East London, the centre of odd jobs and charitable assistance. Dock and waterside employers acknowledge this fact ; for they unanimously assert that after they have taken on the average number of hands they strike a quality of labour which is not worth subsistence wage. As an instance I give a case, for the truth of which I can personally vouch. One day last year a flush of business obliged a labour-contractor to "clear the gates." Two gangs composed of equal numbers were employed on the same job, the one made up of permanent hands, the other of casuals. Working during the same hours, the first gang discharged 260 tons, the second 60 tons. I need hardly add that the one operation, besides yielding a handsome wage to the men (it was worked by the piece), was profitable to the employer; while the work of the casuals was a dead loss to the contractor, forced to pay the minimum wage of five-pence an hour.

In truth, the occasional employment of this class of labour by the docks, waterside, and other East-end industries is a gigantic system of out-door relief—and anyone desirous of studying the inevitable effect of outdoor relief in the East-end should come and live amongst those people. Rise early and watch the crowd at the St. Katherine or the West and East India gates. The bell rings, the gate opens, and the struggling mass surge into the docks. The foremen and contractors stand behind the chain, or in the wooden boxes. The "ticket men" pass through, and those constantly preferred are taken on without dispute. Then the struggle for the last tickets. To watch it one would think it was life and death to those concerned. But Jack having secured a ticket by savage fight, sells it to needier Tom for twopence, and goes off with the coppers to drink or to gamble. Or, if the flush of business forces the employers to "clear the gates," many of those who on a slack morning would be most desperate in their demand for work will "book off" after they have earned sufficient for a pint of beer and pipe of tobacco and a night's lodging. Or take a day which offers no employment—watch the crowd as it disperses. The honest worker, not as yet attracted by the fascinations of East-end social life, will return to his home with a heavy heart: there he will mind the baby, while his wife seeks work; or, if not entirely hopeless, he trudges wearily along the streets searching in vain for permanent work. But the greater part of the crowd will lounge down the water-side and stand outside the wharf and dock gates. As the day draws on the more respectable element will disappear, while its place will be taken by the professional "cadger" and dock lounger. These men would work at no price. They gain their livelihood by petty theft, by cadging the earnings of their working friends, through gambling or drink, and by charitable assistance. From all accounts I very much fear that these are the recipients of the free break-fasts with which the well-to-do West-end, in times of social panic, soothes its own conscience, and calms its own fears. But, apart from this semi-criminal class, the staple of the dock and waterside population subsisting by means of the extreme fluctuation and irregularity of employment is made up of those who are either mentally or physically unfit for worthful and persistent work. These men hang about for the "odd hour" or work one day in the seven. They live on stimulants and tobacco, varied with bread and tea and salt fish. Their passion is gambling. Sections of them are hereditary casuals; a larger portion drift from other trades. They have a constitutional hatred to regularity and forethought, and a need for paltry excitement. They are late risers, sharp-witted talkers, and, above all, they have that agreeable tolerance for their own and each other's vices which seems characteristic of a purely leisure class, whether it lies at the top or the bottom of society. But if we compare them with their brothers and sisters in the London Club and West-end drawing-room we must

admit that in one respect they are strikingly superior. The
stern reality of ever-pressing starvation draws all together.
Communism is a necessity of their life : they share all with
one another, and as a class they are quixotically generous.
It is this virtue and the courage with which they face
privation that lend a charm to life among them. Socially
they have their own peculiar attractiveness ; economically
they are worthless ; and morally worse than worthless, for
they drag others who live among them down to their own
level. They are parasites eating the life out of the working
class, demoralizing and discrediting it.

I venture to think that the existence, and I fear the
growth, of this leisure class in our great cities, notably in
London, is the gravest problem of the future. For we have
seen that the employment offered by the docks and
wharves of East London is of necessity declining. There
is a movement downward in the grades of labour. Permanent men are being everywhere dismissed, while preference men are becoming mere casuals. And as regards
the export trade, the secretary of the Stevedores' Union
informed me that a short time after the opening of the
Suez Canal the Union numbered 2000. To-day the Union
numbers 1700, and he assured me that 500 could do the
work offered.* The case of the non-union stevedores is
still worse. Moreover not only is the direct employment
offered by the docks and waterside decreasing, but the
dependent industries, such as sack-making and cooperage,
have almost ceased to exist : sugar comes packed in bags
instead of casks, and the sacks needed here are manufactured wholesale at Dundee. And yet in spite of this
steady shrinkage of employment we have an unceasing
drift of foreign and provincial labour into London, pressing

* This does not represent the want of employment at the East-end, but
in the Port of London. Stevedores are a compact body of men employed at
the Tilbury, Royal Albert and Victoria Docks, as well as the East London
Docks.

the native-born worker out of the better-paid employments
into the ranks of those who live by unskilled or casual
labour.

It is not difficult to decipher the conditions through
which this leisure class is formed and exists. They
may be summed up in the seemingly paradoxical statement : *the difficulty of living by regular work, and the ease
of living without it.*

Let us take the first condition—the difficulty of living
by regular work. It is evident that the docks and waterside employers cannot augment their business ; the question
remains whether it is possible for them to give more
regular employment—that is, to increase the earnings of
the honest and capable worker, while discontinuing the
outdoor relief to the " casuals by inclination." I think we
may rest assured that if a practical plan were suggested
by which this might be effected, the employer would be
the first to take advantage of it ; for the loss entailed by
the bad work of the casual is a fact unpleasantly realized
in the balance sheet. But anyone who has glanced through
the *résumé* of trade events prefacing this article will have
perceived that the docks and wharves of East London are
about as helpless as the labourers at their gates. In many
instances we are railing at dying men. With a declining
business and rapidly disappearing profits, the docks and
wharves are played off, one against another, by multitudinous
London shipowners and merchants, until, as a wharfinger
pathetically remarked, " We shall soon be forced to pay
them handsomely for the privilege of discharging and
housing their goods." Neither do I wish to localize the
evil one step further up. Shipowners and merchants are,
in their turn, the victims of the dislocated state of metropolitan life. In the " individualism run wild," in the
uncontrolled competition of metropolitan industry, un-
checked by public opinion or by any legislative regulation
of employment, such as the Factory Acts, it seems im-

possible for any set of individuals, whether masters or
men, to combine together to check the thoughtless and
useless caprices of that spoilt child of the nineteenth
century—the consumer. A possible remedy is a kind of
municipal socialism, which many of us would hesitate to
adopt, and which in the case of the docks and waterside
would take the form of amalgamation under a Public Trust
—a Trust on which the trader, consumer, and labourer
would be duly represented.* This would facilitate a better
organization of trade and admit the dovetailing of business.
And supposing the Public Board did not undertake to
provide the labour, they could at least throw open the
gates to a limited number of labour contractors working
under legislative regulations, who would be enabled by
the extent of their business to maintain permanent staffs
of workmen. I believe that the idea of a Public Trust
is not regarded as without the sphere of practical
politics by dock and waterside authorities. But if any
form of amalgamation should be adopted, if any description
of monopoly should be sanctioned by the State, I would
earnestly plead that the true interests of the working
class should not be neglected, and their economic and
social condition entirely sacrificed to the convenience
of the trader and the dividend of the shareholder. The
conscience of the country was awakened to the iniquity of
allowing the whole factory population to be deteriorated
and brutalized by overstrain and absence of all moral and
sanitary regulations. Why should we suffer the greater
evil of a system of employment which discourages honest
and persistent work, and favours the growth of a
demoralized and demoralizing class of bad workers and
evil livers ?

* In connection with this proposed remedy a careful study of the condition
of labour in these provincial Docks which are under the government of Trusts
(though these trusts are not of a representative character), would be of great
value.

The second condition—the ease of living without regular wage—is at once the result and the cause of irregular employment. For supposing low-class labour ceased to exist round about the docks, it is clear that the employer would be forced to arrange his work so as to provide employment for a permanent staff. A limited and high-class labour market would be an "inevitable" before which even the "inevitables" of spasmodic trade and competition would bend and give way. If we cannot make employment more regular, how can we lessen the evil from the other side, and, by discouraging the stagnation of low-class labour in London, force employers to use permanent hands ? For, besides the subsistence yielded by the odd jobs of metropolitan industry, there are other forces working towards the same end—encouraging and enabling the worker to cast off wage-earning capacity and deteriorate into the industrial parasite. First and foremost the extensive charitable assistance doled out in the metropolis. The well-to-do West-enders, unwilling to dedicate persistent thought and feeling to their fellow-citizens, suffer from periodical panic, and under the influence of a somewhat contemptible combination of fear and stricken conscience, fling huge sums of money into the yawning gulf of hopeless destitution. Eighty thousand pounds* dribbles out in shillings and pence to first comers. The far-reaching advertisement of irresponsible charity acts as a powerful magnet. Whole sections of the population are demoralized, men and women throwing down their work right and left in order to qualify for relief ; while the conclusion of the whole matter is intensified congestion of the labour market—angry, bitter feeling for the insufficiency of the pittance or rejection of the claim. And allied to this sin of thoughtless gifts is the desertion of the educated

---

* The amount of the Mansion House Fund for the relief of the Unemployed : 1885.

classes of their posts as leaders of public opinion. The
social atmosphere of the East-end favours idleness varied
by gambling and drink; public opinion is against worthful
and persistent work. Many fall who might have stood,
and in spite of hundreds of unemployed it is hard to find
honest and capable workmen. These are evils which an
awakened conscience and a better understanding of the
conditions of the people among rich and poor alike will
alone cure.

CHAPTER III.

THE TAILORING TRADE *

In this time of burning controversy a description of the
life and conditions of the East End tailors would be
without value if it ignored their exact position in the
metropolitan clothing trade. We might with equal advantage write the history of a country and forget its relation
to other powers. For we have here a new province of
production, inhabited by a peculiar people, working under
a new system, with new instruments, and yet separated by
a narrow and constantly shifting boundary from the sphere
of employment of an old-established native industry. On
the one side of this line we find the Jewish contractor
with his highly organized staff of fixers, basters, fellers,
machinists, button-hole hands, and pressers, turning out
coats by the score, together with a mass of English
women, unorganized and unregulated, engaged in the
lower sections of the trade; whilst on the other side of
the boundary we see an army of skilled English tradesmen with regulated pay and restricted hours, working on
the old traditional lines of one man one garment. The
"new province" is popularly known as the "Sweating
System:" it is the area over which the present inquiry of
the Select Committee of the House of Lords extends (in so
far as it regards the tailoring trade); it is one, though
perhaps not the first, destination of that flood of foreign
immigrant poor which engrosses the attention of a
committee of the Commons. In both inquiries the English

* Republished by the permission of the editor of the *Nineteenth
Century* (date of original publication, August, 1888).

trade union appears in the background as a threatened
vested interest. We have therefore two distinct questions
to deal with—(1) the economic and moral effect of this
class of producers on the English working man; and (2)
the actual condition of these people, judged not only by
our standard of life, but by their own—a question which, I
think, resolves itself into this : Is their condition physically
and mentally progressive? I do not wish at present to
discuss the relative importance, from a national point of
view, of these two questions. But I venture to submit that
in an impartial picture of the East End tailoring trade the
two issues must be kept clear and distinct.

Before I attempt to map out the new province or to
describe the life of its inhabitants, I shall try to indicate
briefly whether it be an industrial discovery or simply an
invasion of the English labour market, and if the latter to
what extent : in other words, whether these two entirely
different methods of production, represented on the one
hand by the Jewish contractor and his Jewish staff, on the
other hand by the English journeyman tailor, are equally
adapted to supply the same demand—whether, as a matter
of fact, they do, or could, execute the same orders.

Take a morning coat made by an English journeyman
tailor for a first-class West End firm (say Messrs. Poole &
Son), and the same article turned out by a Jewish
contractor for the wholesale trade in slop garments.
Lay them side by side. There may be no difference in the
material; that is settled by the taste of the customer.
There may be no difference in the cut, for cutters trained
at good places command high salaries from all classes of
merchant tailors and wholesale clothiers. But look at
each garment closely and examine the workmanship. At
a glance you will perceive that the one is hand-sewn and
the other machine-made. Examine further into the work
of the English journeyman tailor: you will note that in
those parts of the coat that need lining the latter will be

fitted to the material and felled over; while if the coat be lined throughout, the lining will be attached by a slight tack to one or other of the seams of the material and in all cases felled over. There are fewer stitches, yards less thread or silk, and yet in all places material and lining lie compactly together. Now turn to the coat of a Jewish contractor. Take the material in one hand, the lining in the other. Pull them apart. Why, it is not a coat at all —it is a balloon. Snip the two or three hidden tacks at the base of the collar, and even this opens out and loses all individual form. Fill it with light gas and hermetically seal the pores of the stuff—and behold! "the thing" floats up to heaven, formless and without shape, never again to trouble its owner or the English tailor. This garment is not made at all: to use a trade expression, it is "bagged together," material and lining seamed up separately, laid back to back, run round the edges by the heavy-treading machine, the coat turned inside out through an armhole, the machine process repeated. Now the difference to the customer between these two representative coats is, as I said before, not one of material or of cut. In the first place it is one of wear. The coat made by the individual Englishman will wear three times as long as that made by the staff of the Jewish contractor. Still more it is a question of fit. Fit, that one constant test of the art of a tailor or dressmaker, untouched by changes in cut or material, is as much dependent on good workmanship as on the skill of the fitter. A fashionable ladies' tailor knows this when he pays 18s for the making of a lady's bodice fitted by himself. There is no fit—there can be no fit—in a coat made by the machine and by subdivided and unskilled labour. Walk behind the wearer of a sweater's coat; if the material be light, it will sway to and fro with a senseless motion; if heavy, it bulges out first here, then there. The reason is self-evident. With a few weeks' wear the material and the lining stretch different ways, and to a varying extent; and presently the coat hangs on its owner's back like linen on a clothes-line, at the mercy of every movement or gust of wind.

Clearly, then, the order of the gentleman who knows how to clothe himself, and is able to pay for it, cannot be executed by a Jewish contractor. In the making of hand-sewn garments the English journeyman tailor has no rival.

On the other hand the English tailor cannot compete with the Jewish contractor in supplying wholesale houses with ready-made clothing. This is not only a question of the quality and price of the labour; it is, to a great extent, the result of that transformation of a large section of the tailoring trade from a retail to a wholesale business which has taken place within the last thirty years. We may say, if we like, that this transformation was itself effected by the introduction of the sewing machine and sub-divided labour—by the demand for machine-made goods of the balloon type by a middle and working-class public and in the colonial markets. But in a practical discussion of the problems of to-day a Darwinian inquiry as to origin is somewhat out of place. The transformation is an accomplished fact. Wholesale distribution necessitates wholesale production. As the trade at present stands, the English journeyman, even if he were able and willing to make coats at the same figure, could not compete with the con-tractor for orders from wholesale houses. It would be impossible for a firm handling £500,000 worth of cheap clothing annually to give each garment out to an isolated individual working on the principle of one man one gar-ment. The orders of wholesale traders must to a large degree be executed by one or another form of contract—in the case of clothiers, either by provincial factories supply-ing design, cloth, and labour; or by contractors, large and small, organizing labour only. The actual competition here is not between the English journeyman tailor and the Jewish contractor, but between the latter and the provincial factory—not between English trade-unionists and immigrant foreigners, but between Jewish and female labour. With the character and extent of this competition, in so far as it is found within and without the new province, I shall deal later on. At present I will only point out that in so far as the new method of production meets the enormous outgrowth in the demand for cloth-made garments created by the transformation of the tailoring industry from a retail to a wholesale trade, it is not an invasion of the area of employment of the English journeyman tailor, but may fairly be termed an industrial discovery made by the organizers of Jewish and female labour.

I do not wish, however, to deny that there is a debatable land—a battle-field of living competition between the English tailor on the one hand and the inhabitants of the " new province" on the other. The whole of the " bespoke" trade for retail shops might be executed by English journeymen tailors. As it is, only a certain and, I fear, a decreasing proportion of orders are made under the old system. A large number of "ordered" coats are made by Jews; a still larger proportion of "ordered" trousers and vests are made by women. Speaking generally, the West End and City trade in "ordered" garments may be divided into three classes: the first, made on the premises by skilled English tailors, by men who work regular hours (nine to seven) and earn good wages;*

* A journeyman tailor working in a good shop will earn £2 10*s* per week during the busy season; throughout the year he may average £1 to £2 according to his skill. The work is paid by the piece; but the price per garment is based on a time-log of 7*d*, 6*d*, and 5*d* an hour, according to the class of shop. The time-log was constructed many years ago by the Society of Amalgamated Tailors, and was doubtless an attempt to substitute time-work for piece-work, and to equalize wages within the Union. By a calculation of the number of hours taken by a man of average skill to execute a job the payment per garment is worked out and definitely fixed. As, however, the journeyman tailor is paid per garment, the amount of his earnings depends on the

the second class made by English or German tailors * at their own homes, the third class turned out by the Jews and by women.

Now the tailor who works at home is the intermediate step between the shop-worker and the foreign contractor. He takes out work at a lower figure than the statement price paid at the shop: for instance, a frock coat, for which a shop-worker will receive 18s and upwards, he will undertake for 14s. He slips in machine work where it will not be noticed; he employs unskilled labour (his wife or a plain hand to whom he will pay 12s a week) in those parts of the garment in which lack of skill will not be superficially visible. He works for long and irregular hours—the night through if needful to bring the "order" in to time. The workshop is frequently the bedroom and the living room. I have known a home-worker clearing, according to his own account, £5 a week during the busy season, living, working, and sleeping in the same room, with a wife and five children. In bad sanitation, overcrowding, long and irregular hours, the life of the English home-worker too often presents the worst features of the "sweating system." Further, by the introduction of machine-work and female labour, by escaping trade-union regulations as to hours and wage, he deteriorates workmanship, reduces the price of labour, and favours the

rate at which he works, and the fiction of a time-log is probably maintained by the Trade Union as a formal barrier against competition. The master tailors refuse to recognize the Trade Union statement; but there has been no attempt to beat down the price of the best work. In fact, it appears that payment for the most skilled work has risen; but the journeymen tailors assert that their total earnings have decreased owing to irregularity of employment.

* Many of the German tailors employ female hands, and are, to all intents and purposes, small contractors. They nevertheless belong to the Amalgamated Society of Tailors; and apparently they have not attracted the attention of the reformers: a circumstance due to the higher standard of comfort prevailing in their homes and workshops. This is an additional proof that it is not a system of employment which is popularly defined as "Sweating," but certain conditions originating in the character of the workers.

ever-increasing pressure of seasonal employment. The
Society of Amalgamated Tailors have fully recognized the
evil of home work ; and I think every understanding person will sympathize with them in their efforts to check it.
It is to this class of journeymen tailors that the better
class of foreign contractors are becoming every day more
formidable competitors. Certain evils of home-work,
namely, inadequate accommodation, long and irregular
hours, and an indefinite elasticity to seasonal employment,
are stereotyped in the Jewish method of production and
wrought into a system. But, as it will be seen hereafter,
among this class of Jewish workers there is no *sweating*,
either in the price paid by the retail shops to the contractor or in the rate of wages the latter pays to his
hands. The workers are skilled and well paid : the
machinist a first-rate mechanic, the general hand an all-
round tailor, the presser an artist, and the master himself
not infrequently a skilled tradesman. We may consider
the English home-worker a good instrument out of repair,
the Jewish "bespoke" workshop an inferior instrument
sharpened to its highest pitch. From the customer's point
of view, the difference between the coat made by an inferior English journeyman and that turned out by the
superior class of Jewish workshop is somewhat similar to
the difference between bad butter and first-rate butterine.
And in some, though, I believe, rare instances the foreign
contractor manufactures the genuine article, making coats
practically on the old method, with the distinction that the
seams of the material are machined and not hand-sewn,
though the linings are fitted and felled on the English
system. In short, to carry out the former analogy, the
Jewish method of production is an instrument in the
process of perfection, which is cutting its way upwards
through all classes of the coat trade, stopping short only
at the hand-sewn garment made for the gentleman "who
knows how to clothe himself." The comparative demand

for coats made by the three classes of workers will depend
first on the price customers are willing to pay, and secondly
on their capacity for judging and appreciating workmanship.

It is difficult for me to define with the same degree of
exactness the nature and extent of the competition between
women and the English journeymen tailors in the trousers
and vest trade. Whereas the rival coat-making industry
is practically engrossed by a compact Jewish community
resident mainly in Whitechapel, the rival trousers and vest
makers in the " bespoke" trade are distributed all over
the metropolis. They are therefore to a great extent
outside the field of my inquiry, which has been limited to
the East End. I shall simply give the prices paid to
women working (either at home or under contractors) on
the " ordered " trousers and vests which have drifted to
the East End ; and those prices will, I think, be sufficient
to prove that they do not work for bare subsistence wage.
Vests seem to me more suited to female than to male
labour, for after they are cut and fixed there is little
needed but neat sewing. It is probable that vests have
been to a very large extent transferred to women. Entirely hand-sewn trousers are still exclusively made by
men; the making of hunting-breeches is an especially
skilled industry and highly paid ; a Scotch tailor engaged
in it remarking to me: " Our prices are never beaten
down ; if anything, they go up; gentlemen as wears these
will pay anything so long as they fit." This is comforting
to those who were beginning to brood over the vanity of
our national pastimes and the extravagance of our leisured
class, and proves the scientific theory that " compensation"
comes in strange ways. In the trouser trade the female
competition is to a large extent with journeymen tailors of
German birth and extraction ; and, curiously enough, the
contractors who organize this competition are, with few
exceptions, German. That women are formidable and

successful competitors in the making of trousers and vests is, I think, indicated by the census statistics of the entire metropolitan tailoring trade, which show that while the male workers have actually decreased in the decade 1871-81, the female workers have increased in numbers by twenty-five per cent.*

As there is no sign of a decrease of male labour relatively to female in Jewish coat-making, it is evident that it is the English journeymen tailors who are being largely displaced either by foreigners or by women. For this state of things the journeymen working at home are mainly responsible; for home-work has not only been the downward step to the small contractor, but the training-ground for female labour. A man's wife and daughters may be his helpmates; they are other men's rivals.

Such, in briefest outline, are the relations of the new province of production to the old-established native industry. I shall now attempt a picture of the Jewish coat-makers at the East End, as well as a slight sketch of the distinguishing features of the female population engaged in the lower section of the tailoring trade. The sources of my information are, (1) the collectors of the sewing-machine companies,† (2) school board visitors, (3) wholesale

---

* In the census of 1871 we find a total of 38,296 workers—23,516 males, and 14,780 females; in 1881 a total of 41,221—22,744 males, and 18,477 females.

† The sewing machines supplied to the Jewish master tailors, and to the Gentile women engaged in the trouser and vest trade, are almost exclusively purchased on the *hire system: i.e.* weekly instalments, extending over many months, are paid by the customers until they have cancelled the debt. This necessitates a large body of collectors, who visit the customers every week and spend the remainder of their time in touting for custom. Thus the whole of the East End is mapped out into districts; and the past, present, and possible customers in each street scheduled by the thirty collectors who represent Messrs. Singer in East London. Messrs. Bradbury's business, though not so extensive, is organized on the same principle. Through the kindness of Messrs. Singer Mr. Booth's secretaries were allowed to interview each collector separately, and take from him detailed particulars about each individual sweater. Messrs. Bradbury supplied our office with similar information. We were thus able to verify and add to the list of workshops supplied us by the Home Office,

houses, (4) labour contractors, and (5) workpeople of all sorts and conditions. To this I add a slight personal experience of work in the lowest class of coat and trouser shop, and a somewhat extended experience of East End life previous to four months' investigation of the East End tailoring trade.*

The Jewish coat-making industry is practically concentrated within an area of less than one square mile, comprising the whole of Whitechapel, a small piece of Mile End, and a part of St. George's-in-the-East. In this quarter thirty or forty thousand Jews of all nationalities and from all countries congregate, and form in the midst of our cosmopolitan metropolis a compact Jewish community. *Jüdisch* is a language of the streets, and Hebrew characters are common in shop windows and over doorways. Overcrowding in all its forms, whether in the close packing of human beings within four walls, or in the filling up of every available building space with dwellings and workshops, is the distinguishing mark of the district. The percentage of persons *per acre* rises to 227; the highest at the East End. This would seem to entitle the Jewish community to the first place in Mr. Booth's "Tables of Poverty," if it were not that by another test of poverty—rateable value of property per person— this district compares favourably with other East End parishes. These two facts point out two leading features of East End Jewish life—the habit of excessive crowding of dwellings and workshops, and the willingness and ability to pay high rents.

and we were moreover enabled to classify the sweaters according to the number of sewing machines in use, and therefore by the number of persons employed. We took the further precaution of picking out certain streets for a special inquiry by School Board visitors and others : and we were satisfied by the results of these inquiries that our list of small employers was complete, and our classification of them correct.

* I am also indebted to Mr. Lakeman, senior factory inspector at the East End, and to Mr. John Burnett, of the Board of Trade, for general information.

Within the borders of the Jewish settlement we have the names and addresses of 901 Jewish coat-makers employing hands other than their own family, with general information as to (1) the number of sewing machines, (2) the character of the work turned out, and (3) the position and condition of the workshops. In the table given below these shops have been classified according to number of hands usually employed, and cross-divided into sections according to the character of the work done.

CLASSIFICATION ACCORDING TO NUMBERS USUALLY EMPLOYED.

			No.	Per Cent.*
A.	Shops employing over 25 hands	.	15	1·6
B.	„ „ 10 to 25 „	.	201	22·3
C.	„ „ under 10 „	.	685	76·1
			901	100·0

CROSS DIVISION INTO SECTIONS ACCORDING TO QUALITY AND PRICE OF WORK.

			Total	A	B	C
I. Best Bespoke .	.	Morning coat, 12s to 9s / Lounge jacket, 9s to 6s	54	—	28	26
II. Bespoke and stock	.	Morning coat, 9s to 4s . / Lounge jacket, 6s to 3s	192	6	68	118
III. Stock and common		Morning coat, 4s to 1s 6d / Lounge jacket, 3s to 1s	459	8	88	363
IV. Very common (slop)		Morning coat, 1s 6d to 9d / Lounge jacket, 1s to 5d	196	1	17	178
			901	15	201	685

I feel satisfied that our list includes all shops belonging to the classes A and B; but I think it highly probable that a certain number of class C have been overlooked, which would affect more especially section iv. of the second table. It is difficult, however, to establish any exact relation between these two classifications based on broad but rigid lines; as general facts the reader will note that the pro-

---

* These percentages compare very closely with the results of a similar classification of 300 to 400 East End Tailors' workshops prepared for Mr. Booth by the chief of H.M. Factory Department, viz. class A, ·83 per cent.; class B, 18·78 per cent.; class C, 80·39 per cent.

portion of small shops rapidly increases as the work grows commoner; while the contractors employing over 25 hands are, with one exception, confined to the two medium sections of the trade. But our inquiry has brought one fact into strong relief: the sanitary condition and general comfort of the workshop will vary according to its position in the first classification, *i.e.* it will depend more on the importance and wealth of the contractor than on the class of work which he turns out. For the masters who simply superintend and organize the actual workers— they who toil not, neither do they spin—monopolize the best shops of the district; they will secure light (a marketable commodity to the tailor, as it saves artificial lighting), they will substitute the more effectual gas-stove for the objectionable coke fire, and they are more amenable to government inspection in regard to sanitation and space. I have seen workshops belonging to well-to-do contractors which realize a higher standard of comfort than an ordinary provincial factory. I do not wish to credit the owners with any special philanthropic spirit; but while the provincial manufacturer lives in his counting-house or in his own home, the Jewish master spends the day with his workers, helping, encouraging, or driving them, according to his individual nature. The condition of his workshop has therefore a direct effect on his own comfort.

On the other hand, it is in class C (a class which unhappily forms 80 per cent. of the East End trade)—masters who, as Mr. Burnett * tells us, work as hard, if not harder, than their hands—that we discover the most deplorable instances of noisome and overcrowded habitation. The large employer will engage special premises for his work— the better kind of "garden" shop,† or the entire floor of a comparatively large house. The small employer seldom

---

* See *Report to the Board of Trade on the Sweating System at the East End of London*, p. 7.

† Workshop built into backyard—the garden of a past state of things.

knows the distinction between a workshop and a living-
room; if he himself sleeps and eats in a separate room,
some of his workers will take their rest on a shake-down
between the presser's table, the machines, and scattered
heaps of garments. And this living and working in one
room intensifies the evil of the high percentage of persons
per acre which is characteristic of this district. Other
workers who crowd together during the night seek their
day's bread at the dock gates, in the warehouse, the
factory, or along the open streets; but here it is overcrowding day and night—no ventilation to the room, no
change to the worker. Still, there are two stubborn and
incompressible facts in the tailor's shop against which
I would warn the imaginative journalist who calculates
the exact cubic space per person in an unseen and purely
hypothetical "sweater's den." I allude to the presser's
table and the bulky coat machine. These necessitate a
certain minimum space. Moreover, the proportion they
bear to human workers increases in the lowest class of
trade; hence I have seen worse cases of overcrowding
in small "bespoke" shops than among the slop-workers.
But, taking the East End tailoring industry as a whole,
the presence of bulky machinery and the marketable
value of light are physical impediments to the cellar
accommodation and huddled misery of the lowest class of
boot finishers. This comparison does not deny the evil
which exists, but in a picture of East End Jewish life it
changes, by contrast, black into a shade of grey.

In the table on the following page the reader will see
four different types of Jewish coat-shops, with the rate of
wages prevailing in each, together with the customary
hours of labour, not counting overtime. The wages of
the worker are reckoned by the day, but paid weekly.
Piece-work is rare in the Jewish coat-shop; but the more
driving masters insist on a certain stint of work, and the
day, if needful, is lengthened out at the worker's expense

Section I., Class C.—Best Bespoke. One machine ; four hands.

	Wage per day.	Hours of work.	Rate per hour.	Remarks.
Tailor (baster)	7s to 9s	13 to 14	6d to 8d	3 to 4 coats per
,, (presser).........	7s to 9s	,,	,,	day.
,, (machinist) ...	7s to 10s	,,	6d to 9d	Contractor one
Tailoress..................	4s to 6s	12	4d to 6d	of the tailors Tailoress will make button-holes.

Section II.,* Class C.—Bespoke and Stock. Two machines ; eight hands.

	Wage per day.	Hours of work.	Rate per hour.	Remarks.
General tailor	7s 6d to 8s 6d	13 to 14	$6\frac{1}{2}d$ to $7\frac{1}{2}d$	10 to 12 coats per
,, ,, ...	6s to 6s 6d	,,	$5\frac{1}{2}d$ to 6d	day.
Machinist (best)	7s to 7s 6d	,,	$6\frac{1}{2}d$ to 7d	Contractor will
,, (plain)	5s	,,	$4\frac{1}{2}d$	be one of the general tailors.
Presser	7s 6d to 8s 6d	,,	$6\frac{1}{2}d$ to $7\frac{1}{2}d$	ral tailors.
General hand (male)	5s	,,	$4\frac{1}{2}d$	An apprentice
,, ,, (female)	2s 6d	12	$2\frac{1}{2}d$	may be kept at 12s
Buttonholer (girl) ...	3s 6d	Piecework	4d	per week to fell sleeve linings and sew on buttons, and learn trade.

Section III.,* Class C.—Stock and Common. Two (or three) machines ; eight or nine hands.

	Wage per day.	Hours of work.	Rate per hour.	Remarks.
Machinist (best)	6s to 7s	13 to 14	5d to $6\frac{1}{2}d$	15 to 25 coats
,, (plain)	3s to 4s	Indefinite	2d to 3d	per day.
Baster....................	4s to 5s 6d	13 to 14	$3\frac{3}{4}d$ to 5d	Contractor will
Presser	6s	,,	5d	be baster or first
General hand (female)	3s 6d	12	$3\frac{1}{2}d$	machinist.
Feller (girl)	2s 6d	,,	$2\frac{1}{2}d$	The general hand
,, ,, ...	2s	,,	2d	will probably work
Buttonholer (girl)......	3s	Piecework	$3\frac{1}{4}d$	a third machine when needed, or there may be third machinist and wife as general hand.

Section IV.,* Class C.—Very Common. Two machines ; five hands.

	Wage per day.	Hours of work.	Rate per hour.	Remarks.
Machinist (best)	6s	13 to 14	5d	15 to 20 coats per
,, (plain)	3s	Indefinite	1d to $2\frac{1}{2}d$	day.
Presser	6s	13 to 14	5d	Contractor will
General hand (female)	1s 6d	Indefinite	1d to $1\frac{1}{2}d$	be presser or first
Feller (girl)	Nominal	,,	Nominal	machinist. Indef. hrs. May employ "greener" as second machinist at nominal wage. Buttonholer: outdoor hand, $1\frac{1}{2}d$ to 2d per hour.

* The following are actual examples of other classes of shops :—
Section II., class B. Contractor, baster ; wife, buttonholer. First

in order to accomplish it. Otherwise a day's work for a man is thirteen to fourteen hours; half a day seven hours; a quarter of a day four hours. The wages of women are based on a twelve hours day; but since the partial enforcement of the Factory and Workshop Act (which allows only ten and a half hours' actual work) one and a half hours for meal-time is deducted from the daily wage as it appears in our table. There are, however, two important qualifications to a paper rate of wages: the question of overtime (whether it be paid or not) and the average number of days worked per week throughout the year. Overtime may be accounted for in two ways: it may be paid extra, or a very long day may be married to a short day—seventeen hours' work on Thursday may be compensated by the early closing of the Sabbath Eve. Now, in regard to overtime, our inquiry leads us to this conclusion: that it is paid or otherwise compensated for to all classes of hands in the shops of large contractors, and that it is accounted for to all skilled hands throughout the trade. But among the imperfectly taught workers of the slop and stock trade, and more especially in the domestic workshop, under-pressers, plain machinists, and

machinist, 8s 6d ; second ditto, 6s; fixer, 9s ; presser, 8s 6d ; under-presser, 5s ; gen. hand (male), 5s ; gen. hand (male), 4s ; gen. hand (female), 2s 6d ; feller, 2s ; buttonholer, 3s 6d ; apprentice, 9s per week (thirteen hands in all).

Section III., class A. Contractor superintends ; son-in-law manager, £3 per week. Fixer, 7s per day ; presser off, 8s ; under-presser, 7s ; seven machinists, (male), first, 9s ; second, 8s, 8s, 7s ; (female), 4s 4d, 4s, 2s 6d ; general hands (female), four at 18s per week, one at 16s per week, two at 15s per week ; fellers (girls), one at 12s and one at 9s per week ; buttonholers, six, earning 2s 6d to 3s 5d per day (twenty-six hands).

Section IV., class A. (This contractor works on 3s to 1s coats). Contractor himself superintends. Fixer, 8s 6d ; four basters,6s 6d, 6s, 5s, 5s ; thirteen machinists (male) 8s, 7s 6d, 5s, 5s, 6s, 4s, 4s, 3s 6d, 3s, 2s 6d, (female) 4s 9d, 3s 6d per day; (apprentice) 7s 6d per week ; four pressers (male), 8s, 7s, 5s, 3s 6d per day ; seven general hands (female), 4s, 3s, 3s, 2s 6d, 2s 6d, 2s 6d, 2s 6d per day; two fellers, 2s, 1s, per day ; two apprentices, 5s, 4s 6d, per week; six buttonholers earning 1s 6d to 3s 6d per day. (Thirty-nine hands.) This contractor is said to drive his hands.

fellers are in many instances expected to "convenience" their masters, *i.e.* to work for twelve or fifteen hours in return for ten or thirteen hours' wage. We must, however, in noting the scanty earnings of unskilled labour in Jewish coat-making, recognize one striking distinction— I mean the difference between permanently low wage and what may be considered a form of trade apprenticeship. Machinists and pressers receiving less than five shillings for thirteen hours' work may be regarded as learners— a state from which they are bound to rise if they have the average strength and capacity. For instance, a "greener" will work three months for a nominal wage in a slop-shop: in six months he will be earning three to five shillings for an "indefinite" day: in a year's time he may be earning (according to the class of trade for which he is fitted) 6s to 10s 6d per day of thirteen to fourteen hours; or he may be himself a small master. Female fellers working in shops turning out coats from 2s 6d and upwards are termed apprentices if they earn less than 9s, and "improvers" if they earn less than 12s for a full week's work. From the position of feller they rise to that of "general hand," and will receive in that capacity 2s 6d to 5s a day, according to the quality of work they are equal to. But this is emphatically not the case with the general hand of the small slop-shop, who helps in the manufacture of 1s to 1s 6d coats. She will be expected to "convenience" her master, and her maximum pay will be 1s 6d a day. And the sewing needed in this class of garment is in no sense a training for better work; indeed it unfits her for it. Therefore we have a limited class of women working in the Jewish coat trade whose earnings can never exceed 1s 6d, and frequently fall below 1s, for twelve hours' work. But, excluding the general hand of the domestic slop-shop, we may consider that in East-End coat-making a rate of 4½d per hour for male workers, 2½d per hour for female workers, is the low-water mark of ordinary but mature labour; while 9*d* an hour for men and 6*d* an hour for women may be regarded as the high-water mark of exceptional skill.* The full significance of this distinction between permanently unskilled and imperfectly trained labour will be appreciated by contrasting the greener of the coat-trade, with his foot on the ladder of a rising scale of earnings, with his brother in the lowest class of boot finishing, whose labour, like that of the general hand of the slop-shop, cuts out no step to better things. The distinction is broad indeed—it is the difference between hope and despair.

The second qualification to a paper rate of wages, namely, the number of days' work actually secured throughout the year, varies greatly according to the class of shop and the position of the worker. In the best bespoke shop the work is fast and furious during the busy season (from March to August, from October to Christmas), and tends to heap itself up at the latter end of the week, frequently extending through the better part of Thursday night. On the other hand the workers are locked out for weeks together, and they are often unfitted to take work, even if they could get it, in other sections of the trade. It is, therefore, most difficult to calculate their average earnings. In the manufacture of stock and slop coats the current flows more smoothly, and I am inclined to think that its irregularity is caused quite as much by the competition between small masters as by seasonal demand. But undoubtedly the larger contractors offer the most constant employment; for owing to the heavy rent and other standing charges of their workshops they must obtain orders or fail. Again, skilled workers stand, in regard to continuous employment, at a

---

* It would be well to contrast this rate with that of the trades-union statement (given in note to p. 41). The Jewish contractor saves, not by "sweating" skilled labour, but by employing imperfectly trained workers, or a lower grade of workers, for that part of coat-making that needs little or no skill.

great advantage; for during the slack season the staff of the workshop contracts, and throws off the less skilled and more incompetent worker—the master endeavouring to provide work for those of his staff without whom he cannot execute an order if it should fall to his lot; while during the busy time first-class machinists and pressers will be actually bribed by one master to leave another, and will, to some extent, dovetail employment at different shops. I think it would be fair to state the average work per week throughout the year as four to four and a half days in the shops of large contractors and for the most competent and skilled hands throughout the trade; three days for medium shops and average labour; and two and a half days and under for the great majority of permanently unskilled or imperfectly trained workers.

In constructing the four different types of Jewish workshops we have taken class C (shops employing under ten hands) as being the most typical of East End tailoring, the class in which the contractor is invariably one of the staff, and worked it out in the four different sections of the trade, adding in the notes three actual instances of classes A and B. But the difficulty of clear-cut generalization, in Jewish tailoring, is extreme; for beyond the elementary facts that the male workers are exclusively Jewish and the female workers principally so, that the use of the sewing machine and the importance of the presser's table vary inversely with the quality of the work turned out, I have discovered no distinct organization peculiar to the different sections of the trade. For instance, *a priori* reasoning would have led us to suppose that subdivision of labour, the characteristic feature of the Jewish as compared with the English method of coat-making, would be most elaborate in the cheapest branches of the trade. But this is not so. Subdivision of labour increases with the size of the shop, and not with the cheapness of the garment turned out; and as the large contractor cannot take the very best, and will not take the very worst, kind of work, it is developed in its most perfect form in the medium shops of sections ii. and iii., shops working on 2*s.* to 6*s.* coats. Here you not only find fixers, basters, machinists, pressers, and fitters, but, as Mr. Burnett says, " of every branch enumerated it is difficult to find two of the same branches who are paid at the same rate." For instance, it needs less skill to machine the linings than the material of a coat, a lower grade still for sleeve linings, while the machinist who makes cuffs and sews in pockets must be a first-class mechanic ; hence we have already four machinists receiving different rates of pay, and exercising different degrees of skill. The work is honest and good of its kind; but the art of the English tailor has been exchanged for the perfect mechanism of Jewish organization. In a typical Jewish workshop a razor is never used to cut wood ; the hatchet is sharpened.

But on either side the line of good medium work sub-division of labour exists only to a very limited extent. In the best bespoke shops the staff are all, or nearly all, skilled tailors ; they will stop the machine, or lay down the iron, to baste, fell, stitch, or make buttonholes. Their work may be specialized, but their skill is uniform. On the other hand, the lowest slop trade drifts into the domestic workshop with its small and imperfect staff of workers : the same man may baste out and "press off" the 1*s* coat; a mere machinist may pick 5*d* jackets from off the heap by his side, run up the seams and round the edges, the garment flying back-ward and forward to the general hand who will do all the soaping, felling, and buttoning that is required. I place soaping first in the list; for soap replaces the needle in the lowest slop trade ; and it needs little but muscle to soap the seams of shoddy cloth, or the face of the coarse canvas which lies between material and lining, and lends to the coat its temporary form. And lower still we find the Gentile women—the fringe of the coat trade—who make coats throughout for 7*d*; who will take bundles across the

counter of the wholesale house which have been indignantly
refused by the smallest Jewish sweater. Thus subdivision
of labour, yesterday the fetish of the economist, to-day the
bugbear of the trade-unionist, is, in the tailoring industry,
innocent alike of art or fraud; incapable of producing the
coat for "the gentleman who knows how to clothe himself,"
but utterly disdainful of the soaped-up garments which lose
shape and substance in the first London fog. Honestly
made balloons, adapted to the wear of a tasteless middle
class, are its only, but its numerous, progeny.

I now pass to the relation the profit of the contractor
bears to the wages of his hands, together with the general
condition of all classes engaged in the tailoring trade. But
I wish first to dispel an illusion which, judging from articles
in leading papers, seems to have taken firm hold of the
public mind.

Besides the labour contractor we are told that there are
a class of middlemen who stand between the wholesale or
retail house and the master of the workshop—a series of
parasites all of whom "sweat" profit out of the actual
worker at the bottom of the scale. This class of middlemen
was a fact of the past; with equal certainty we may assert
that it is a fiction of the present. That there exist isolated
instances of middlemen who are not superintendents of
labour, I could hardly deny, unless I knew every coat-shop
in London; but we have overwhelming evidence that these
individuals (if they exist at all) do not constitute a class, for
though we have full particulars of shops in all sections
of the coat-trade, we have in every case traced the work
direct to the retail or wholesale house. I have heard of an
overflow of work, of instances in which a labour contractor
has taken out too great a quantity for his own staff, and has
retailed it to his friend; but that is simply a trade accident
and not a trade custom. If, therefore, the term "sweating"
be limited to sub-contract, there is no sweating in the Jewish
coat-trade, unless you choose to regard the wholesale houses

as the first contractor. But this would lead us to the conclusion that all descriptions of merchandise are made under the "sweating system"; for throughout our industrial organization the wholesale house stands between the producer and the retailer, and the cloth manufacturer becomes as much a "sweater" as the Jewish coat-maker. Even in the working men's co-operative movement—that shortest cut between the producer and the consumer—we have watched the rise of two great wholesale societies, under distinct management and with a separate profit and loss account, buying from the manufacturers and selling to the retail stores.

There is, however, one curious exception to this absence of middlemen in the coat trade, namely, in Government work. The wholesale orders given to Government contractors are sublet to labour contractors, who either work on the premises of the first contractor or in their own workshops. It is questionable whether, in this peculiar case, we ought not to regard the first contractor as the wholesale house and the Government as a body of consumers. But any way the reason for this exception is obvious, and is moreover intimately associated with the explanation for the present absence of sub-contracting from the coat-trade at large. In Government work there is a margin between the price at which the work is given to the first contractor and the price at which he can get it executed, with profit, *to the satisfaction of her Majesty's viewers.* Part of his margin of possible profit the Government contractor hands over to a labour contractor; it saves him the personal supervision of a workshop, and he secures through contract a cheaper and more efficient superintendence than through a salaried foreman. Now the middleman, who formerly existed in the coat-trade at large, lived on the margin between the price to the wholesale house and the cost of labour in an unexplored labour market. This margin has been absorbed by the enterprise of rival traders. The prices at which stock

and slop garments are given across the counter of wholesale
houses are 25, some say 50 per cent. lower than they were
twenty years ago.   In fact the nineteenth century patent
sounding-machine   of   competitive   trading   has   pierced
through the series of middlemen and has at length struck
the low level of the actual rate at which labour is willing
to sell itself in the East End market ; and any unusual
variation produced by an additional depression of wage, or
by a temporary inflation of price, will in many cases be
handed over by the so-called " sweater " in the form of a
bribe to the foreman of the wholesale house by whose favour
he secures the work.   Hence, if there exist middlemen in
the Jewish coat trade, they pass under the disguise of the
salaried foremen of large trading firms.   Bribery has replaced sub-contract, in so far as the keen-eyed profit instinct
of the wholesale trader permits it.   But the position of the
actual maker of the garments is in no way affected by the
change.   Neither would it be altered if to-morrow the
principal of the firm himself stepped into the position of the
corrupt foreman.

Closely connected with the bribery of foremen and the
low prices current in the stock and slop trade lies the
question of the actual profit of the contractor compared
with the wages of his hands.   First let us distinguish
between the different classes of contractors, as we have
distinguished between different classes of workers.   The
typical sweater—" the prince of the sweating system "—
the man who employs over twenty-five hands—has been
narrowly watched by the representatives of comic and
sensational papers.   He is pictured sauntering about his
workshop with his hands in his pockets, with a cigar in his
mouth, and with the East End equivalent to an orchid in
his button-hole—though in a workshop which " reeks of
the smell of human flesh, and in which thirty or forty
workers are huddled together like cattle in a pen," even
this must be an unpleasant and, I should have thought, a

somewhat needless, occupation for a man who "sweats" a
large income out of the labour of his "hands." No doubt
the representatives of these journals have had opportunities
of analyzing his year's balance-sheet that I have been
unable to obtain. All the information that I can give
about a master of this class—and I fear it will sound
prosaic and lacking in the picturesque—is that his workshop realizes a greater degree of comfort, that his hands
are more regularly employed, and are more secure of the
payment of overtime and of their wage at the end of the
week, than is the case with the small master who gains
himself a precarious and uncertain livelihood. From what
I have seen of the private apartments, and from what I
have noticed of the personal expenditure of this class of
contractors, I should imagine that they made a very fair,
perhaps, in one instance, a large income relative to the
turn-over of their business. Men in a large way escape
the blackmail of foremen, for they deal direct with principals
of the wholesale firms; and I am told that one of these
contractors has himself a share in the capital and direction
of the business of his chief customer. Still there is a
paradoxical fact which the creators of the typical sweater
will find hard to explain. If contracting on this scale be
so lucrative and so easy, how is it out of 900 Jewish coat-
makers at the East End there are only fifteen who employ
as a rule twenty-five hands. And in striking opposition to
this enigmatical fact we see the eighty per cent. of small
masters employing under ten persons; while there remains
nineteen per cent. of the intermediate class belonging more
especially to the better paid sections of the trade. Clearly,
then, the small master who manufactures, with the help of
imperfectly taught and permanently unskilled labour, the
balloon and soaped-up garment for the working class home
and colonial markets—the man "who works himself as
hard or harder than any of his employés"—is the typical
sweater of East End coat-making.

In truth it is exactly the absence of the capitalist employer, independent of, and distinct from, the wholesale
trader, able, to some extent, to resist the constant pressure
of competing firms in the direction of cheap, intermittent,
and low-class production, that is the curse of the East End.
Unhappily, the large and responsible employer is severely
handicapped by the economic conditions of the metropolis
as compared with those of the provinces—the extravagant
rent for factory or workshop, the heavy rates and taxes,
the high price of gas and coal, and, intensifying all these
inequalities, the irregularity of the London trade, which
leaves him with serious liabilities during the slack seasons
of the year.

And while the large contractor is placed at a serious
disadvantage, two circumstances tend to an indefinite
multiplication of small masters in the Jewish coat trade,
competing vigorously with each other, not only for the work
of the shops, but for the services of the most skilled hands:
the ease with which a man becomes a master, coupled with
the strongest impelling motive of the Jewish race—the
love of *profit* as distinct from other form of money-earning.
The ease with which a man may become a master is
proverbial at the East End. His living-room becomes his
workshop, his landlord or his butcher the security; round the
corner he finds a brother Israelite whose trade is to supply
pattern garments to take as samples of work to the wholesale house; with a small deposit he secures on the hire
system both sewing machine and presser's table. Altogether it is estimated that with 1*l.* in his pocket any man
may rise to the dignity of a sweater. At first the new
master will live on "green" labour, will, with the help of
his wife or some other relative, do all the skilled work that
is needed. Presently, if the quantity of his work increases,
or if the quality improves, he will engage a machinist,
then a presser. His earnings are scanty, probably less
than those of either of the skilled hands to whom he pays

wages, and he works all hours of the day and night. But the chances of the trade are open to him; with indefatigable energy and with a certain measure of organizing power he may press forward into the ranks of the large employers, and if he be successful, day by day, year by year, his profit increases and his labour decreases relatively to the wage and the labour of his hands.

In the East End tailoring trade the characteristic *love of profit* in the Jewish race has a two-fold tendency; to raise the workers as a mass of individuals, and to depress the industry through which they rise. Contractors and workers alike ascend in the social scale; taken as a mass they shift upwards, leaving to the new-comer from foreign lands the worst paid work, the most dilapidated workshop, and the dirtiest lodgings.

On the other hand, the prices at which work is taken are constantly reduced by a race of workers who have neither the desire nor the capacity for labour or trade combination, and who are endowed with a standard of life that admits of an almost indefinite amount of work in the worst possible conditions.* At present, however, the comparative scarcity of *skilled* labour, joined with the growth in all directions of Jewish tailoring, both in an increased export trade and in the partial invasion of the bespoke work of the City and West-end—this combination of a limited labour market (as regards skill) and trade growth checks the downward tendency of cost of production and maintains a level of good wage and fair profit in the higher branches of the trade. Thus whatever may be the effect on the English working man, and whatever may lie hidden in the future for a race of producers with an indefinitely low standard of life and apparently without the capacity for combination, the present condition of the

---

* Portions of the article published in the *Nineteenth Century* have been omitted in the present chapter, as the characteristics of the Jews are fully dealt with in the chapter on the Jewish community.

East End Jewish tailors may be fairly stated as "mentally and physically progressive." If they alone were concerned, no inquiry would be needed.

An account is given in the chapter on "Working Women," of the manufacture of trousers, vests, and juvenile suits by Gentile women. The workers in this case are the wives and daughters of the irregularly employed and of the purely parasitic population of East London. I have described this population in treating of the Docks. If the Jewish community is like a reservoir continuously rising and overflowing, the mongrel population surrounding it may be compared to a stagnant pool; the worthless and the unfortunate of all districts, of all industries, of all classes, trickle into it; as a mass it sinks downwards; infants, young children, weaklings are pressed out of existence by the struggling mass above; while individuals once floating on the surface are sucked downwards by currents of drink, vice, or sheer misfortune, and drop into the nethermost place.

The women have been fitly termed the Chinamen of this class: they accept any work at any wage. They grasp after the leavings of the Jews in the coat-trade; in some instances they act as general hands in the Jewish slop-shop; and they monopolize the East End trouser and juvenile suit trade. And when Jews and Gentile women come into direct competition (as they do in vest-making) they accuse each other loudly of ruining the trade. I think as a general fact the Jews carry off the best paid work, while the struggling wives and mothers of drunken husbands and starving children slave day and night for a pittance which even a greener would despise, except as apprenticeship to better things. But notwithstanding this, the striking feature of the female labour engaged in the East End tailoring industry is the extraordinary range in the earnings. For, even if we exclude the best bespoke work (corresponding to section i. of the Jewish coat trade), which in the case of trousers and vests is accidental to, rather than characteristic of, East London, we find women in the shops of German contractors, working on second-class order or good stock trousers, who will clear 5s for 10½ hours' work, either as machinists or as finishers. The rule of the trade is piece work; the wages of women in the better class trouser and vest trade (corresponding to section ii. of the coat trade) vary from 3d to 6d an hour according to the rate at which they work. On the other hand, directly we lose sight of garments requiring neat and skilful workmanship and descend into the permanently unskilled work of the vast majority of the trouser, vest, and juvenile suit hands at the East End, if we leave the workshop and step into the home, we may watch women and girls straining every nerve, who cannot earn more than 2d, and must frequently content themselves with ¾d, for an hour's labour. This sudden fall is partly due to the vigorous and growing competition of the provincial factories—a competition most acutely felt in the juvenile suit trade, which, by the way, is the only section of metropolitan tailoring that suffers from foreign as well as from provincial competition. The provincial factory cannot undertake "ordered" goods, neither can it turn out garments with "form." Hence the Jewish coat-shop is very slightly affected by the rival factory system; for with a coat style—"form" as it is called in the trade—is of the first importance, and female labour (whether at home, in the workshop, or in the factory) has always been found fatally deficient in "form." But for strong and sound work, the provincial factory with its greater sub-division of labour, with its superior machinery, excels in all ways (except cheapness) the slipshod output of the demoralized and poverty-stricken home. Therefore trousers and juvenile suits corresponding to the honestly made balloons of the large Jewish contractor are chiefly manufactured in the provinces; while the women at the East End who are not skilled or fortunate enough to secure

" order " work are for the most part engaged on trousers, vests, and juvenile suits for the working-class home and colonial markets—garments that are " flattered " into temporary shape by the presser's iron, and in the making of which soap largely replaces the use of thread —fit companions for the soaped-up coat of the domestic sweater.

The women engaged in this lowest branch of the tailoring industry work either direct for a wholesale house or for a distributing contractor. The latter are more especially characteristic of the trouser trade ; they may be Germans or English women ; in rare instances they are Jews. They take large orders from shipping or wholesale firms, form centres of employment throughout the East End, give the work out, first to be machined, then afresh to be finished, while they press the garments either themselves or see it done on their own premises. In other cases women will take small quantities from a wholesale house or from one of these contractors, machine the garment either alone or with help, and give out the finishing to their neighbours. Thus, I have known a shipping order pass through the hands of a series of individuals before it reached the homes of the finishers. We have, therefore, clear evidence of sub-contract in the trouser trade. But while sub-contract exists to a small extent, distributing contractors, as a class, are being swept away. Small wholesale trading firms are springing up in all parts of the East End, turning dilapidated barns or old stables into workshops for indoor workers, and distributing far and wide their commoner work in the homes of the women.

And I have analyzed carefully the earnings of women working on exactly the same class of garments for a contractor or sub-contractor on the one hand and for a wholesale house on the other, but I have failed to discover any difference in the price paid per garment; while undoubtedly the worst paid work is made under the direction of East

End retail slop-shops or for tallymen*—a business from
which contract, even in the equivocal form of wholesale
trading, has been eliminated. Here again the sweeping
away of the contract system has in no way lessened the
evils of the so-called " sweating system " ; the position of
the actual worker remains unchanged.

These are the main facts of the East London tailoring
trade, the leading features of this new province of production. Each year adds to the number of its inhabitants,
not only at the East End, but throughout the United
Kingdom.† The Jews occupy one portion of it, the Gentile
women the other—both alike constantly shift their boundary
further and further into the domain of the English journeyman tailor ; while on the opposite side the factory system
(also a province of women) competes vigorously with the
female home-workers in the trouser and juvenile suit trade,
but makes little headway against the Jewish industry of coat-
making. Within the boundary, the new province may be
mapped out into sections according to the skill of the
workers and the quality of the garments turned out. In all
cases a definite class of producers, receiving certain rates of
wage, corresponds to a definite body of consumers paying a
certain range of prices. Thus the highly paid staff of the
Jewish or German contractor, working on ordered coats or
trousers, manufactures for well-to-do commercial or professional customers ; the makers of first-class balloons,
with their subdivided labour and sliding scale of earnings,
supply shopkeepers, clerks, artisans, and the better class
colonial markets ; and lastly the small master of " green "

* The tallyman takes orders direct from the actual wearer, and is paid for
the garments in small instalments. He usually manufactures on his own
premises, and takes the measurements of the customer himself. He
unites in his person the functions of a credit-shop and a sweater.

† At Leeds the ready-made clothing industry has attracted some 8000
Jews within the last twenty years. In the Stroud Valley (a newly formed
centre of the trade), two hundred Jews have recently settled. They confine
themselves almost exclusively to coat-making in both instances. In Manchester, Birmingham and Bristol Jewish coat-making colonies are to be found.

labour and the permanently unskilled female home-worker, struggling and striving for bare subsistence wage, serve the African gold-digger, the East End lounger, or the agricultural labourer with soaped-up garments of shoddy cloth.

In regard to the lowest class of trade, it is needless to remark that it is dependent for its existence on the presence in the labour market of a class of workers—such as Jews or women—*with an indefinitely low standard of life.* Without a constant supply of destitute foreigners and of wives forced to supplement their husband's irregular earnings, the low-class tailoring trade would cease to exist. This would be no great evil, for while the workers are starved, the consumers are defrauded. No one profits by this extreme form of sweating except the more grinding wholesale house and the unknown landlord who secures, through the transformation of backyard or living-room into workshop, a double rent. The real "sweater," therefore, has a threefold personality—an ignorant consumer, a grinding and fraudulent wholesale or retail slop trader, a rack-renting landlord; in some instances, we might add a driving labour contractor. This is the body of the sweater; the soul is the evil spirit of the age, unrestrained competition.

[The 900 shops tabulated and classified in the foregoing paper are all situated in Whitechapel or in the parts of St. George's or Mile End Old Town, lying contiguous to Whitechapel and inhabited by the Jews. The boundary to the east in St. George's is Cannon Street Road, and is continued as New Road through that piece of Mile End which intervenes between St. George's and the northern part of Whitechapel; the boundary to the south is Cable Street. This district is the seat of the coat-making trade, and to this district our investigations were chiefly directed. To complete the information for the whole East End, I append a table showing the total number of shops on our list and their character so far as we were able to ascertain it :—

Source of Information.	Whitechapel.	St. George's (part)	Mile End Old Town (part)	Total.
Factory Inspectors	614	125	124	863
Other Sources	89	48	15	152
	703	173	139	1015

Coat and General shops.........................	901
Vests..	10
Juvenile Clothing	7
Trousers	97
	1015

Remainder of District.

Source of Information.	St. George's (part).	Mile End Old Town (part)	Stepney	Poplar	Bethnal Green.	Shoreditch.	Hackney.	Total.
Factory Inspectors	17	23	14	22	20	51	20	167
Other Sources	9	33	3	32	11	1	1	90
	26	55	17	54	31	52	21	257

Coat and General shops...................................	57
Vests	1
Juvenile Clothing	65
Trousers	61
	184
Unclassified (Shoreditch and Hackney)	73
Grand Total 1272	257

Classification according to Size.

	A 25 workers and upward.	B 10 to 25 workers.	C Under 10 workers.	Total.
Whitechapel Section :				
Coat and General	15	201	685	901
Vests, Trousers and Juvenile Clothing	6	35	73	114
	21	236	758	1015
Remainder of District :				
Coat and General shops	6	4	47	57
Vest, Trousers, and Juvenile Clothing	15	25	87	127
	21	29	134	184
Unclassified (Shoreditch and Hackney)				73
Grand Total...............1272				257

In addition to these shops, there are a large number of domestic workshops, occasionally employing outside labour and entirely escaping the notice of the factory inspector. This is particularly the case in the eastern portion of Mile End Old Town, and Stepney and Poplar, the districts in which the slop trouser and juvenile suit trades are principally located.

It will be seen that to arrive at our total of 1272 shops, we add 242 as to which information came to us from other sources than the factory inspector's books. It is probable that many of these 242 shops represent removals or change of name or the rapid springing up of new concerns. It is not possible for the factory inspectors to keep fully abreast of their work in so fast growing and shifting a trade. We believe our numbers to be somewhat swollen in this way.

On the other hand, it is probable that some of the smaller shops have escaped notice, especially in Bethnal-green, in which direction the trade is extending. We do not think any of the larger shops can have been omitted, and but few even of the smaller ones in the older districts. To test this we made a special inquiry as to seven selected streets, and the results show a rather smaller number than on our lists, especially in the Whitechapel district.—C. B.]

CHAPTER IV.

BOOTMAKING.

WITHIN the district dealt with in these pages (East London and Hackney) the large majority of the London boot-makers reside, and in many parts of it form a considerable fraction of the total population; as will be seen by the following figures, based upon the occupation returns of the last census (1881).*

| — | Total Population. | Not engaged in any oc-cupation (including children and other dependent persons). | Engaged in the Boot Trade.† | | | | | Engaged in other occupa-tions. | Percentage of occupied persons who are en-gaged in the boot trade. |
| | | | Males. | | Females. | | | | |
			Under 20.	Over 20.	Un-der 20.	Over 20.	Total.		
Tower Ham-lets‡.........	439,186	250,945	645	3,620	422	789	5,476	182,765	Per cent. 3
Shoreditch andBethnal Green	253,552	138,574	1,036	5,613	945	1672	9,266	105,712	8·77
Hackney	163,681	87,110	287	1,733	178	376	2,574	73,997	3·48
Total...	856,419	476,629	1,968	10,966	1545	2837	17,316	362,474	4·78

* These figures include manufacturers, factors, dealers, artisans of every description, warehousemen, packers, &c., vendors and makers of lasts, boot-trees, laces, tags, bows, tips, pegs, &c., repairers, and "translators" (who patch up for sale cast-off boots).

† The figures obtained by Mr. Booth point to an increase of about 2,000, or nearly 12 per cent., in the number of persons engaged in the boot-trade in our district at the present time, while the whole population is supposed to have increased by 52,000, or about 6 per cent., with the result that rather over 5 per cent. of the present employed population may be considered to gain their livelihood in this industry.

‡ Including Whitechapel, St. George's-in-the-East, Stepney, Mile End Old Town, and Poplar.

It will be convenient to treat first and separately of the hand-sewn trade, which is chiefly concerned with the production of "bespoke" goods—goods ordered by and specially designed to fit a customer. Suppose, then, that the reader has been measured by the shopkeeper or his manager. The next thing to be done (by the measurer or by a subordinate under his supervision) is to produce a copy in wood of the customer's foot—the last.* The boot is then built up by the workmen upon the last, much as a plaster cast is formed by a sculptor upon the features of his subject.

The construction of the boot is commenced by the "clicker," who makes in paper a pattern from which he proceeds to cut out the leather required for the upper— that is, all that part of the boot which is above the sole. The upper in most cases consists of several distinct parts, each of which has to be cut out very nearly in its final form, while great waste can easily be caused if the skin is not divided in such a manner as to yield the greatest possible number of these pieces. The clicker is therefore required to possess a high degree of skill.

The average earnings of an experienced clicker in City shops doing a bespoke trade are generally from 30s to 35s a week, his hours of employment seldom exceeding ten in the day (including meal-times), with the usual Saturday half-holiday.

The clicker having done his work, the different parts of the upper, together with the fitted last and with the pattern, or some other indication of the measurements, are given out to the workman whose duty it is to put these parts together—the "closer."

When the closer has brought back the top of the boot

* In former times the shopkeepers made their own lasts; but last-making is now a separate profession, and all that is done by the shopkeeper or his "last-fitter" is to take a last already modelled on normal lines and by careful alterations to make this accurately represent the idiosyncrasies of the customer's foot.

completed, this, together with the last and the necessary materials for the lower portion, is handed over to the "maker," who has to put on the sole and heel.

The description which has just been given will explain the number of different workmen required to make a boot under the orthodox system of boot-making. But, in the City, even more than in the West End of London, this system is fast dying out. There are now, even in the good-class bespoke trade, but few masters who get their tops cut out and closed in the primitive manner by men working in their homes.* More and more it is becoming the custom to make use of uppers made up in a factory carried on upon a wholesale scale.

If we watch the closer at work, we shall find that the preparation of the different parts for being sewn (called "fitting") is done to-day in much the same manner as fifty years ago. But the sewing, which was then done by hand by the closer himself, or, very often, by boys working for him, is now in most cases performed with the sewing-machine. The part of the boot-closer's profession which has suffered the smallest amount of disturbance from the novel instrument of production is that which is concerned with what is technically known as "long work," *i.e.*, riding boots and "Wellingtons." Still, even in the case of the long work closers (for this branch is for the most part in the hands of a special class of men), although some few dispense almost entirely with the aid of the machine, it is more common to find that only about one half of the closer's task has been performed by hand.

Probably the average long work closer in the City, employed by shopkeepers and working single-handed, may be taken to earn, one week with another, at least £1. 5*s* (nett).† There are, however, some closers who do

---

* The total number of the closers working in our district does not exceed 50.

† The manager of a shop in the City, which has an excellent reputation among the workpeople, assured me that their long work closer takes only 18*s*

long work for wholesale firms manufacturing uppers for the hand-sewn trade. These men get "stock" to make when the bespoke trade is slack, and in some cases, as I was informed by an employer and can well believe, receive an average of from £2 to £2 5s per week, from which totals we must, in calculating the nett remuneration of the men's labour, deduct from 2s 2d to 2s 5d for grindery* and repairs to machine, and—since a closer of this type seldom works without more or less assistance—a further sum in respect of the value of the work done by wife or daughter.

Turning now to the short work, we shall find that the average weekly earnings of a closer, working single-handed on good bespoke work, amount to about 33s (nett).† As to those who get their machines worked for them, the men paying regular wages to a machinist (a woman of this class generally receives from 18s to 21s a week) are, for the most part, men with a good "seat of

(gross) even in a good week. Another closer, employed principally upon long work, gave me very full details as to his work and earnings. I find from his work-books that during the past twelve months his average nett weekly gains, after he has paid for his "grindery"—this is the trade name for materials such as, in this case, thread, silk, bristles, &c., supplied by the workman—amount to £1 2s 10d. This man is a first-class craftsman, but is advanced in years, and, therefore, slower at his work than formerly. He has now no children dependent upon him, and works, say, an hour a day less than most long work closers. He is also too conservative to avail himself, except to the smallest extent, of the labour-saving machine.

* For the meaning of this term see the last note.

† That some of these closers make an income much above this amount is proved by the instance of a man who informed me that in 1887 (which was the worst year that he has ever had), he received a gross sum of £117, and that in the current twelve months (of 1888) he expected to take £140. This would give him in that year, after allowing for grindery and repairs to machine, a nett average of £2 10s 9d per week. On some few occasions this man has earned as much as 18s (nett) between 6 P.M. on one day and the same hour on the next; and in the same way another closer, also working single-handed, boasted to me that he had "in the Jubilee week of 1887" made £3 15s 8d nett. But it is quite exceptional for a man to get such a quantity of work in so short a time; nor could he long continue to work at such high pressure.

work," taking £3 gross per week, leaving the closer, after
he has paid the cost of his grindery, wages, and all other
expenses, a nett remuneration of 36s to 39s. More commonly the closer will be found to avail himself, from time
to time, of the assistance of some member of his family.
The position of a closer of this type may be illustrated by
the earnings of a man whose work-books I have analyzed.
His wife is a good machinist, and helps him when he has
work enough on hand to require her assistance. He
makes about £2 1s (nett) per week throughout the year.
Being specially quick, this man devotes rather less than
nine hours a day to labour; most closers, however, when
in full work (say for five months in the year) seldom work
less than eleven hours in the day.

Forty years ago—as I am informed by the secretary of
the City (Closers') Branch of the Amalgamated Society of
Boot and Shoemakers, himself an old man and the son of a
closer still living—men could not earn more than £1 a
week. When the sewing-machine was introduced, the
price paid per pair fell greatly; but the men found that
their output was much increased, and the earning power of
those who could obtain plenty of work was not injuriously
affected. Of late years many closers have left the trade;
no one is learning it. Those who remain admit that the
price paid for the work is well maintained, but say that it
is now difficult for closers living in our district to obtain
full employment.* For, although there are some closers
(doing long work) living in the West who are employed by
City firms, yet few, if any, West End shops give work to
closers living in the East. Unfortunately, the hand-sewn
trade in the City is in a languishing condition; and the
shopkeepers, in many cases, instead of employing closers
working at home in the manner which has been described,

---

* On the other hand the employers complain that on account of the
scarcity of closers they find great difficulty in getting their tops made with
anything like reasonable expedition, especially in the case of long work.

prefer to get their "tops" supplied by a wholesale manufacturer, and so avoid the expense of keeping a stock of leather.

So far we have been dealing mainly with the *bonâ fide* bespoke boot—that which is made throughout to the order of the customer. But a very large number of boots in our district are constructed with ready-made uppers, though these are joined to the sole, and the boot is completed by makers working upon the fitted last. The vast majority of these ready-made uppers for the hand-sewn trade are made, not in the homes of the workers, but in factories, mostly in Wellingboro', Northampton, and other places out of London. There are, however, several of these establishments in our district, and a few details in regard to one of the best-conducted of them may be of interest. In this factory, which has an extensive *clientèle* both in London and in the country, from one thousand to eleven hundred pairs of uppers are turned out every week, of which about one hundred and fifty will be "special orders," *i.e.*, made specially for the customer of the shopkeeper, who sends a ticket indicating the character of the leather to be used, the mode in which it is to be made up, and the necessary measurements, together, in some cases, with the fitted last; the other eight hundred and fifty or nine hundred and fifty are "stock." Long work is given out by this manufacturer to be made by men working in their own homes; the uppers of "short" boots are made in workrooms on his premises.

The earnings of the workpeople in this factory, their hours of employment, and the terms of apprenticeship, closely resemble those prevalent in the workshops of a manufacturer of goods of the better class in the machine-sewn trade, with which we shall deal later on, and need, therefore, no separate description. The manager of this closing factory, who, in addition to general supervision, also attends to the fitting of the "special orders," is not a foreman in receipt of time-wages, but undertakes with his employer to get the work done at a fixed sum per pair, his remuneration consisting in the difference between the aggregate price of the output and the total amount of the wages of the operatives employed in its production.

Turning from the conditions to the nature of the employment, in these workrooms we note the novel features which the wholesale scale of manufacture has introduced. Sub-division of labour is carried further than before. Here not only is the pattern-cutter a distinct man from the clicker, but, instead of the closer working alone or with a single machinist, we now find (*a*) fitters* who prepare the work for the machine, (*b*) machinists, (*c*) button-holers, and (*d*) table hands who sew on buttons, &c. And the workers of all four classes are female. Male labour is too costly a luxury to be employed by the manufacturer when he can get the work done well enough for his purposes by women willing to accept wages much lower than those demanded by men.

We will now suppose the shopkeeper to have his uppers ready; the next step is to give these out, together with the leather required for the construction of the soles and heels (the "bottom stuff"), to the maker. It is the duty of the maker to cut out the inner and the outer soles and the stiffenings, puffs, shanks, and other minor portions, to add all these to the upper, and to complete the structure by building the heel and giving the final touches known as "finishing."

The makers do their work either in their own homes or in what may be termed associated workshops—places where a rent of 1*s* per week is paid for a seat.† There are

* The full title of these operatives is "paste-fitters"; they are so called from the material used in putting together the surfaces, which are then sewn by the machine.

† These workshops—it will be understood—are not provided by the men's employers. The landlord who lets accommodation of this kind is generally

very few (I know of only one) such common workshops
in our district; but in the West they are numerous, and
are a great convenience to men living at a distance from
their shops, as is the case with some makers in our district
who work for West End employers.

Like the closers, the makers are paid by the piece,
and the amount of the men's earnings varies widely
according to the industry and dexterity shown by each,
there being a difference of quite 25 per cent. between the
maximum possible out-put of different men of the same age
and doing work of the same class. But an investigation
embracing a large number of instances shows that the main
factor in the financial position of these workmen is the
greater or lesser continuity of their employment. There
are men in our district who—as I know from the statements of both employers and employed—frequently earn
from £2 2s to £2 5s (nett) in a week, and who, if they work
with reasonable steadiness, can average from £1 16s to
£1 18s throughout the year.* These, however, are quick
workers, unusually fortunate in the regularity of their
employment. Most of the makers living in the district
get full work for five months or less in each year; and an

---

himself one of the makers working in the place. Neither closers nor
makers, as a rule, can be induced to work in a workshop provided by the
employers. The men like to work when they please and as they please,
without restrictions as to hours or otherwise. Those who work at home in
some cases do so for the sake of occasional assistance rendered by their wives.

* The men in question work for a City shop. As a rule, the complaints
as to irregularity of employment are greater among makers working for
City than those employed by West-End masters. By the work-book of a
steady man, working for a West-End shop, now before me, I find that he
made £1 18s 3d (nett) in his best week; but his weekly average for the
year is only £1 4s 3¼d. Another industrious maker (working for a different
master) is shown by the wage-sheets of his employer to have earned in one
exceptionally busy week £2 4s (nett), while his average through the year
is only £1 5s 3¾d. There are, however,—I have reason to believe—among
the men working for West-End shops a considerable number who average
more than this.

industrious man will have reason to think himself fairly fortunate if he averages £1 3s to £1 5s (nett) per week. Not a few take less than this. But some of those who earn an average smaller than £1 3s could, beyond question, increase their actual takings if they were less unsteady in their habits.

When in full employment, most makers work eleven or twelve (occasionally thirteen or fourteen) hours in the day, often snatching their meals without leaving the seat. Few work during these hours day after day without a break. And, indeed, the severe nature of this sedentary occupation makes occasional relaxation a necessity. In the busy season—I can say from my own knowledge— the time spent in actual labour is, in the case of many men, not less than seventy, and, I believe, in most cases about sixty hours in the week.

The industry of the hand-sewn makers has been very materially affected by the introduction of the sole-sewing machine. Not that the price paid per pair is lower now than in the old days. For years past very few youths have been put to this trade,* and many of its former devotees have gone into the machine-sewn trade. So that, although the demand for hand-sewn boots has fallen off in a marked degree, yet an important diminution in the supply of labour capable of producing this work has also taken place, and the strong Trade Union which exists among the makers has been able to put considerable pressure upon the masters. The price paid per pair is, in fact, higher to-day by more than fifty per cent. than in 1860 (in the pre-machine era), by far the greater part of this improvement having been gained within the last fifteen years.

It is, however, proper to observe that this increase in

* The hand-sewn makers appear to deliberately discourage the entry of youths into their trade, hoping in this way to keep down the supply of available labour, and so make it more easy to maintain the present level of wages. Compare Leno on *Boot and Shoe-making*, 2nd ed., p. 210.

price does not imply a general and proportionate augmentation of the men's weekly earnings. One maker says that his actual average to-day is £1 18s 9d per week (nett), while in 1860 he would have received only £1 1s 3d (nett) for the same amount of work. This is a man with an exceptionally good "seat of work." But in the majority of instances the increased difficulty of obtaining full and continuous employment has done much to counteract the increase in the wage-scale.* The causes of this difficulty among the hand-sewn makers of our district are not far to seek. The substitution of the peg or the rivet for the stitch has done much to drive the cheapest class of hand-sewn boots out of the market; and each year brings into existence some new variety of screwed, "combination" (*i.e.* partly screwed, partly sewn), or other travesty of the genuine hand-sewn article. More and more every day does the sole-sewing machine (first introduced into our district in the year 1866) take the place of the maker's awl. And while the demand for hand-sewn boots is everywhere diminishing the makers of our district are especially affected by the changed conditions of the trade. The cheaper class of bespoke goods, now sold in the London shops, are made, for the most part, out of London; nor is the case different with the ready-made hand-sewn boot of every grade. While in former years the London maker used to fill up the slack season in the " custom" trade by working on stock goods, the manufacture of ready-made hand-sewn boots—an article still much in demand for men's wear —has almost entirely abandoned our district, the chief

---

* This statement refers principally to men employed by City shopkeepers, and making high-class work at the rate of wage accepted by the trade union. The number of boots of this class sold in the City has for a long time been steadily decreasing. Some makers in our district working for City or suburban shops at less than the recognized piece-wage obtain full employment nearly all the year round. In the West-End a first-class maker can often still get employment as regular as thirty years ago; but he can, as pointed out in the text, no longer fill up his slack time with stock work.

sources of supply being the provincial seats of the boot industry. As for women's boots, the vast majority of purchasers are nowadays content with the machine-sewn boot, generally ready-made. But it is by no means an uncommon thing for a shopkeeper to send the order of his customer of either sex, even for bespoke goods, to be executed by the wholesale manufacturer with the aid of the sole-sewing machine.

It will be seen that the hand-sewn makers have to contend against a host of adverse influences; all the same, it appears to be certain that their average earnings exceed those received in 1860 by something like 20 per cent.

We have so far been considering what may be termed the normal organization of the hand-sewn industry in our district. The simplest form of the trade, that in which one man manufactures the boot throughout and sells it to the customer, is practically defunct in London. The nearest approach to this primitive type is made by a class of workmen scattered through the metropolis, who carry on business in their own homes upon a diminutive scale, acting as both producers and vendors. They buy their uppers from a warehouse (generally ready-made, but occasionally to order), and put the sole and upper together themselves. These men also take job-work (repairs). I have found it impossible to ascertain, even approximately, the average profits made by men of this class, who, of course, have no work-books to show, and who seldom, if ever, keep accounts. Next in order comes the ordinary shopkeeper, whose establishment we began by examining. With this trader, who, in most cases, takes but a small part in the actual labour of production, differentiation of function commences. The shopkeeper is a middleman between producer and consumer. Not infrequently, indeed, he is only one link in a chain of middlemen. In addition to the wholesale manufacturers who supply to the shopkeeper, not alone uppers, but also in many cases complete boots, there exists in relation to the hand-sewn trade a special class of sub-contractors, members of which may be found in different parts of our district. These are the " chamber-masters," men who seldom make stock, and whose business it is to carry out orders for bespoke work, which the retail vendor passes on to them for execution. A chamber-master of this type will probably act as his own clicker, his family assisting him in his work. He will get his uppers closed by machinists in his own house or by women who do the work (sometimes with the assistance of subordinate labour) in their homes. The completion of the boots is entrusted to makers, mostly inferior workmen, to whom they are given out at prices usually much lower than the piece-wage fixed by the trade union.*

When we pass from the hand-sewn to the other branches of the boot-making industry—branches mainly concerned with the production of ready-made goods—the organization of industry becomes in a marked degree more complex, both by the multiplication of middlemen and by the increased tendency to specialization of function in the worker. The purchasers of stock goods being less wealthy and less fastidious than the fortunate few who can afford to pay for an article specially designed to correspond with the idiosyncrasies of the customer's foot, cheapness is, in the ready-made trade, an indispensable element ; and, since the profit of the vendor, under whose supervision the work is done, upon the sale of each pair is, as a rule, much smaller in the case of ready-made than of "custom" boots, an increase in the scale of production becomes almost a necessity. The retailer of these ready-made goods has nothing to do with

---

* The description given relates only to chamber-masters in our district, most of whom are in a small way of business and make very meagre profits. In the West End there are some chamber-masters working on a larger scale, some of whom pay the highest rate of wages specified in the standard of the union.

their production, but is a mere middleman,* a distributor, whose wares, however conspicuously his name may be stamped upon them, are purchased from the wholesale manufacturer. What is more, the wholesale "manufacturer" himself is very often no more than a middleman. When a wholesale vendor finds that, for one reason or another, some other manufacturer can produce an article at a lower cost than himself, he "buys in" this article in order to re-sell it to the shopkeepers or other dealers whom he supplies.†

In addition to the "manufacturers" who themselves make a part, at any rate, of the goods which they sell, there exists a class known as "factors,"—men who do not own a manufactory, but buy up the produce of manufacturers, generally of the smaller manufacturers, and re-vend it. The factor is, of course, a middleman pure and simple.

To turn now from distribution to production, we shall find that in the industrial organization of the wholesale trade, the "saving" of labour occupies an all-important position. The "saving" of labour—that is to say, the reduction of the cost of labour by the utilization of labour to the greatest possible advantage—may be attained in several distinct modes. Thus it was discovered that a boot could be made up sufficiently well to satisfy a not too critical wearer if its component parts, instead of being sewn, were put together with wooden pegs or metal rivets. Now a man can knock in pegs or rivets much faster than he can sew stitches. Here we have the substitution of one operation for another. But a method of "saving labour" of

---

* In certain cases the middleman retailer is dispensed with; for some manufacturers sell part of the goods which they produce, or which they purchase from other manufacturers, in shops owned by themselves; but this is exceptional.

† This practice of buying in will be further alluded to when we come to deal with the question of the wage-scale established by the trade unions, which makes it practically impossible for certain firms to produce the inferior grades of boots.

much greater importance is the substitution in relation to operations practically identical of a better for a worse instrument of production, the simpler instruments being called tools, while the more complex are, in many cases, referred to as machines.* We have seen how, even in the bespoke trade, the sewing-machine has to a very great extent supplanted the closer's awl; in the ready-made trade we shall find that machinery plays a part still more remarkable.

Another and a potent method of utilizing labour to the greatest possible advantage remains to be considered. This is known as the division of labour. Subdivision of labour affects production in two distinct directions, qualitative and quantitative. By allotting to each of several workmen a single part of a task, that task may be done better than if one man did the whole. " Jack of all " parts of a trade is often " master of none."† And thus, in regard to hand-sewn boots, as we have seen, the " all-round " workman, who can " box the trade," is, and has long been, replaced by the united forces of workmen of four, or (if we omit the comparatively unimportant operative by whom the bottom stuff, for the soles and heels, is cut out, and reckon only the clicker, the closer, and the maker) of three distict types. It is, however, rather as increasing the quantity than as improving the quality of the output that division of labour is adopted in the wholesale trade. A worker whose whole life is spent in performing one particular class of operations will attain a rapidity of performance rarely to be met with

* In numerous industries, of course, labour is further saved by the substitution of gas or steam for human energy as the motive power of the instruments of production. But in the boot trade of East London and Hackney very little use is made of either gas or steam in driving machinery.

† Specialization of function is incidental to all skilled industry. Thus we find closers who devote themselves exclusively to the making of uppers for men's or for women's boots, as the case may be ; and makers who, if " men's men," can only make a lady's boot with difficulty and cannot make a lady's slipper at all ; and *vice versâ*.

in the man whose work embraces a wider range.* Even in the bespoke hand-sewn trade we have observed that in the production of the upper the old-fashioned closer is being driven from the field by the subdivided industry of fitters, machinists, button-holers, and table hands; while in the construction of a complete machine-sewn boot we may find, each engaged upon a distinct operation or small group of operations, as many as twenty different workers.

The visitor whom the courtesy of an employer allows to examine the details of labour organization in a boot manufactory will count in the clicking-room perhaps ten men and youths at work. The principal of these cuts out in cardboard or zinc the patterns for the different parts (some fourteen in number) of the upper, which are then cut out by clickers working from these patterns, and taken to the machine-room.† Here from twenty to thirty girls and women are employed under the supervision of a foreman. Most of these are fitters, machinists, or table hands; possibly there will be one or more whose special vocation it is to work button-holes by hand or with a button-holing machine, or an "eyeletter," whose duty consists in inserting metal eyelets by means of a simple machine into holes made by a punch. Bows and buckles are put on at a later stage by another class, the "trimmers." Young untaught "room-girls" are employed to carry the work about and do odd jobs.

Our upper is now complete, and we must look after our bottom stuff. At one end of a room we shall see a man cutting out the outer soles by means of a sole-cutting press;

---

* In fact the ideal workman—from the point of view of rapidity of performance—is one who never has to pause to think what he is going to do, but works on with the steady speed of a well-regulated machine. The nearest approach to this type of perfection is, of course, made by a man who day after day performs the same fraction of the total processes necessary to the production of the complete article.

† The sewing-machines used in making uppers can be driven by steam. But the application of motive power to these machines is very uncommon indeed in our district.

a second may be similarly cutting out the inner soles; next
to him stands a third " rough-stuff-cutter," turning out from
yet another press the pieces required for the heel; while a
couple of boys, each working a separate machine, produce
the minor portions necessary to the completion of the base
of the boot. These several fragments and the upper to
which they correspond are collected by the fitter-up (there
will probably be two of these men) and given to the laster.
In the lasters' workshop some twenty or five-and-twenty
workmen are engaged under the supervision of a special
foreman upon what among themselves they call " the tap-
ping." The upper is drawn over an iron last, and the inner
and outer soles are joined to the upper and to each other by
nails; after which the soles are further fastened together
by the sole-sewing machine. This is generally worked by
a treadle moved by the foot of the operator, but in some
instances by a gas engine.

We shall already have observed that the laster, before
adding the outer sole, took it over to a boy, who placed it
between the grooved surfaces of a " channelling" machine,
and, after turning a handle, handed back the sole scarred by
a deep furrow, destined, we now remark, to receive the
stitches of the machine. At a subsequent stage the edges
of this furrow are pressed together so as to close over
and conceal the stitches. In some instances the " channels"
are " put down" by a boy, who commences his industrial
career as a specialist in this work.

We must not forget our heel. This is generally added
by the laster. But boots of the inferior descriptions now
often have their heels built, attached, pared, and breasted by
machines invented to perform these distinct processes, and
demanding special operatives. The boot is now completed in
the rough. " Finishing"—that is, trimming into their
proper shape the sole and heel, colouring these black, yellow,
or white, and adding the final polish—is, in this wholesale
trade, in the hands of a separate class of workmen, who

(with very rare exceptions) are employed, not upon the premises of the manufacturer, but out-doors. When the finisher has brought back the boot, it is placed in the drying-room, where efficient ventilation, superintended by a careful attendant, soon gets rid of a certain amount of moisture imbibed during manufacture. Nothing now remains except a final brush-up; when this has been deftly given by the young women of the cleaning-up department the boots are deposited in the neat cardboard boxes in which they are forwarded to their ultimate destination.

The hours of employment in most boot factories are from 8 A.M. to 7 P.M., with an hour allowed for dinner and half an hour for tea; on Saturdays from 8 A.M. to 2 P.M., with a short interval for lunch. Overtime is occasionally worked, and, in most cases of time-wage, is paid for at about the same rate as ordinary work. The men employed on piece-wage not infrequently take less than the normal time for meals.

Our inspection has made us acquainted with the different classes of workers engaged in the construction of a machine-sewn boot. But it must be clearly understood that what we have seen is typical of but a small percentage of the boot factories to be found in the metropolis. Most of the London manufacturers, instead of getting all the work (except the finishing) done in their own manufactories, give much of it to out-workers. The work of the clickers and that of the rough-stuff cutters is always done on the premises; the closing of the uppers is, in the large majority of cases, performed by outside workers; the lasters, in very many instances, work out-doors; the sole-sewing machine is also very frequently dispensed with, that part of the work being also given out. Even where the output is of considerable dimensions, the factory itself may be so minute that a few rooms in an ordinary dwelling-house suffice to accommodate staff, plant, and stock. As we descend the scale we rapidly leave behind the giants of the trade—men who turn out ten thousand and more pairs in a week*—and find ourselves among manufacturers of Lilliputian proportions,† whose weekly output is limited to a few gross, and whose tiny workrooms contain little more than a sole-cutting press and a table for the clicker; until at last we reach the lowest level of all, the owner of a couple of rooms in a tenement house‡, who buys his leather, cuts his uppers, gets his wife or daughter to close them, and lasts and finishes the boots himself, selling a gross or a gross and a half at a time to a large "manufacturer" or to a "factor."

This explanation having been made, the reader is invited to examine the financial position of the principal among the different classes of workers. A good pattern-cutter gets 60s per week; a first-class clicker earns from 42s to 38s; less experienced men 37s, 36s, 34s, down to 28s; young hands 25s to 14s. Apprentices (seldom regularly bound)§

* For many reasons the practice of giving work to out-workers tends to produce industrial conditions less advantageous to the workers than those which prevail when the work is carried on in large factories. But there is something to be said in favour of a method which enables the working-man who has saved a few pounds to start as a manufacturer, and, if he has the necessary business ability, to rise step by step. I borrow this remark from a gentleman who commenced operations as a manufacturer with a capital of £12, put by out of his wages as a workman, and who now turns out his eight hundred pairs weekly. A not inconsiderable number of the manufacturers in our district have in a similar manner risen from the ranks of the employees or are the sons of men who rose in this way.

† These very small manufacturers correspond to the chamber-masters in the hand-sewn trade. In the branches with which we are now dealing the term "chamber-master" is chiefly applied to those who work with the assistance principally of members of their own family.

‡ Much of the work done by these small men is rivetted work, generally for children's wear; some of it is "needle-and-thread" work (for infants' use).

§ When serving under indentures, clicker apprentices, for whom a premium of £10 has been paid, usually get 4s to 5s a week in their first year, rising to 12s—15s at the end of three, or 15s to 17s 6d at the end of four years; exclusive of bonus.

serve for five (sometimes for four) years, generally beginning at from 3s to 5s a week, with a rise of about 1s every
six months. In addition, a bonus of about 2s 6d a week is
often given to industrious pupils. The earnings of clickers
are reduced, if full work cannot be found for them,
but increased if overtime is worked. On the whole a
thoroughly competent clicker is not much affected by
irregularity of employment. Less experienced men, however, are taken on as extra hands in the busiest season
(say from the middle of February to the middle of July)
and discharged at its close.

In the machine-room the foreman or forewoman is an
important person and well-paid. A first-class foreman
will get 50s a week. Among the hands in this room, who
are all female, first-class machinists or fitters earn from 18s
to (exceptionally) 22s; less experienced hands generally
get 14s to 16s a week. Apprentices or learners serve for
three years, giving their time for three months, and then
rising gradually to 7s or 7s 6d. Button-holers can make
from 16s to 18s.* The earnings of table hands vary
greatly: some are experienced workers, who take 10s to
12s, 12s 6d, or even 14s; many are young girls receiving
from 6s upwards, according to ability. Eyeletting is done
by young hands getting 6s to 9s. Trimmers may earn 12s
to 14s on good work, but on common goods less competent
and experienced girls will receive 5s to 10s. Room-girls
get 2s 6d to 3s 6d. These figures represent the normal
wages of the hands, wages increased when overtime is
worked and diminished when work is slack. Their actual
average weekly earnings (ascertained from inspection of
pay-sheets and the statements of employees) are never
much more than 90 per cent. of the normal wage, of which,
in some factories, as the hands assert, not more than 85 or

---

* Button-holers are paid in some cases by week-wage, in others by piece.
Button-holes worked by hand seem to be generally paid for by piece-wage.

80 per cent. can be earned, one week with another, through the year.

While the better class of uppers is generally manufactured upon the premises of the manufacturers, the commoner work, by far the larger part of the whole output of the trade, is given out to persons (generally women) who do the work in their homes,* in some instances single-handed, but in most cases with the assistance of subordinate employees, varying from one or two to twenty in number. Establishments on this larger scale are, however, rare; staffs of five or less are much more numerous. The women employed by these sub-contractors being, as a rule, far less skilled than those who work in the machine-rooms of the manufacturers, their wages are on a lower scale. A machinist or fitter† of this type, may, if thoroughly efficient, take 15s to 18s, but as a rule receives from 12s to 14s a week; girls just beginning to know their business will get 9s, 10s, 10s 6d, while novices, mostly unable to do more than machine linings, will take 5s to 8s a week. Hands of "general utility" (frequently combining the functions of table-hand, room-girl, and porteress), earn from 4s 6d to 8s. The regular working-day in these work-rooms is longer as a rule by half an hour, in some cases by about one hour, than in the factories.‡ Overtime (say one

---

* Parts of the work are occasionally given out again by these sub-contractors. Thus they sometimes get the eyelets inserted by a woman owning a machine for that purpose. The paste-fitting is in some cases given out to a woman who works in her own home. When the uppers are ornamented with an elaborate pattern, the sub-contractor may get this put on by a "flowerer" who does this part of the machining at home. The making of the button-holes is also sometimes given out in this manner.

† Among these out-door hands machinists seem to be usually paid by time; fitters are sometimes paid by the piece.

‡ That longer hours are not worked in these work-rooms does not appear to be the direct result of the operation of the Factory Acts. For there are hundreds of these places into which the Factory Inspector has never set his foot and of whose existence that official is probably unaware. Still, the

or one and a half hours) is occasionally worked, and seems
to be generally paid for; on the other hand, their normal
earnings are much diminished by slack time, the irregularity of employment among these out-door upper-makers
being very great indeed. The standard of wages current
among the operatives has fallen about 6 per cent. in the last
few years; but the profits of the sub-contractors by whom
they are employed seem to have suffered to a far greater
extent. Many of these sub-contractors are married women
or widows with household duties to attend to as well as
their work; and these appear to earn but little more than
their own machinist or fitter. It is a saying among these
subordinate employers that 2*s* 6*d* per week ought to be
gained upon the labour of each machinist or fitter; and, if
an employer of this class devotes her whole time to the
work and can get enough to do to keep her hands employed with some little regularity, this calculation is—I
believe—fairly correct. But, now that it is so easy to hire
a machine, the number of these contractors is continually
being augmented. The competition among them is keen;
the prices paid to them are constantly falling; and every
year the amount of slack time tends to increase.

To give an idea of the profits made in a fairly busy
week, I have, after making careful inquiries, framed two
typical balance-sheets, based upon the actual receipts and
expenditure of two of these small contractors. A. is the
wife of a hand-sewn maker who does not live on very
good terms with her, and does not give her enough money
to keep up the family establishment. She was the widow
of a sea-captain and has two children, a girl of 15 years
and a boy of 12 years. She only took up the trade after

regulation of labour in the large factories has had a beneficial effect by
setting up a standard to which the " out-door" workers conform from a
natural dislike to work much longer hours than their more fortunate friends
employed " in-doors."

her second marriage. She has three machines, of which
she herself works one. Her profit and loss account for a
week in last May is as follows :

Gross Receipts   ...   ...   £2. 15s 5½d.

		£	s.	d.	£	s.	d.
Expenses.—Wages :	1 fitter	0	13	0			
	1 machinist (improver) ...	0	9	0			
	1 machinist (daughter, only } able to machine linings) }	0	6	0			
	1 shop-girl (table-hand } and room girl) ... }	0	8	0			
					1	16	0
	Grindery and repairs to machines ...				0	9	0
	Rent (say)				0	3	0
	Light				0	0	4
	Railway fares of shop-girl taking } work to warehouse ... ... }				0	0	6
					£2	8	10

		£	s.	d.
Gross Receipts	2	15	5½
Expenses	2	8	10
Nett Earnings	£0	6	7½

Thus this woman's nett profit, which includes the remuneration of her own labour and interest on her capital (three
machines bought for cash for £18) is 6s 7½d for the week.

B. is a single woman, a brisk, business-like person of
some 22 years, who understands her trade thoroughly.
She has three machines purchased on the hire system (two
are paid for already at £8 each, the third is being paid for
at 2s 6d per week). But she has, at present, only work
enough to keep two machines going. B. is employed by
the same firm as A.; but has a second string to her bow;
the prices received by her from both employers are similar
to those which I found in the work-books of A. Taking her
receipts and expenditure for the same week, we find
this :

				£ s. d.	£ s. d.
Gross Receipts	...	...	£3 3 0		
Expenses.—Wages : Machinist	...	...	...	0 14 0	
Fitter (sister)		...	...	0 13 0	
Shop-girl (can do no part of the work except the inking)	...	...		0 4 6	
					1 11 6
Grindery and repairs to machines			...		0 9 9
Rent (say)	...	...	...	...	0 2 9
Light	...	...	...	...	0 0 2
Omnibus fares of shop-girl		...	...		0 0 6
					£2 4 8

			£ s. d.
Gross Receipts	...	...	3 3 0
Expenses	...	...	2 4 8
Nett Earnings	...		£0 18 4

B. therefore gets, over and above the value of her own work, something like 5s as her contractor's profit (out of which she has to pay 2s 6d to the sewing-machine company) ; and I think that these figures may be taken to show the earnings of a competent woman, managing one of these small upper-making businesses, during the busy part of the year. But the irregularity of employment in this department (as I have ascertained both by the statements made to me by some scores of these small mistresses, and from figures which I have examined both in the work-books of the employed and in the pay-sheets of the employer) is so great that their takings on the average, one week with another through the year, are generally less than one-half of what they receive in a busy week; while in slack and busy seasons alike the rent of the work-room has to be paid, and the claims of the sewing-machine company for the hire of machines satisfied.* However, notwithstanding

* Here are some figure from the pay-sheets of a manufacturer as to the takings of his out-door machinists. It should be observed that it is impossible to say whether or not these women work for this employer alone,

the severe competition, a few of the larger contractors still
earn considerable profits.

The houses in which these upper-makers carry on their
trade are, as a rule, ordinary dwelling-houses (not erected
with a view to being used for manufacturing purposes)
scattered through Bethnal-green, Hoxton, Hackney, and
other parts of our district. Some of these work-people are
going to Clapton, Homerton, and other localities on the north-
eastern and northern fringe of the boot-making quarters, but
find it a far cry to the warehouse. The houses get larger and
more pleasant to the eye as you get away from the centre.
The sanitary condition of the abodes of these upper-makers
is neither better nor worse than that of other dwellings
in the same locality; but their workrooms are not, of
course, large enough to provide the same amount of air-
space per worker as exists in those of most wholesale firms.

and the figures are stated to show, not the total receipts from all sources,
but the degree of irregularity of employment :—

Machinists (sub-contractors).	Number of weeks in the year in which work was taken out.	Maximum weekly takings.			Average weekly takings for 52 weeks.			Average weekly takings for weeks in which work was taken out			Remarks.
		£	s.	d.	£	s.	d.	£	s.	d.	
A	51	2	13	6½	1	8	8	1	9	7	
B	49	4	11	4	1	15	2	1	17	4	This is a sub-contractor working on a relatively large scale and employed by 3 or 4 manufacturers.
C	47	1	19	6½	0	16	4	0	18	1	
D	45	2	7	9½	0	19	3½	1	2	3½	
E	45	1	9	3	0	11	2	0	12	11	Gets a low class of work.
F	23	2	0	9	0	8	8½	0	19	8	

But, with some exceptions in the lowest department of the
fancy shoe and slipper trade (which is dealt with separately
later on), the standard of comfort among these out-door
upper-makers is by no means low.

Passing to the rough-stuff department, we find that a
good fitter-up takes 30*s* to 35*s* a week; the presses are
worked by hands who, if very competent, receive as much
as 24*s* or 25*s*, but who more generally take from 20*s* to
22*s*, while youths and boys get from 17*s* to 18*s*, down to
5*s* 6*d*, according to ability.* In the laster's workshop the
foreman will probably get a weekly wage of about 40*s*
(I came across one large workshop in which the foreman was
paid by results, agreeing with his principals to get the
boots lasted at a fixed price, and taking as his remuneration the difference between that price and the actual cost
of the labour employed),† and a few other lasters may also
be found doing bespoke work at from 35*s* to 40*s* a-week.
But, with insignificant exceptions, piece-work is the rule.
A slow worker will often turn out only three pairs, while
in the same time his neighbour will have produced four.
But, here again, the factor which exercises the greatest
influence upon the amount of a man's income is the greater
or less regularity of his employment. As a rule, lasters
may be taken to get full work for only five or six months
in the year. In one representative manufactory I find,
by referring to the pay-sheets of the employer and the
wage-books of the men, and by taking an average of the
wages of six men, that a laster, if steady at his work, can

---

* The principal hands in the rough-stuff cutting department are required
to possess a considerable degree of judgment, without the exercise of which
their work cannot be properly done. It seems agreed on all hands that the
remuneration received by rough-stuff cutters is somewhat unduly low.

† It is proper to remark that this form of sub-contract does not appear to
exercise an injurious effect upon the earnings of the workpeople, which in
this instance are very high (I saw the men's work-books). In the parallel
case of the upper factory above mentioned, the wages paid to the hands
working under the sub-contracting foreman were also good.

earn in his busiest week £1 18s 3½d, but, taking one week with another for a year, only averages £1 5s 8¼d per week. In another factory the figures (average of earnings of six men) are, maximum weekly wage £2 2s average for year £1 9s 10¾d. Among the men working for a third firm one man takes £1 18s 11d in his best week, but only averages £1 5s 0½d through the year; another laster can earn as much as £1 18s 6d, but does not actually average more than £1 3s 5½d. (These figures are given nett, i.e. after deducting cost of grindery—nails and other materials supplied by the workmen.)*

It is necessary to point out most distinctly that the figures here submitted represent the *minimum* and not the average extent of the irregularity of employment among lasters and finishers in our district. The men whose earnings we have examined are indeed fair samples; but the circumstances of their industrial position are superior to those of very many among their compeers. Our statistics are, of necessity, confined to the cases of men who had worked for their employer throughout the whole year. These are the permanent staff, the picked *noyau*. When the busy season is over the manufacturer will probably be unable to find employment for a large fraction (perhaps one-third) of his lasters, and these unlucky workmen will have to pick up what work they can, where they can. While, therefore, the figures given prove that competent workmen on the regular staff of a factory can average about £1. 7s† a week, this amount must be taken to be materially in excess of the actual average earnings of the whole of the London lasters. It is, unfortunately, true that

* The details upon which these figures are based may be of interest and are given on the next page ; the earnings stated are nett.

† It will be observed that these figures are calculated on the basis of the number of weeks actually worked. In the factories in question, as in many others, work is suspended during one or two weeks in the year ; so that the actual average weekly income, even of men on the permanent staff, is somewhat lower than their earnings in their average working week.

Employer.	Remarks on Employer.	Laster.	Number of weeks in the year in which the man worked.	Total earnings for one year.			Maximum weekly earnings.			Average weekly earnings for weeks in which the man worked.			Remarks on Laster.
				£	s.	d.	£	s.	d.	£	s.	d.	
X	Pays wages according to agreement with trade union at nearly the highest rate of piece-wage. Does a good class of work.	A	51	62	10	5½	1	13	6½	1	4	6¼	Generally steady at his work; a good worker; on women's boots; middle-class all-round work.
		B	51	80	10	9½	2	4	7	1	11	7	Always steady, but takes a day's holiday in the country occasionally.
		C	51	61	5	2½	1	11	5½	1	4	0¼	Always at work: a good craftsman, but slow.
		D	51	65	5	10	1	14	10	1	5	7¼	Very steady; on girls' boots of good quality.
		E	50	52	11	2	2	1	6½	1	1	0¼	Very steady; on girls' boots of middle-class quality.
		F	49	67	4	0½	2	3	8	1	7	5	Generally steady; on women's boots of middle-class quality, all-round work.
Y	Has no agreement with trade union, but pays what wages he thinks fit. Does medium to common work.	G	50	74	7	5¾	1	17	4	1	9	9	
		H	50	74	0	4¾	2	13	0	1	9	7¼	
		J	50	73	0	2½	2	2	10½	1	9	2½	
		K	50	65	10	9½	1	13	4¾	1	6	2½	
		L	50	81	3	1	2	3	8	1	12	5½	
		M	49	79	13	3	2	1	10½	1	12	6	Steady, but works rather short hours; lost one week through illness.
Z	Ditto.	N	50	58	12	11	1	18	6	1	3	5½	Very steady.
	Two only of the lasters employed by this manufacturer are taken as examples in this table; because most of his lasters employ a certain amount of assistance. These men, however, work single-handed.	O	43	53	16	9½	1	18	11	1	5	0½	Very steady; has been a soldier, and has a pension.
	Average of 14 men......			67	16	7¼	1	19	11¼	1	7	3¾	

some hundreds of these lasters—men often of considerable skill in their craft—can for many, and those the bitterest, months of the year obtain little or no employment, and frequently suffer great privations.*

To revert, however, to our figures, it must be noted that these refer to the earnings of men working single-handed. Many of the out-door lasters, especially of those engaged on common work, increase their income by employing subordinate labour. The English lasters seldom have more than one assistant, often the man's own son, and hardly ever an adult.† The learners employed under this method of working are not regularly bound as apprentices, no such thing as apprenticeship existing among lasters.‡ Where

---

* The irregularity of employment in the London boot trade is to a great extent accounted for by the fact that the London artisan, though unexcelled in making light boots for women's wear, cannot compete with the provincial workmen in heavy goods, whether men's boots or those fitted for out-door use in winter by women. It must be borne in mind that a manufacturer, as a rule, only begins to manufacture when he has received an order, and manufactures only the quantity ordered. If it were possible to anticipate the demands of the busy season by making up " stock " goods in the slack, the work could, of course, be spread more equally over the year. Several reasons have been given to me by manufacturers showing why this course cannot be adopted. (1) Stock deteriorates by being kept; (2) fashions change so rapidly that it would not be safe to reckon on being able to sell to advantage goods made up some time before sale ; (3) a manufacturer who makes stock is, of course, unable to know beforehand what price he will get for his goods, and could guard against possible loss only by paying for their production somewhat lower wages than he pays in the busy season on boots, his profit on which he knows beforehand ; but the payment of lower wages at one time in the year than are paid at another would meet with resistance on the part of the operatives, who would fear that the lower prices of the slack season would not be raised when the busy time came round.

† In London few English boys are put to the work of lasting ; the ranks of the lasters are for the most part recruited by men who migrate to the metropolis from the provincial seats of the boot-making industry.

‡ I find from an old work-book (1886-87) that an out-door laster and his son (of fifteen) made an average of £1 8s 6d per week for twelve months ; while the pay-sheets of one manufacturer prove a specially steady man working with his son (of eighteen) and assisted by his wife to have averaged £2 3s 9d ; a third laster, who employs a boy during the greater part

these inferior workers are employed, a special subdivision of the work is necessitated. Thus the laster himself will put on all the bottom stuff except the heel; to build and pare the heel and to open the channel is the unskilled balance of the task which can be entrusted to the tyro. These boys and youths, who, when they know enough to be of service, get from 5s to 10s a week, work about the same hours as their masters, as a rule about ten in the day, usually knocking off work at tea-time on Saturday.* While the out-door lasters who work single-handed will frequently be found working in associated workshops, where their stand costs them from 6d to 1s a week, those who employ boys usually work in their own homes.

The employment by lasters of subordinate labour (except in the case of father and son working together) is strongly discouraged by the trade unions; but the system under which adults are thus employed is doubly obnoxious. In the first place it is a "team system," a novel subdivision of labour introduced with the special object of lowering the technical qualifications necessary in the worker, and so bringing into the trade unskilled labour. The supply of available labour being thus increased almost indefinitely, the endeavours of the skilled craftsman to maintain the present level of wages are hampered, if not frustrated. The key-note of the team system is that a series of operations, formerly entrusted collectively to a single artisan, is split up in such a manner that one part of the work—that which requires the greatest degree of skill—is performed by a workman who, possessing a relatively high degree of ability, is fairly able to insist upon an adequate remuneration, while the remainder of the work is placed in the

of the year (when engaged on very common work), is shown by the books of another manufacturer to take an average of £2 1s 5d. These earnings are stated clear of grindery.

* Some of the lasters who work in their own houses appear to work longer hours than those stated in the text; but the practice of working for more than the normal hours is condemned by the public opinion of the men in the trade.

hands of men whose greatly inferior competence in their craft forces them to accept a much lower rate of wage. The head laster rounds the insole and gets it and the upper into their correct position on the last. When he has done this, he "drafts" the boot by putting in the first nails at the toe, collects and prepares the various pieces required for its completion, and hands over the remainder of the task to be performed by his subordinates, who, provided that their superior has done his part properly, can with but a small amount of skill successfully accomplish the laborious, but incomparably less difficult, balance of the work, all the more so as this balance is, in many cases, parcelled out among them, each performing only a fraction of the task.

Then, again, the adverse tendency of the team system, regarded as an instrument for lowering wages, is further emphasized by the fact that, with few exceptions, the men working under it are of foreign race—men possessing in an exceptional degree the qualities of industry, perseverance, frugality, and temperance, capable of working, and willing to work, from fifteen to seventeen, or even eighteen hours in the day at a rate of pay which to English eyes appears altogether inadequate, and contriving to get a living even out of the most meagre and precarious earnings.

The competition of the Hebrew operatives cannot, indeed, be said to have diminished the earning power of the majority among the English lasters (all the best men among whom obtained in 1872-75 a substantial increase in their piece-wage which they have since maintained). But the introduction of the team system has, without doubt, exercised an influence anything but beneficial upon the position of the English lasters employed on common goods, and has also, by enabling cheap boots* to take the

* The uppers of many of these common house-boots are of German manufacture, but, as I am informed, very often of English material made up abroad.

place to a great extent of the low-class shoes and slippers formerly sold for house wear, seriously affected the hands engaged in producing this grade of "sew-rounds"*—hands, for the most part, also belonging to the same foreign race.

This "team" work is carried on under what is known in the trade as the "sweating system." The "sweating master" is a fairly skilful laster, who takes out work from the warehouse and gets it done in his own house with the assistance of other less skilled men employed by him. These men receive, in some cases, weekly wages (reduced in slack time), in others a proportion of the price paid by the warehouse. The master in addition to "fitting up" the work for his men in the manner described, fetches it from the warehouse and returns it (these journeys involving much loss of time and often the hire of a barrow), and pays for grindery, gas, and rent of workshop. In a busy week a comparatively competent "sweatee" may earn from 18s to 25s; less skilful hands may get 15s or 16s; but boys and newly-arrived foreigners take 10s, 8s, 7s, or less, while the masters, after paying all expenses, would, according to their own estimates, make not less than 30s, and must in many cases net much higher sums. Owing, however, to the irregularity of their employment, the average weekly earnings of both masters and men through the year fall very greatly below the amount which they can earn when in full work.†

Glancing now at the process which immediately follows the lasting, we find that the sole-sewing machine demands in the operator the possession of considerable skill, and (except when motive power is supplied) of great strength. A first-class sole-sewer is by no means easy to get, and will command as much as 43s or 42s 6d, less skilled operators receiving from 36s to 28s a week.

* The sew-round trade is described in detail later on, p. 112 *et seq.*

† I append two estimates for a workshop on the team system in full work. The first is that of an out-door laster working with one man and one

The earnings of the sole-sewers are in most cases affected
by the slack time, though I have known a man to be so
valuable that his employer was glad to give him his 42s 6d a
week through both slack and busy seasons. But, as a rule,
a sole-sewer must expect to be put upon three-quarter wages
when trade is dull; or, if, as is frequently the case, he receive
a fixed *minimum* wage with an extra sum in respect of all
boots over a stated number sewn in the week, the operator
will lose this bonus in the slack season. This latter method
of payment is often adopted by the owners of out-door sole-
sewing machines. For, when a manufacturer does not
possess a sole-sewing machine, he gets this part of the work
done by " sole-sewers to the trade," who own machines
conveniently scattered through the regions where the outdoor lasters most do congregate. Some of these machines
belong to men in a large way of business, often also carrying on the trade of dealer in leather and grindery, others
are the property of small men, each of whom works his own
machine; and an owner of this class finds his earnings
seriously diminished by the stagnation of the slack season.
The price paid per pair for sewing has fallen to a marked extent

boy, and is, I believe, fairly accurate, being based upon the statements of all
three workers :

							£	s.	d.
Week's out-put.—9 dozen at 4s ...	...	...	...	...			1	16	0
9 „ 3s 9d	...	...	...	...			1	13	9
Gross receipts...		...	...	...	...		£3	9	9

		£	s.	d.		£	s.	d.
Expenses.—Wages of man ...	...	1	5	10½				
„ boy ...	...		6	0		£	s.	d.
						1	11	10½
					Grindery ...		6	0
					Rent.. ...		1	6

		£	s.	d.			
Gross receipts	...	3	9	9		£1 19	4½
Expenses ...	...	1	19	4½			

Nett earnings of master... £1 10 4½

My second estimate is based upon information supplied to me by a sweating master in the presence of his staff of three men and two boys, all of

of late years; on the other hand, the cost of the machines is less than when they were first introduced, and few of them are now subject to the royalty upon each boot sewn which was formerly paid to the patentee. The machine in general use costs some £62, and it will be understood how great a convenience it is to a small manufacturer to save, not alone the cost of a machine which his own work could not keep fully employed, but also the wages of the operator, and the space required for the sole-sewing machine with its attendant channel-making machine by giving out his sewing to a sole-sewer to the trade.*

whom acquiesced in its accuracy. I am not inclined to place implicit confidence in these figures, but think them approximately correct:

		£	s.	d.
Week's out-put.—12 dozen at 4s 6d		2	14	0
,, ,, 4s		2	8	0
,, ,, 3s		1	16	0
		£6	18	0

	£	s.	d.	£	s.	d.
Expenses.--Wages of 3 men... ...	3	6	0			
,, 2 boys... ...		15	0	4	1	0
Grindery					12	0
Hire of barrow for porterage					1	2
Rent					3	6
				£4	17	8

	£	s.	d.
Gross receipts ...	6	18	0
Expenses	4	17	8

Nett earnings of master... £2 0 4

It will be observed that nothing is in either case put down for firing or for light; for my visits to these workshops were paid in the height of summer; nor have I reckoned interest on capital; the sweating master finds all plant and tools required. In both the cases cited the adult sweatees are paid by the piece. No. 1 gives his man the price which he himself gets from the warehouse less 1s per dozen in all cases; No. 2 deducts as follows; from 4s 6d — 1s 6d; from 4s — 1s 3d; from 3s 6d—1s; as far as I am able to ascertain, this appears to be the scale most generally in force. The boys in both workshops are paid by the week.

* I am informed that sole-sewing establishments of a similar nature are to found scattered through the boot-making villages round Leicester and Northampton, villages in which boots are lasted and finished by men working in their homes.

Coming now to the finishers, we shall find that the introduction of the team system has transferred into the hands of the foreign workmen the greater portion of the work in this branch of the trade. The Englishmen now engaged in it are, for the most part, the *élite* of their craft, finishers employed upon goods of a fairly high-class, and receiving, as a rule, the full rate of wages fixed by the trade unions in 1872-75. A man of this type works at home, frequently assisted by a boy (for the employment of a boy is, in the case of a finisher, not discouraged by the unions), and sometimes by his wife, or pays rent to a chum for a seat in his room. With regard to the earnings of these finishers I have not found it possible to obtain from the pay-sheets of their employers information sufficiently exact to justify the statement of precise figures. For in each case it is necessary to know, and not always possible to discover, what money, if any, the finisher has paid out of his gross takings in respect of assistance.* On the other hand, a finisher is often employed by more than one firm, so that, in order to arrive at the total earnings of a number of men of this class, with a view to stating a fair average, an amount of investigation would be required which the circumstances of the case make practically impossible. On the whole, after an examination of the wage-sheets of several representative employers, and after making minute enquiries among a large number of finishers engaged upon different grades of work, I believe that the nett gains of a finisher working upon the orthodox system will, in most cases, be found to be very similar to those of a laster of similar competence, employed upon boots of the same grade. Among the finishers, as among the lasters, there are some men who obtain work much more regularly than others; these are thoroughly good and reliable workmen who are kept fairly well employed all the year round. But, for the most part,

---

* These finishers pay their boys from 7s to 10s a-week; the boys do not appear to be bound as apprentices.

these finishers are quite as much affected by slack times as the lasters.

Finishing includes one series of operations requiring a moderate degree of skill—"knifing"—and a host of subordinate processes which are within the meanest industrial capacity. Under the team system the knifing is placed in the hands of a special workman. When this man has trimmed the edge of the sole and the surface of the heel into the required shape, he passes the boot on to a much inferior worker, by whom these parts are rubbed down, coloured, and polished. The sock—*i.e.* the lining of the insole —is then put in, as a rule, by yet another person, a worker lower still in the industrial scale. In the team system we have thus a further extension of that fundamental principle of competitive enterprise—the saving of labour. In this case labour is saved (*i.e.*, the labour-cost is reduced) by the utilization to the greatest advantage of the superior ability of the knifer, no part of whose energies are now thrown away upon work, which, under this system, is performed by labour of the most unskilled, and therefore of the cheapest, description—labour which, under the old-fashioned methods of the trade, could not have been used at all. The introduction of the team system into the finishing industry accompanied the adoption of improved tools, which, while greatly diminishing the difficulty, materially augmented the speed of the knifer's work, and thus enabled the number of subordinate workmen "following" him to be increased. In this way the gates were thrown open, and the flood of foreign labour rushed in.

Only in the very rarest instances (I am acquainted with but one such case) is this team-work finishing performed "indoors" by men employed directly by the manufacturer. Almost always the work done under this method is performed by out-workers under the sweating system. The master finisher, who takes the work out from the warehouse, in most cases himself knifes the boots, his team of three (less often four)* journeymen finishes them; his wife cleans the linings, and (unless a socking hand is employed at the factory) puts in the socks. Some of these sweating masters, however, employ knifers under them (among whom the knifing itself is sometimes subdivided),† and can then keep going a much larger team (say from four to eleven journeymen finishers). In this case much of the master's time is taken up by the supervision of his workers and by the search for work wherewith to keep them employed—a task involving many weary hours of patient waiting, and a lavish expenditure of tact, and also, in many cases—it is alleged—the bestowal of a certain amount of *douceurs* upon the manufacturer's foreman.

The normal length of the working-day among the foreign finishers is, during many weeks in succession, from seventeen to eighteen hours on five consecutive days of the week, and some twelve or thirteen hours‡ on another. The Jewish Sabbath, commencing at sunset on Friday, puts an end, in most cases, to the work of the week; and brings to the journeyman, at any rate, a period of repose which lasts until the following Sunday morning. But Saturday evening is very frequently devoted by the master finishers to knifing the boots upon which their men are to start work on the following day.

It is worthy of notice that the wives of the masters have to stop up, even after the working-day of the journeymen is ended, in order to sock the boots which the men have finished, in order that the goods may be ready for delivery next morning.

* There are some knifers who are unable to work with sufficient rapidity to keep pace with more than two or even one subordinate worker.

† Thus one of these subordinate knifers will be found to occupy himself exclusively with the heel, being incompetent to undertake the more difficult work required for the knifing of the "forepart."

‡ It may occur that a small part of these hours is spent by the journeymen in waiting for work to be brought back from the warehouse by the master: but very frequently their labour is carried on without intermission.

Residing, for the most part, in those squalid and over-crowded quarters of East London in which the foreign population has centred itself, in houses often, like the majority of the homes of the East London artisans, replete with sanitary defects, the master finishers provide for their men and themselves workrooms (some of which are also used for sleeping in) frequently devoid of the requirements of comfort, or even of health. The journeyman finisher, and his master divide equally between them the price per pair paid by the manufacturer, the master paying the rent of the workshop and providing lasts, tools (which he gets ground and sharpened at frequent intervals), gas for heating the irons and for lighting purposes, all materials required, and porterage, and giving his hands coffee in the morning and tea in the afternoon to wash down the scanty food which, in very many cases, they eat without leaving their work. For a journeyman thinks himself exceptionally lucky if, in the busy season, he can spare the time to run home for his mid-day meal.

The earnings of these finishers vary very greatly according to the amount of dexterity possessed in each case. Those masters, upon whom the manufacturers can depend to bring back the boots finished in a manner thoroughly satisfactory, not only get better prices for the work, but obtain employment much more regular than the majority; and the position of these better-class sub-contractors and of the journeymen whom they employ forms a strong contrast to that of those engaged upon the common and low-priced work. Yet, even where the prices received by the master finisher are good, and, by consequence, the piece-wage which he pays to his hands is fairly high, the earnings of the journeyman, if he is a slow worker, may be very low. It is no uncommon thing to find one of these journeymen unable to work much more than half as fast as his neighbour in the workshop.* In some cases this

* Here are some figures as to the earnings of three men employed in the

arises from want of experience; for many of these foreigners enter the trade without any previous knowledge of the craft in any form. Even when a man has been working at the finishing for several years, he will, in some instances, be found to work with very little more rapidity than in his novitiate, owing either to the want of natural aptitude for the work or to the deteriorating effects produced by the hard life, which is destructive of energy.

Few of these master finishers keep systematic accounts; while if a journeyman possess anything in the shape of a wage-book (and many of them have none), it will generally be found to indicate receipts for a few weeks only. For these reasons it has been impossible to arrive at any general statistics as to the financial position of the operatives engaged in this branch of the trade. To the best of my belief, which is based upon inquiries made among both master and journeymen finishers of all classes and upon an examination of a number of their pay-sheets and wage-books, the general average earnings of an ordinary competent hand in the busy season are about 26s a week. This season, however, lasts for little more than four months; in the remaining part of the year the dearth of employment is so great that a man taking 26s when in full work, will —according to the statements of these journeymen— average, one week with another through the year, no more than 16s. Some of the finishers, both masters and journeymen, fill up the slack time in this industry by working in another department of the trade (see post, p. 120), and so obtain continuous employment almost throughout the year. But the men who have no other source of livelihood than the finishing must be very hard pressed in the slack season.

same workshop in three successive weeks taken at random from their wage-books. All three work the same hours:—

		£	s.	d.	£	s.	d.	£	s.	d.
A	made	1	9	0	1	18	11	1	8	0
B	„	1	6	9	1	8	6	1	6	2
C	„		18	3		18	9		17	8

The figures last stated refer to the financial position of a journeyman of average capacity engaged on moderately well-paid work. As an instance of what can be earned by a quick man upon a good class of work, I have known a journeyman to take as much as 12s 9d as the result of one day's work.* A very quick and steady man was found to have gained in four successive weeks, taken at random, £7 1s 0½d, showing an average of £1 15s 3⅛d, with a *maximum* of £2 0s 5d. From the wage-book of another capable journeyman I find that between the middle of May and the middle of December (a period embracing more slack time than busy) he earned £47 6s 3d in 29 weeks, giving an average of £1 12s 7½d per week; the earnings of his best week being £2 16s 7½d. Another competent journeyman in the same workshop as the last made, in the heart of the slack time (9 weeks ending middle of December), a weekly average of £1 4s 9d with a *maximum* of £1 10s 8d.

On the other hand, while there are certainly some among the journeymen who, as we have seen, can earn more than our representative finisher, yet there are others who take much less. The price paid by the warehouse in the case of the man earning 26s in a busy week may be taken to be from 4s to 5s per dozen pairs. But there are men engaged upon work for which no more than one half of this price is paid by the manufacturer; and, although this very common work can be executed with somewhat greater rapidity than the better-priced boots, yet the earnings of a journeyman employed upon work of this kind, even if he be a fairly quick workman, are much smaller than those of our typical finisher; while if he be slow and incompetent, he will—as I

* This is an exceptionally quick man; but said by his master to be a great gambler, to have been known to come to work without coat or boots, having pawned these articles, and to be in the habit of not working more than four days a week. Even so, his earnings for six successive weeks amount to £10 3s, giving an average of £1 13s 10d per week, with a *maximum* of £1 17s 5d.

have ascertained from the statements of both masters and
men—earn, even in a busy week, no more than from
10s to 15s.

Much that has been said concerning the financial circumstances of the journeymen will apply equally in the case of
their masters. The general ratio between their respective
earnings may be illustrated by the case of a sweating
master supposed to employ three journeymen, each of whom
earns 26s in a busy week. After deduction of all expenses
the nett gains of this master will be found to be £3.*

Of this sum the master may fairly claim about 39s as
earned by his knifing,† and, say, 5s more for his wife's

---

* The actual receipts and expenditure of our representative sweating
master will be as follows :—

	£	s.	d.
Gross receipts—24 dozen at 5s per dozen	6	0	0
9 „ „ 4s „	1	16	0
	£7	**16**	**0**

	£	s.	d.
Expenditure.—Wages of 3 journeymen at 26s ...	3	18	0
Rent		4	0
Grindery		3	6
Benzoline (for cleaning linings) and packing paper...			9
Kit-cutting (sharpening tools)... ...		2	0
Interest on and depreciation of plant...		1	2
Porterage		1	6
Gas (for heating irons and for light) ...		4	0
Coffee and tea (supplied *gratis* to journeymen)		1	1
	£4	**16**	**0**

	£	s.	d.
Gross receipts (as above)	7	16	0
Expenditure...	4	16	0
Nett gains ...	**£3**	**0**	**0**

† It is, of course, not easy to say what is the fair value of the work
performed with his own hands by the master. The remark in the text is
based upon the price allowed for knifing by two manufacturers whom I found
to get part of their finishing done upon their own premises by men employed
by themselves without the intervention of a sub-contractor. This price

labour (socking, cleaning linings, sewing on buttons, and packing); so that his remuneration for seeking work, "shopping" the boots, and supervision is 16s per week. But the master suffers at least as much as his men from the long months of slackness; and, taking the calculation made by the journeymen of the ratio borne by the amount of their own earnings in a busy week to that of their weekly average through the year to be correct, this small employer and his wife will between them net (taking one week with another) no more than 34s or 35s a week, which includes the remuneration of their labour as well as all profit whatever.*

(one-fourth of the total sum paid for the double operation of knifing and finishing) is identical in each case, and in one case was settled by the manufacturer in agreement with the trade union of the journeymen finishers. The indoor finishers employed by the last-mentioned manufacturer have—it may be noted—since left his service, having been withdrawn by their trade union, not, however, in consequence of any dissatisfaction with this arrangement, or, indeed, of any dispute as to wages.

* The figures as to the actual average gains of the sweating master and his wife, one week with another through the year, upon the above basis are as follows:—

	£	s.	d.
Average gross receipts ($\frac{1}{26}$ of £7 16s)	4	16	0

Average expenditure.—

	£	s.	d.
Wages of 3 journeymen at 16s ($\frac{1}{26}$ of £3 18s)	2	8	0
Rent		4	0
Grindery ($\frac{1}{26}$ of 3s 6d)...		2	2
Benzoline & packing paper ($\frac{1}{26}$ of 9d)			5½
Kit-cutting ($\frac{1}{26}$ of 2s)		1	2¾
Interest and depreciation		1	2
Porterage (say)...		1	0
Gas ($\frac{14}{26}$ of 4s)		2	5½
Coffee and Tea...		1	1

	£	s.	d.
Average gross receipts	4	16	0
Average expenditure	3	1	6¾
Average nett gains ... £1	14	5¼	

Total expenditure: £3 1 6¾

The figures just stated relate to the financial position of a sweating master engaged upon a class of work fairly high-priced. The earnings of a master employed upon boots, for which the low prices, of which we have spoken, are paid by the manufacturer, are in a marked degree more meagre. And it is proper to observe that the smaller payment per pair diminishes the profits of the master even more than the wages of his men. For, whether the price paid for getting a boot finished be 2*d* or 10*d*, the cost of the grindery and other expenses incidental to the work (all of which are defrayed by the master) is much the same ; so that, as the price gets lower, the proportion of the moiety of this price taken by the master which is absorbed by these disbursements must be a constantly increasing fraction.*

Those, however, among the master finishers who get work at prices higher than the average, and whose

---

* The actual character of the budget of a workshop in which the work is of the lowest-priced class may be illustrated by the case of A. B. who was found to be in possession of a set of books very well kept, which he was good enough to hand over for inspection. His total takings for the year 1888 were £81 7*s* 4¾*d*, giving a weekly average of £1 11*s* 3½*d*. A. B. was, up to the end of 1887, a journeyman finisher, and is a novice at the knifing. He is too slow to keep more than one journeyman "following" him ; but he has more work than this journeyman can finish, so that A. B. not only knifes all, but also finishes some of the boots. He also "shops" the work, and his wife socks the boots, and cleans the linings. In an average week the journeyman would earn about 11*s* 3½*d*. We cannot allow A. B. less than about 5*s* for grindery, rent, hire of barrow, and the other expenses indicated in the preceding tabular estimate ; and 3*s* is scarcely too large a sum to fix as the value of his wife's work. Thus the nett remuneration received by this sweating master, including his profit as sub-contractor, will average 12*s* per week. On the second of the two occasions on which this man was visited he had begun work before 5 A.M., and was left with an hour's work still to do at 11.30 P.M. He had devoted two hours out of this long day to "shopping the work," and another interval of the same duration to sleep. This was upon a day not specially busy, and in the slack time. A. B. has been working at the trade for four years (three of which he spent as a journeyman). No doubt, when he has improved in skill, he will be able to get better work, to employ a larger team, and to earn more money.

employment is comparatively regular in character, make, of course, considerably more money than the 34s or 35s per week of our typical sub-contractor. But the number of these better-paid masters does not appear to be large.

There exists—it should be observed—a class of sweating masters whose financial circumstances are generally superior to those of their rivals. These are the men, already alluded to, who employ subordinate knifers,* and are in consequence able to take on a large number of journeymen, and to produce an out-put much in excess of that possible where a smaller team is engaged. While the gains of a master working upon this larger scale are considerably in excess of those made by the smaller men, it is of much importance to him to secure an abundant supply of work with which to keep all his hands fully employed. With this object he—it is alleged—underbids his rivals; and it is in a great measure to the competition of these larger sub-contractors that the present depressed condition of this industry is attributed by the men in the trade. Whatever may be the cause, it is certainly asserted on all hands that the prices paid for finishing by the manufacturers have within the last few years fallen to a serious extent.

We have now concluded our investigation of the machine-sewn trade, by far the greater part of the boot-making industry of the metropolis. Neither the pegged boot nor the rivetted demands any detailed treatment in these pages.

---

* I have found it impracticable to ascertain with exactness the average earnings of these knifers. Some of them are paid weekly wages which are subject to diminution in slack time; while some masters assert that in certain instances the knifers are engaged at a fixed sum which is not reduced when work is scarce. These wages seem to range from 30s a week for a really competent all-round knifer down to 20s for a man who can only pare and breast heels. Other knifers are paid a part of the price received from the manufacturers. Thus a knifer, only able to knife heels, was said to receive out of 10s per dozen, 10d; out of work below 10s and above 6s 6d per dozen, 9d; from 6s 6d to 5s per dozen, 8d.

The makers of pegged boots* are few and far between in our district. I know one man who some little time back had continuously for two years a "seat of work" of pegged boots, which brought him in a wage of 42s or 43s nett per week. But regularity of employment such as this is—my inquiries lead me to believe—very exceptional; and the figures are cited as showing, not what the "pegged" men in general actually average, but what a good worker can earn, if only he can get the work to do.

Rivetted boots are made in considerable quantities in different parts of our district, especially in the eastern part of Bethnal Green. These boots are in demand for the children of the working-classes and, to a certain extent, for women's wear. Few boots of good or middling grades are in our district made with rivets; and the men who are principally engaged upon rivetted work appear to be, for the most part, somewhat inferior craftsmen; though a really good workman may be driven to this work when the machine-sewn trade is slack. As to their earnings, men on rivetted work seem to take much the same wages as men of similar industrial capacity engaged upon sewn work of a corresponding grade. These remarks apply to the men by whom a rivetted boot is put together; as to the finishing, there is no distinction worthy of note between rivetted and machine-sewn boots, whether in regard to the nature of the work or the wages of the workers.

There remains for consideration the class of goods called "sew-rounds," goods in the manufacture of which a large number of persons are engaged in our district, which, indeed, is the principal centre of this industry in England. Sew-rounds are fancy shoes and slippers, and are distinguished from all other kinds of boots and shoes by certain peculiarities in the process of joining the upper to the

* Some men can make either a pegged, a sewn, or a rivetted boot; but this is not always the case.

sole which it is not necessary to describe technically in this place.*

In dealing with the sew-round trade it is necessary to distinguish between the different grades; for the industrial conditions of the workers vary greatly according to the quality of the work.

First, as to the manufacturers by whom the sew-round hands are employed, the very best goods are made chiefly for large firms; but the inferior grades are often made up by men in a very small way of business, whose produce is "bought in" by the great houses or by factors. Some of these miniature manufacturers sell part of their slippers to hawkers; indeed, I came across one man who saved all intermediate profits by himself hawking his own goods; and you may find a man "manufacturing" sew-rounds one season and working as the employee of a "manufacturer" the next.

As to the industrial position of the workers, before noticing the points of difference between the operatives engaged upon different classes of work, we may note one important circumstance which affects all alike. The busy season in the sew-round trade lasts for only about six months in the year. Some few houses keep all their hands fairly well employed, even in the slack season. But this is quite the exception.

Dealing in detail with the position of the workers, we will take first those who "bind" the uppers of these goods. These uppers, which, as a rule, are much simpler in construction than those of any other foot-gear (though often elaborately decorated with beads, etc.), are made in the work-rooms of the manufacturers only in the case of the very best goods. The binding of all other sew-round

---

* The sew-round has no welt, and its construction is begun by lasting it inside out, after which it is "turned," with its inner surface now next to the last, the position in which all other boots and shoes are lasted throughout.

uppers is given out to be done at home by persons, in some cases working single-handed, in others employing subordinate labour. These sew-round upper-binders resemble in their industrial circumstances the out-workers who make the uppers of boots (as described *ante*, p. 88 *et seq.*)*

Some of the work given out in this manner is of fair quality and not badly remunerated. Thus a woman who is working single-handed on the uppers of satin shoes tells me that in a busy week she can earn (after paying all expenses except the hire-purchase instalment of 2*s* 6*d* due on one of her two machines) about 28*s*. But there do not appear to be many women of this more fortunate type.

In the case of the lowest class of goods the prices paid by the manufacturers appear to have fallen greatly in the last few years and to be steadily diminishing, a fact which—as far as I have been able to ascertain—has affected the profits of the sub-contractors even more injuriously than the rate of pay of the subordinate workers. A paste-fitter engaged on the lowest class of work can still earn 2*s* 6*d* a day; a machinist similarly employed says she gets 2*s* a day; a few years back she could get 2*s* 6*d*. For the uppers upon which she is working 7*d* per dozen pairs was paid only one year ago; now the middlewoman is only getting 5*d* (this reduction I know to be general; and one manufacturer tells me that he gets work of this class done for 4½*d* per dozen). The sub-contractor in question calculates her profit upon this kind of work to be between 1*s* and 1*s* 2*d* a day; and since she has to pay, not alone wages, but also rent of workroom and hire of sewing-machines (these two items having to be paid in busy and slack times alike), and to provide grindery, light, and firing, it will easily be understood that not very much of what she receives for these 5*d* per

---

* In the higher branches of the sew-round binding the workers appear, like those who close the uppers of boots, to be almost exclusively English women. In the lower branches some of the work is done by foreign operatives, in some cases by males.

dozen uppers remains at the end of the week as the reward of her own labour (she works one of her four machines) and of her supervision.*

So far we have been speaking of leather uppers, which are sewn with the machine. Felt and carpet uppers are generally bound by hand, for the most part by women who are partially supported by their husbands; and indeed no one could get a living out of this work; for, even if a woman give her whole time to the work (most of them only ply the needle in odd half-hours), she cannot earn more than about 1s 3d per day.

To turn now to the operatives engaged in making the soles of sew-rounds, joining the uppers to these, and finishing the shoes, we shall remark that, while the better class of work is almost exclusively in the hands of persons of English blood, the operatives engaged upon the inferior work are mainly of the Hebrew race, most of them foreigners who have arrived in this country within the last few years.

Of the sew-round makers engaged upon best to middling work a few work upon the premises of the manufacturers, but the majority in their own homes. The indoor hands, in some instances, do the whole of the work (lasting, sewing, and finishing) single-handed, but in others have the shoes sewn for them by a sew-round machine; there are, however, but few of these sew-round machines in London. The outdoor hands get their sewing done by some member of their family, or employ a boy, girl, or young woman to sew for them. In many places you will find that the services of several persons are called into requisition, not only for the sewing, but also for cutting soles, making socks, and for finishing. These subordinate

---

* The hours of work in this upper-binding workshop are 8 A.M. to 8 P.M.; overtime is rarely worked, and is paid for at 1d per hour above the normal rate. The sub-contractor is a married woman, and carries on this trade in order to supplement the earnings of her husband.

workers are often called in only for occasional hours or half-hours during the day. The principal operatives (who last the shoes) in some instances work long hours. Those whose employment is most regular spend about eleven hours a day at the seat. But when a man is without work for half the year, he has to make up for lost time, and in the height of the busy season will work from twelve to fourteen hours a day for many consecutive weeks.

As to the rate of pay earned by these operatives, their weekly takings naturally vary greatly, not alone by reason of the difference between the piece-wage paid for different qualities of work, but still more because the amount of assistance received by each is so diverse. When in full employment, a man engaged on best goods, with help, say, from his wife and daughter, will (as the pay-sheets of the manufacturers show and the men agree) be able to earn from 50s to 70s (nett, *i.e.*, after paying cost of grindery) per week; on *medium* grades he might earn from 35s up to 55s (nett). But in order to gauge the earning power of the hands it will be best to take the case of those men who work with no other assistance than that of a single sewer, employed at a fixed wage—from 8s up to 15s a week, according to competence. These sewers are sometimes girls or young women, but often boys, who in due time become full-fledged craftsmen, competent to last and finish as well as to sew. They do not appear to work more than about ten hours a day, even when, as is most often the case, their employers work longer hours than these.

A sew-round hand working with one sewer can, after paying for his grindery and the wages of his assistant, earn about 28s in a good week; but some men, being quick workers, undoubtedly earn much more, especially if engaged on a good class of work. One man says that, working on *medium* goods in a factory, with his sewing done for him by the machine, he has earned up to 33s 6d (nett) a week (with a working day of between ten and eleven hours); while a first-class craftsman, employed upon a good quality of shoe, tells me that he has in twelve and a-half-hours earned as much as 18*s* 6*d* gross (say, after deducting cost of grindery and assistance, fully 15*s*). This man insists—and I am inclined to agree with him—that many sew-round hands are anything but steady workers, so that their actual takings are no certain indication of the wages possible to be earned by a steady man.

As already stated, the sew-round trade in all its departments is, in general, a six months' trade only; but here again (as with the men in the machine-sewn branch) a certain number of workmen, selected on account, partly of their ability, but even more of their steadiness, are kept fully employed nearly all the year round. But the majority among the sew-round hands must through the slack six months of the year endure very considerable privations; unless, indeed, they are able to turn their hand to some other branch; I have met with men who can do this; but such versatility is not common.*

Up to this point our attention has been directed to the operatives engaged in making sew-round work of best to middling quality, all of whom—we have noted—are of English blood. The inferior classes of sew-round shoes are made chiefly by Jewish workpeople, whose industrial condition can only be described as wretched in the extreme. These shoes are made by men, boys, and women who work together in groups, somewhat analagous to those engaged in lasting or in finishing under the team system. Residing, as they do, in the most densely populated quarters of East London (principally in Whitechapel, Spitalfields, and the western portion of Bethnal Green), these foreign sew-round hands are crowded together in small workrooms, which, in some cases, are occupied also as sleeping-rooms; some of these places are underground. Here these operatives toil

---

* I am told that some sew-round hands belong to militia regiments, and supplement their trade earnings by their pay.

frequently for fifteen, sometimes for eighteen or even more hours out of the twenty-four during the first five days of the week. On Fridays work generally ceases at dusk, often (in cases in which the work has to be shopped by midday, and no fresh work is given out until next evening) before noon. But it will be best to state exactly the particulars observed upon visits paid to a few representative workrooms of the type in question.*

In a top room of a tenement house—a room of fair proportions for Spitalfields—I came across a group of nine workers. The principal of the establishment is a fine looking man who has seen service in the Russian army; he and his son perform those parts of the work which require the greatest amount of skill. Four other men are chiefly occupied in sewing, but devote part of their time to certain other minor operations, no one of them possessing sufficient competence in his craft to be trusted with the more important processes.

The fifth man is a raw " greener" who has only been in England for six months. He came to this country absolutely ignorant of any trade, and is cheerfully working his way upwards. At the present time his services are employed, partly in carrying the work from and to the warehouse, partly in some extremely elementary operations in connection with the shoes.

The two remaining members of this group are women. One is an English sewer, a respectable-looking workwoman who seems to know her business fairly well. The other is a Jewess of magnificent proportions and evidently possessing no ordinary degree of intelligence and energy. This is the wife of the principal, who appears to leave to her a large share in the management. Besides making the socks for the shoes, she sometimes carries the heavy baskets of work

---

* As already remarked with regard to the finishers, these hours include the time during which the hands are waiting for a fresh supply of work to come in from the warehouse.

from and to the warehouse; and at all times exercises a general supervision, the good effects of which are manifested in the prosperous condition of the business. For this is, as things go, a flourishing concern, the nett profits of which—without professing to know enough of its details for complete accuracy—I should roughly estimate at about £3 per week, of course only during the busy season.*

This sum of £3 represents the joint remuneration of three persons (father, mother, and adult son) as well as all subcontractor's profit.

The English female sewer, who works about four and-a-half days in the week (Friday is a short day, Saturday is the day of rest of the principal), earns (on piece-wage) from 3s 1½d to 4s per day according to the class of work. Four out of the five men (also on piece-wage) earn each about 15s a week; but they are not quick workers, or might earn up to about 18s or 19s. The fifth (the greener) is content with a week-wage of 10s; and I am convinced that this rate of pay is considerably above the market value of his work.†

The English woman comes to work about 10 A.M. and leaves off about 9 P.M. The other hands work, during five days out of seven, from about 7 A.M. to about 10 P.M.; the principal, his wife, and son from 7 A.M. to midnight. During a great part of Friday and the whole of Saturday, as already explained, no work is done.

The head of this workshop declares that he is busy with sew-round work from the beginning of August to the end of November only. I believe that he can get a fair amount of work through the first three weeks of December also, but at reduced prices; for in this low-class trade not alone are

---

* The principal supplies all necessary materials (grindery), lasts, and tools, gets all tools sharpened, pays rent and cost of light and firing, provides porterage, and gives the hands tea and coffee *gratis*. This man's lasts are of good quality, and it costs £3 to £4 annually to renew his stock.

† This work was of the simplest nature, and was learnt by him in eight days. In the six months that he had been in England this man had saved 30s; he appeared well pleased with his life, and confident that he would soon rise.

prices falling steadily from year to year, but the manufacturers cut down the price which they have been paying
in the busy season, as soon as the slack time commences.
From Christmas until Easter this sub-contractor can find no
employment for himself or for his hands. Then he turns
master finisher until the middle of July. One of his present
hands also takes to the finishing (as journeyman), when the
sew-round season is over, and can earn, he says, in that
branch from 28s to 30s a week, about twice as much as he
is now taking.

Not only does the sew-round sub-contractor turn into the
finishing sub-contractor, and the journeyman sew-round hand
into the journeyman finisher, but you may find a man working as a journeyman finisher through the spring and summer
and taking out sew-round work during the rest of the year
as himself a sub-contractor, employing subordinate labour.

This was the case with the principal of another workshop which I visited in two successive weeks. At the
close of the last finishing season this man had applied to
the Board of Guardians for the Relief of the Jewish Poor
for a loan with which to purchase a stock of lasts required
for the sew-round trade, and, the master finisher for
whom he had been working having volunteered to stand
security for him, his application had been granted. The
room in which I found P—— at work with a group
or team of five men, all recent accessions to our foreign
colony (his wife coming in from time to time to lend
a helping hand), is about 9 ft. in length, 6 ft. in width,
and 7 ft. in height. He sends his socks out to a woman
who makes them at home. According to the detailed
calculations of the men, in which their master acquiesced,
the wages that they can earn (they can never get work for
more than five days out of the seven) are as follows : *

* These figures seem low; but it must be remembered that these men are
very incompetent. I do not think that these greeners earn much more than
as stated in the text.

			s.	*d.*	
A	can earn by sewing.....................		13	1½	per week.
B	,,	partly by sewing, partly by cutting soles .... }	7	3½	,,
C	,,	chiefly by lasting, but partly by sewing .... }	10	2½	,,
D	,,	chiefly by sewing, but partly by finishing ...... }	11	3	,,
E	,,	by sewing.....................	13	1½	,,

The man and his wife appeared to be able to net between them about 35*s* per week. But this amount they will have continued to earn so long only as they could get this "line" of patent shoes on which they were working on the occasion of my second visit. The week before I had found the principal at work with two subordinates only upon a cheaper shoe; and his profits were then much smaller.

The hours worked in this workshop seem to be longer than in the previous case, some of the men declaring that they come at 6 A.M. and often stay until 1 A.M. The principal assures me that he generally works from 6 A.M. until 2 A.M. or even 3 A.M.; this is not easy to believe; but I have heard very similar accounts concerning other men in the same position. He seems to regard the finishing, to which he will return when the busy season in that department comes round, as much lighter work; but he asserts that he is so slow a workman that he cannot earn more than 18*s* a week as a journeyman finisher.

There appears to be no doubt that many of these sew-round sub-contractors earn less, rather than more, than their own hands. This may be exemplified by the case of a man to whose small cellar workshop I paid two visits, finding him, his wife, his son (about 14 years of age), and four subordinates, mostly greeners, at work, and two children lying asleep in their clothes upon a bed in the room. His estimate for a day's takings and expenditure (which I have tested as well as I could, and do not believe to be very inaccurate) is as follows :—

Gross takings.—

	s.	d.
2 dozen at 3s 6d	7	0
2 dozen at 3s	6	0
	13	0

Expenditure.—

	s.	d.		s.	d.
Wages* A (sewing and edging†)... ...	3	1½	per day.		
B (sewing and other work) ...	3	1½	,,		
C (sewing and buffing†) ...	1	9	,,		
D sewing	1	0½	,,		
				9	0½
Grindery				1	4
Tea and Coffee					2½
Paraffin and Coke					3
				10	9¾

	s.	d.
Gross takings	13	0
Expenditure (not including rent)	10	9¾
Nett gains ...	2	2¼

This sum of 2s 2¼d per day, in reckoning which no allowance is made for rent of workroom, includes the remuneration of the labour of this sub-contractor, of his wife, and of his son, as well as his middleman's profit, which it will be seen is a *minus* quantity. What the man has to gain by being a sub-contractor instead of a journeyman is, of course, an increased chance of continuous employment; for the subordinates are taken on or discharged as work is plentiful or the reverse. This man says that in the finishing season he earns a little more than he can on the sew-round work. He is then a sweating master employing one journeyman, who himself employs a "learner."

The hours worked here during the five busy days of the week are said to be from 6 A.M. until midnight for all the men but one, who stops up with the principal until 2 A.M.

* The men here are raw and incompetent.
† Edging and buffing are parts of the finishing.

The last class with which we have to deal is the makers of felt, imitation worked,* and carpet slippers. This trade, which for thirty years has been principally in the hands of Jewish operatives, is a decaying industry, these slippers having to a great extent been driven out of the field by the cheap house-boots already referred to.

The busy season in the slipper trade lasts for some seven months; but some men get work for nine or ten months in the year, and a few may be met with who are seldom without a fair share of employment.

It is of interest to note that, while the prices† obtained for their goods by the slipper manufacturers have fallen enormously,‡ the piece-wage paid by them has fallen very slightly, and in some cases has not fallen at all. The slipper-makers, however, assert that, in some instances, the materials now supplied to them are of so coarse a nature that it takes nearly twice as long to make a slipper as in days gone by.

Some of this work is done upon the premises of the manufacturers, but the bulk of it in the homes of men who take the work out from the warehouse. In some instances the work is performed by associated groups in much the same manner as in the case of the cheap shoes last mentioned; but very frequently you will find the slipper-maker at work with a single sewer, who, probably, also assists in the finishing. I have heard of, but have never seen, men who could "work up to" two sewers, and I have come across a man working single-handed; but this is not common.

As to the men working in groups, a method which seems

* The uppers of these are imported from Germany.

† In certain classes of slippers the importation of German and other foreign goods has contributed to bring down the price.

‡ It must be added that the price of carpet has also fallen considerably, and that leather of inferior quality and lower price than ever is used for the bottom stuff.

to have been practised in this trade for the last thirty years, the description given of the operatives engaged on common sew-round shoes will—I believe—apply in this case also, and need not be repeated. The hours of work and the earnings of the men are much the same in both departments.*

With regard to the slipper-maker who has one man to sew for him (and this seems to be the most common arrangement) a fairly competent maker ought in a moderately busy week to earn about 22*s* (less rent, light, and firing, but clear of grindery), while his subordinate should take about 12*s*. This 22*s* represents the remuneration of the labour of the maker, and also of a certain amount of assistance rendered by his wife (who cuts the shapes for the socks).†

TRADE ORGANIZATIONS.—No account of the industrial circumstances of the boot-makers of our district would possess the smallest claim to completeness unless it offered to the reader some description of the Trade Unions under which a considerable part of the labour engaged in this industry is organized. By far the most important among these Unions are the Amalgamated Society of Boot and Shoe Makers, and the National Union of Operative Boot and Shoe Rivetters and Finishers. The City Branches‡ of the Amalgamated Society number some 400 members; the London Metropolitan Branch of the National Union about 1,800. The former comprises

---

* The slipper hands, however, do not, as a rule, get tea or coffee given by their employer.

† It is extremely difficult to arrive at an average statement as to the earnings of the slipper-makers, and still more so of their sewers, on account of the great difference in the industrial capacity of different men. For example, a quick sewer can sew and turn 4 dozen in a day; most of them, however, only do 2½ dozen; and I have come across men who could only do 1 dozen. Many of the sewers are raw and very incompetent hands. I have known a man working with his son (of 25 years) and his daughter (of 30 years) to make 7 dozen of slippers (labour-price 3*s* 6*d* per dozen, cost of grindery 6*d* per dozen), between 8 A.M. and 2 A.M. But this speed is exceptional.

‡ Some men (makers) residing in East London and Hackney belong to the West-end branches of the Amalgamated Society.

a few closers, a number of makers of hand-sewn boots, and a somewhat larger number of men engaged on sew-round work; but the majority are lasters and finishers employed in the machine-sewn and rivetted trade, the proportion between lasters and finishers being as two to one. The latter includes twenty to thirty clickers and two or three rough-stuff cutters; but is principally composed of lasters and finishers (say two lasters to one finisher). In addition to their primary function of trade combination, these Unions partake of the character of provident societies (both sick and burial), and are collectively responsible for the honesty of their members, making good to the employer materials intrusted to a workman and not returned. It is, however, principally in their relation to the regulation of the wage-standard that the Unions require to be noticed in this place.

The three City branches of the Amalgamated Society comprise, respectively, closers, "men's men" (*i.e.* makers of men's boots), and "women's men" (*i.e.* makers of women's boots). The members of the City (Closers') Branch are only eleven in number, and some of them are no longer employed as closers (one, for instance, was found to be foreman in an upper-making factory; another is clicker in a bespoke shop). The City Closers have no general agreement as to wages with the employers at large; but a certain number of the better-class shopkeepers pay their closers according to a special wage-standard agreed upon in each case between the individual master and the Union. In some instances a first-rate workman will make for himself with his employer an agreement upon terms more favourable than the Union wage-standard.

The organization of the makers* in the City (Men's), and

---

* Of the sew-round hands in the Society a very small number work under a shop statement (*i.e.* an agreement between a particular employer and the Trade Union); but the large majority make the best terms they can for themselves without the intervention of the Trade Union. I have not heard any

City (Women's) Branches of the Society is much more methodical than that of the closers. The whole of the Society makers work under a general wage-standard fixed by the Union in agreement with a number of the best employers in the City hand-sewn trade. This standard is embodied in a "statement," the present statement dating from the year 1882. The basis of this wage-scale is the *minimum* price to be paid for making the simplest possible form of boot—the "ground-work" price. If any additional work is required to be put into a boot, or if certain materials are used in its construction, then there will be a charge of, *e.g.* 9*d* for putting on a double instead of a single sole, or 6*d* if patent instead of ordinary leather is employed, the amount of every conceivable "extra" being specified in the statement. It is, however, recognized that in different classes of boots different degrees of good workmanship are required; and in order to regulate the labour-price in conformity with the varying quality of the work, a distinction is made in the ground-work prices. Not that the actual quality of each pair of boots determines whether the maker shall be paid first-rate, second-rate, third-rate, or fourth-rate wages. The rate of wage to be paid in each case depends upon the class to which this man's employer is held by the Union to belong. The Society knows the character of the goods principally sold by each shopkeeper, and fixes the scale of the wages which he has to pay for all work done for him accordingly. Thus the ground-work price* paid by an employer may be 7*s* 6*d*, 7*s* 3*d*, 7*s*, or 6*s* 6*d*, according to the category within which he has been placed by the Union, the City statement being in force in some twenty-one shops, of which about twelve are first-

complaints as to the insufficiency of their piece-wage. These men possess a considerable degree of skill, and there is so great a demand for their labour in the busy season as to ensure its adequate remuneration.

* The extras are the same, in whatever class the employer may be placed.

rate, two second-rate, six third-rate, and one fourth-rate. For these twenty-one employers, the members of the Amalgamated Society are not allowed to work at a lower rate than that fixed by the statement; nor is the employer allowed—under penalty of losing the services of such of his men as belong to the Union—to employ any maker (whether a member of the Society or not) at less than this regulation labour-price. For any other shops the Union allows its members to work at a lower ground-work price, *e.g.* 5*s* 6*d*, 4*s* 6*d*, or even less, the men accepting such terms as they can obtain in each case. However, the efforts of the Society, to which most of the best workmen in the hand-sewn trade belong, have been able to secure for a large number of makers the recognized rate of remuneration.

At the same time it must be remembered that the rate of a man's piece-wage is not in all cases an infallible index to the amount of his actual average weekly earnings. In the first place there is so much less work put into a 5*s* 6*d* boot, as compared with one at 7*s* 6*d* (ground-work price), that a man can make 6 pairs of the former in the same time that it takes to make 4½, or at the most 5, of the latter. Then again, while the heavy labour-cost of first-class hand-sewn boots makes the price of this article almost prohibitory, except to a comparatively small number of wealthy customers, the inferior grade of boots, on which the lower piece-wage is paid, commands a ready sale, and can even compete successfully with the machine-sewn goods. The result is that a maker who is willing to accept less than the statement wage can very often get full employment and earn good wages all the year round, while the man who insists on his proper rate of pay is frequently only half-employed.*

* I have come across several instances of men employed at a rate below the Trade Union scale, who were making far more money than the general run of the makers remunerated according to the wage-standard of the statement. Thus one of these makers, working at a piece-wage considerably below

When the attempt was made for the first time (in 1872) to regulate by combination the wages of the workmen employed in the wholesale trade upon machine-sewn and rivetted work, the arrangements between masters and men were drawn up on the lines of those which had prevailed among the hand-sewn boot-makers—with this exception, that the employers working under the provisions of the new (wholesale trade) statement were no longer classified into first-rate, second-rate, &c., but each was at liberty to pay a rate of wages varying, to a certain extent, with the actual quality of the workmanship demanded in each individual pair of boots. It was felt that, in the nature of things, it could not be expected that any manufacturer should turn out one grade of work and one grade only. But how to determine, once and for all, the actual quality of workmanship exhibited in the out-put of a workshop was the problem. The solution was found in the classification, no longer of the employers, but of the work, boots being classed in grades as "best," "seconds," or "thirds." This classification—it is important to note—was based upon the material used in each case. Thus, *glacé* kid was, at the time when this statement was adopted, put only into boots of the best quality, being too expensive a leather to be used in making inferior boots. Therefore all boots in which *glacé* kid might be used were to be paid for as "best work."

When this statement was introduced,* the firms (some

---

that fixed by the Trade Union, tells me that he is earning a trifle over £1 16s (nett) per week through the year; another that he seldom clears less than £1 12s 6d. I have known a man give up his "seat of work" at a "first-rate" shop (paying 7s 6d ground-work) to work at 5s 6d per pair for a non-statement employer. He could get only three pairs a week while working for the former, but got six pairs from the latter. Compare with these figures those stated *ante*, p. 249.

* It should be observed that the first-class statement now in force is not exactly identical with that of 1872, some modifications (not affecting any question of principle) having been introduced since that date.

fifteen in number) included in its operation were the only houses making really first-class goods. But soon some of their non-statement rivals (assisted by their freedom from the regulations and restrictions of this wage-scale) began to turn out boots of a quality very nearly as good as theirs. Then, in 1875, a new " second-class " statement, with a scale of piece-wage slightly lower than the "first-class" statement, was brought into force, and under this some twenty-five houses are now working, while by special agreement with the Trade Unions some half-dozen others are paying a wage intermediate between the first and the second-class statements. It may be observed, in passing, that this second statement, while it agrees with the first-class statement in treating the material used as the criterion of the quality of workmanship required in a boot, yet concedes something to the manufacturers, for the specified grades range down to " fourths."

As a matter of fact, the old test of material is quite out of date. Formerly all *glacé* leather was very costly, and boots made of this material were worn only by persons who could afford to pay a high price. Nowadays *glacé* kid (the skill of the leather-dresser having discovered novel methods of imparting the *glacé* finish to inferior and much cheaper skins) is used for boots of a low grade, in the manufacture of which first-rate workmanship is no longer required. The rigid maintenance of this test (material) by the Unions is a serious impediment to the trade of the houses working under the provisions of the first and second-class statements. At the same time, just as in 1875 the first-class houses had, in the race in which they were so severely handicapped, been almost over-taken by their competitors, so a few years later it was found that the most enterprising among the non-statement houses were close upon the heels of the second-statement firms. That the workmen should be doing for these outside houses work almost as good as that done for the statement firms at a rate of wages considerably lower than was paid by the latter, was thought to suit the non-statement employees as little as it suited the statement employers. Accordingly, in 1884, a third or *minimum* statement, with a piece-wage inferior to the second-class statement, was served by the Unions upon the non-statement masters; and, after some thousands of men, working for about 300 different firms, had been for five weeks out on strike, an agreement upon this basis was come to between the representatives of the masters and of the men. This arrangement, however, was at the last moment upset by the opposition of the men working for the statement houses, who feared that the introduction of the *minimum* statement was but the thin end of the wedge, and would ultimately drag down the level of their own wage-standard.

The position has remained virtually unchanged up to the present time. A certain number of individual employers have been compelled by the Unions to adopt special agreements as to wages ("shop statements"), with a wage-scale lower than that of the second statement. But no arrangement embracing the whole of the trade has as yet been adopted. The result is, that the firms working under the provisions of the first and second statements are greatly hampered in their business, which is of necessity confined to the manufacture of the very best goods, since these, and these alone, can be produced at a profit by employers obliged to pay a scale of wages so high as that imposed by the Unions upon these houses. To be forced to employ his expensive plant (as well as his hands) upon one sort of work only is an obvious disadvantage to any manufacturer, but especially to one engaged in the boot trade. For a boot manufacturer the two essential elements of economy in regard to his raw material are, first, to purchase it in large quantities, good and bad together, and, second, to use up the inferior leather in making boots of the commoner sorts. Now,

while it is open to the non-statement houses to buy whatever leather they like, and to use it in any manner they
like, the statement manufacturers, being practically prohibited from making any but goods of a high class, are
forced to buy only picked leather, to use only the best
portions, and to sell the " roundings " (inferior portions),
frequently at a considerable loss.

Forced to forego economy in the purchase of their
materials, these firms are at the same time heavily
handicapped by the necessity of paying the high piece-wage
fixed by the statement, while (with the exception of the
very few who work under shop statements) the whole of
the London manufacturers not included in the operation of
the first and second statements, nearly 400 in number, are,
under the existing arrangements, entirely free from all
control on the part of the Unions. A statement firm must
not employ a single laster (whether a member of either
Union or not) at lower wages than those prescribed by
the statement under which this firm works. The non-
statement houses may—for all the Unions can do to stop
them—pay, even to members of the Unions, any wages
that the men choose to accept; and may, indeed—and
sometimes, it is said, do—pay one of their men at a
lower rate than another.

With regard to the position of the operatives who work
for the houses unrestricted by the Union wage-standard,
it is not asserted that the non-statement masters, as a
body, treat their men badly. No doubt the piece-wage
ruling among these outside manufacturers is lower by 30
per cent. than that obtaining in the statement workshops;
but then, the quality of workmanship exacted being also
lower, the men's out-put is considerably augmented, and
they can in very many cases earn at least as much as the
recipients of full statement wages, and that without working
longer hours. From the inquiries which I have personally
made among the workmen, and from inspection both of

their wage-books and of the pay-sheets of employers, I
have been able to compare the earnings of the men working
under the statements with those of the operatives who
are employed by the non-statement houses; and certainly
the lasters whom I have found to be receiving the highest
wages, not only in the busy time, but on the average
through the year, have been men working for non-statement
manufacturers.* There are, however, among the manufacturers who escape regulation by the Trade Unions some
who avail themselves of the frantic competition for
work among the less skilled hands employed upon work
of a low grade, especially among the sweating masters,
in order to cut down wages to the lowest possible figure;
while even the better-disposed among the non-statement
employers, finding their position adversely affected by
having to contend against these less considerate rivals,
must, however unwillingly, end by reducing the piece-wage
of their own "common" work. Nor are there wanting cases
—let us hope rare cases—in which non-statement houses
have behaved with what their men consider to be the most
reprehensible harshness.† And there can be no doubt that
the fact that the statement houses are practically incapaci-
tated by the restrictions of the Trade Union wage-standard

* If the reader will turn back to p. 95, he will find this statement borne
out by the figures there tabulated.

† An instance of this description may be seen in the account given in
Appendix B of the first report of the Select Committee of the House of Lords
on the Sweating System of a case in the Shoreditch County Court in which
a laster unsuccessfully sued his employers for money deducted from his
wages by virtue of an agreement signed (without however, as he alleged, being
understood) by him, which allowed the defendants to deduct from each
weekly payment of wages 2s 6d, to be retained by the firm as a deposit and
forfeited by the workman if he should leave their employment within twelve
months. The object of this document (which these manufacturers stated
that they require all their workmen to sign) is, of course, to compel a man
coming to them in the slack season at a low rate of wages to remain working
at the same wage throughout the busy season, instead of seeking work elsewhere at a higher rate.

from themselves manufacturing any but high-class boots, on which a high labour-price is paid, while it does not in any way tend to check the production of inferior goods at lower wages, yet does tend to drive the low-class trade into the hands of employers whose dealings with their workpeople are not always as satisfactory as could be desired— employers who supply with the inferior descriptions of boots and shoes, not only the retail trade, but also these very statement houses. For, naturally, if a firm has to defray the salary of a traveller and to keep up a connection with shopkeepers and dealers in all parts of the world, it does not pay that firm to offer none but high-class goods ; the requirements of customers in respect of inferior boots, shoes, and slippers must also be satisfied ; and this the statement houses have to do by " buying-in " these goods from the non-statement manufacturers. Under these circumstances the profit of an additional middleman must, obviously, be provided for—a profit which, in all probability, has to come out of the labour-price of these goods. In many instances, however, the London statement houses, in order to be able themselves to manufacture common and *medium* as well as best work, are either removing their business to Northampton or establishing branch factories in that place ; for in Northampton the shackles of the London statements no longer fetter their operations.

At Northampton there has recently been introduced an arrangement which constitutes a fresh departure in the organization of the boot industry. The test of material is no longer applied with rigidity ; in fact, the only restriction as to material is that *glacé*, glove, or bronze kid must not be used in boots lower than " thirds." In all other respects the manufacturer is free to make boots of any conceivable grade or description ; for the Northampton statement includes no less than seven qualities, in addition to an " extra quality to meet special requirements." This arrangement—which applies to the entire home trade of Northampton, without any invidious class distinctions among the different firms in the town—certainly relieves the employer from much embarrassment. Nor, unless the information given to me by persons in a position to know the facts is incorrect, does it enable him to take advantage of his men by getting best work made at the price of thirds, or of seconds. The interests of the men are guarded by a tribunal upon which both employers and employees are represented, and which determines in case of doubt the category within which a boot ought in fairness to be placed, its decisions being assisted by reference to a sample show-case containing an assortment of boots classified according to quality. If a dispute arises between a master and his men as to the price to be paid upon a novel description of boot, the sample from which the men are to work is submitted to the Board of Conciliation, who, comparing it with the exemplars of the show-case, determine whether the boot is to be rated as "seconds" or "firsts," according as it more nearly resembles the "seconds" or the "firsts" among the boots of a similar general character in the standard show-case.

It will be seen that the Northampton statement introduces into the boot trade a principle which, in its adaptability to the ever-changing conditions of industry, somewhat resembles the sliding-scale as it is applied in the case of miners' wages. The hard and fast lines drawn by the London statements disappear; and in their place we have a wage-standard which claims to be flexible enough to suit the requirements of the manufacturers, but rigid enough to protect the interests of the men.

It is not surprising that the adoption of the Northampton statement in 1887 (which has been followed by the introduction of a similar arrangement at Kettering) should have suggested to the London manufacturers the advisability of renewed negotiations with the Trade Unions, in order, if possible, to obtain for the metropolitan trade a statement of wages on the lines of that in force in Northampton—a statement doing away with the distinctions between first-class, second-class, and non-statement houses, and embracing the entire trade, and giving in future to all the London manufacturers, without exception, a great degree of freedom as to the quality or description of goods to be made by them. These negotiations, commenced in the latter part of 1887, are not yet* concluded.

This much seems certain; the arrangements hitherto in force are such as to cause grave prejudice to a number of the principal employers of labour in the trade, employers against whom, certainly, no lack of fairness in dealing with their hands can be alleged, and at the same time to tend to the serious disadvantage of many of the operatives. In fact, while some of the most reputable of the London manufacturers are over-regulated by the Trade Unions, the large majority, including all the most grinding tyrants to be found among the employers, escape all regulation whatever.

It remains to speak of the trade organization of the operatives working under the team system, which is distinct from that of the general body of workmen. Until within the last year or two such a thing as trade organization was unknown among the operatives of the former class. Now they have two special Trade Unions. These are the Jewish Mutual Boot Finishers' and Lasters' Trade and Benefit Society (a combination of sweating masters), and the International Journeymen Boot Finishers' Society. According to the statements† made to me by their respective secretaries, the former society numbers some 250, the latter about 300 members. The Union of the sweating masters

---

* March, 1889.

† I have no means of checking the accuracy of these statements.

has induced a few among the non-statement manufacturers
to make agreements fixing the prices to be paid by them
for the work; the Union of the journeymen has, as yet,
taken no steps to secure from their employers an increase
in the remuneration of its members.

[*Note to Edition of* 1892-3.—Since the account of the
boot trade given above was compiled, changes, some of
them important in character, have taken place in the
conditions of this industry. Many of the workmen engaged
in the production of hand-sewn boots (the makers working
for the City shops, and both the makers and the closers
working for the West End shops), have received a material
advance in their Trade Union piece-wage. In 1890 a
strike took place affecting the wholesale trade in East
London, and having for its object the abolition of outdoor
work (whether done in the workshops of sub-contractors or
in the homes of the men) in the lasting and finishing
departments, so far as concerned the manufacture of boots
(as distinguished from sew-rounds). After a conflict, which
began on March 31st and ended on May 5th, a settlement
was arrived at, the manufacturers undertaking to have all
their boots lasted and finished upon their own premises by
workmen all employed directly by themselves. A Board
of Conciliation and Arbitration for the wholesale boot trade
in London has been formed; and a statement of wages has
been adopted which applies to all firms other than those
working under the provisions of the first and second-class
statements, and which is framed in a manner suited to
prevent much of the inconvenience experienced prior to the
adoption of these new arrangements. In the sew-round
branch a strike took place in September, 1890, the result
of which is thus described in the Report of the Board of
Trade on the Strikes and Lock-outs of 1890 (p. 63):
" Statement compiled at a meeting of masters and men.

Result was an advance of about 12½ per cent. Some of the employers granted the men's demands early in the strike "; see also the remarks by an employer at p. 180 of the same Report. The concessions obtained appear to have affected the position of the workers engaged in producing sew-round shoes of the superior grades, but to have created no alteration in that of the persons (mostly of foreign birth) employed in the manufacture of the low-class varieties.

The clickers in the wholesale trade have organized a Trade Union, which, according to the evidence given before the Labour Commission, has 1,650 members in "London and district," including Croydon and St. Albans. The two Jewish Trade Unions have become absorbed into the National Union (now termed the National Union of Boot and Shoe Operatives).

The effects in regard to the industrial position of the workpeople and otherwise caused by the changes referred to in this note it is not practicable to examine upon the present occasion.]

CHAPTER V.

TAILORING AND BOOTMAKING IN CENTRAL LONDON.

The following notes on Tailoring and Bootmaking outside of East London and the Women's work connected therewith may be of interest.

(1.)—COMPARISON WITH EAST LONDON.

In both tailoring and bootmaking, we have in Central London the "West End" trade, that is the work done for the fashionable shops of Regent Street and the neighbourhood. The general characteristic of this trade is high-class work, commanding a good price, and those who get enough of it do very well. It is the irregularity of the work which brings poverty; and which may usually be coupled with irregularity of life. The best and most trustworthy workmen, both tailors and bootmakers, are hardly ever without work, and setting long hours in busy times against some enforced idleness in slack times, working when they can and only playing when they must, may average full work the year round. From this satisfactory condition of things there is a sliding scale downwards till we come to those who can only count on having work when no one in the trade is idle. It may be that these unfortunate men have not the capacity, and that their work will only pass muster when the standard is somewhat relaxed, as it comes to be in the busier season; or that, either from illness, old age, drunkenness, or idleness, they are not to be counted on for doing regular work, and so lose their chances. Possibly it is their own fault, or perhaps not, but it remains in any case the fact that there are many who are very poorly off.

If all were equally good workmen, and all shared equally among them the work as it comes in, it must be said that none would be very well off, for none would average anything like full work. It is only by monopolizing nearly all the work in slack times that the steady and capable men make up a tolerable average earning. Their prosperity has as its shadow the poverty of the less capable or less steady; and it must be admitted that, on the whole, the rate at which the work is remunerated is none too high. But it is not easy to raise it, for, it will be seen, there is a vicious circle out of which it is hard to get. A rise of wages, if obtained, goes mostly to those who need it least, while the necessities of those who, even with an increased wage, have not enough to live upon, undermine the position of the workers and rob combination of its power. It follows that to diminish the numbers of the incapable, and so strengthen the possibilities of combination, is the only policy which promises permanent success.

Both in tailoring and bootmaking, the best "bespoke" work, which is the kernel of the West End trade, has a limited and perhaps a rather shrinking sphere, but the supply of first-rate workmen is as limited as the trade, and to make themselves into a close corporation, pushing all

who are not capable workmen and good unionists into other
branches of their trade, would seem the most hopeful
plan.

The " Factory system," which involves the utmost use of
machinery; the " Sweating system," which by division of
labour makes use of workmanship of all qualities at varying
prices ; and the employment of individual artisans who
themselves perform all parts of the work, may roughly be
taken as representing the " Provincial," the " East End,"
and the " West End " methods of production respectively.
They of course overlap a little; there are factories in East
London, and there is some sweating in the West End, and
work is done on all three plans in the provinces; but
speaking generally the division holds. Each system is
capable of good as well as of evil, and those employed
under each must work out their industrial salvation
according to the circumstances of their particular case.

Bootmaking, which in East London is divided into six or
eight different operations by as many classes of workpeople,
has only two divisions in West End work. There is the
" closing" or putting together of the upper portion of the
shoe or boot, and there is the "making," which includes
all the rest of the work connected with making and finishing the boots or shoes. Closing is done either in the workshops of the employers or in the homes of the work-people.
When done at home, a man will very commonly have the
assistance of his family ; his wife, or a daughter, or perhaps
a son will work with him, and he may have two or even three
sewing machines. There are instances in which family
work of this kind degenerates into sweating, and even into
" sub-contract," but such cases are not usual, safe-guarded
as the trade is in this direction by the fact that the quality
of the work must be very good to satisfy the West End
employer and his customers. "Making " is either done at

home (each man working alone or possibly with an apprentice, who will most likely be the workman's son), or in "co-operative workshops." There seems no good reason why the workshops in this case should be provided by the men and not by the employer, as is, I think, invariably the plan in other trades—but so it is. To work at home is often not convenient, and the work is not such as wife or children can assist in, so the men often club together, subscribe a shilling a week a-piece, and hire a room where each has his seat and his bench. There may be 12 or 15, or as many as 40 or 50, in one of these workshops, and altogether perhaps 150 or 200 workmen are so accommodated in the district, drawn from about 600 members of the Trade Union. None but members of the Union are admitted to the workshops. The government of these shops is by committee, like a club, and one member usually acts as secretary, and receives a small remuneration. The subscription provides cost of firing (in winter) and newspapers, in addition to the rent. Rents for such shops are high, and it takes a well-filled room to leave any margin over expenses, out of the shilling subscribed. Any surplus is divided from time to time, and on the other hand if the room is not full, an extra three-pence or so a week may be levied to meet the weekly payment of the rent. The men naturally sort themselves; there are quiet and respectable shops, and others of a faster sort. If men are too fast or too slow for their companions they are pushed out, and some discretion is used in admitting new members. Political feeling runs deep rather than high, for there is not much difference of opinion—almost all are Radicals, only some go further than others, towards Republicanism or Socialism. The hours kept are irregular, and mostly so when work is slack, as after half a day lost in waiting, the work is often needed in a hurry, and the time wasted must be made up by working late at night or coming early in the morning. There are two keys to the shop, one of which any member wishing to stay late or come early can take for the time, the other remains with the doorkeeper, who is chosen for living conveniently near-by. Every man provides his own lamp for lighting, and his own spirit-lamp for heating the irons needed in the finishing, and also finds his own " grindery," a term which covers wax, thread, &c., as well as tools. Meals may be brought to the shop from home or from a cookshop—but most of the men go out or home for dinner. Those who work in these shops do not all live in the neighbourhood, as working in this way makes it easier to live elsewhere—at Battersea for instance.

In *Tailoring,* as in bootmaking, the West End system involves comparatively little division of labour—for although in the tailor's shops two men work together, they work as partners. Of the life led in such a shop and the conditions of the trade, there follows an account written by one whose daily life it is. I wish I could hope to lay before my readers as vivid and true a description of the internal working of every industry in London :

(2.)—West End Tailoring—Men's Work.

A Tailor's Workshop.—Few workpeople in what are termed the organized Trades of the West End, spend more time in their workshops than the journeyman tailor. He ordinarily begins work at 8 A.M. (although many start at 5 and 6 o'clock), and scarcely leaves the workroom until 8 P.M., thus usually putting in fully 12 hours' continuous work in the day, which is often stretched to 14 and 16 hours in busy times. His food, which is generally partaken of in the workroom, may be put down as follows :—*Breakfast* at 8 or half-past, consisting of tea or coffee, bread and butter, with an occasional rasher of bacon, bloater, haddock, or couple of eggs; *Luncheon* at 11 A.M.: beer, bread and cheese; *Dinner* at 1 o'clock: beef or mutton, vegetables, pudding and beer; *Tea* at 4 o'clock, with bun or bread and butter; this, with an occasional glass or two of beer, constitutes his day's food, and is nearly always taken by the tailor sitting on the board, with his work lying at his side and the newspaper in front of him. Of course many make it convenient to go out to their meals, but in the West End shops they are the exception. This is especially the case in the busy seasons, which are supposed to extend from March to August, and from October to December. In the matter of dress, tailors have always been considered the best off among working men, and certainly the younger members of the trade keep up their reputation in that respect. Many of the supposed West End mashers are nothing more or less than our friend the tailor.

A number of different tradesmen go round supplying the men with food, beer, cloth, boots, hats, &c., in fact nearly all the necessaries of life can be had in the shops by the payment of weekly instalments. In many of the shops the men have a loan society (called a boot fund) to which the men pay in one shilling per week, the money being loaned out at the rate of a halfpenny or penny in the shilling per week. These societies generally last about six months, when they are broken up, the principal and interest being shared out between the members.

There is in all shops a kind of unwritten code of laws that all must act up to, one of the most general being that all new hands must pay their footing—called "standing their ale." This generally costs the new-comer 1s 4d, the price of half a gallon; those who wish to drink with him subscribe enough among them (called "bears") to bring in ale sufficient to give one or two glasses all round, with which they pledge each other's healths. Births, birthday and marriage anniversaries, and other like events, are made the occasion of having ale from the individual interested therein, and in many of the workshops to be seen walking with a female friend costs the unlucky individual no end of annoyance until he pays his ale for her (called "putting her in the pitcher"); after that, should anyone in the shop speak disrespectfully of her, he is at once fined for so doing. One of the most amusing incidents that takes place in a shop is a trial, which is arranged in this way: Let us suppose that A has said or done something that B considers to be insulting to him: the latter places 1s in the hands of a member of the shop who has been appointed judge, and states his complaint; A is then called on for his defence, after which the jury, consisting of all the men working, retire and consider the question; returning to the shop they inform the judge of their verdict, which is invariably one of guilty; the judge then puts on his judicial robes, consisting of a sheet of white wadding over his head, and in most solemn tones pronounces the sentence, usually "I fine you in one gallon of good old ale, and confiscate the shilling lodged by B as court expenses." If A refuses to pay he is "put out the pitcher," i.e. boycotted, until he does. These mock trials have been at times used as a means of dealing out well-merited punishment to individuals who have been guilty of mean or harmful actions towards their fellow-workmen; but the new race of tailors will scarcely stand all the nonsense of the good (?) old times—in fact, the tension of their work hardly allows it, except in the slack season; and then they have no money to spare for such foolery.

The irregularity of employment in the trade is responsible for a deal of the gambling—such as dice, domino and card playing—that goes on in the workshops; the system of working being piece work, it is no loss to the employer should the foreman keep a man sitting idle for hours, or even days, through his bad management, and very few firms make any attempt to arrange their work so as to secure greater regularity of employment for the journeyman.

Coatmaking, which is considered to be the principal branch of the trade, is usually carried on by two men working together as partners; one makes the left and the other the right fore-part. The left man is the captain of the job; he is responsible for seeing the work put fairly together; he marks with cotton thread all the outlets left on the job by the cutter, cuts all the pockets and linings, makes the left side of the coat, makes and puts on the collar, and gives the work the final press off. The right man makes the right side of the coat, both sleeves, and joins the halves together. Partners generally take rights and lefts alternately. Vests and trousers are made by separate and single individual workmen.

The foreman, who cuts and gives out the work, has a great deal to do with making a shop good or bad for the workers. Some are petty tyrants, who never get on well with their workmen, others the reverse, but in nearly all instances where the employer is himself the cutter the men are better treated and more considered. In all firms the garments are fitted on at least once, but some cutters require their work fitted on the customer three or four times, while in other cases the customer himself insists on having his clothes tried on again and again, and when finished is never pleased until they have been altered and re-altered times out of number. But whether it is the fault of the cutter or the customer, to the journeyman it is not only a source of great worry, but is an actual loss of wages as well. Alterations, although very worrying jobs, are generally paid for at the rate of sixpence per hour—that is, one penny per hour less than other work, and as it is in the interest of the cutters to keep down the cost of alterations and baisting, he squeezes down the worker to the very lowest possible point in the charging for time on these jobs !*

Often when the cutter feels a bit lazy, and the work is in no particular hurry, he will keep a man sitting about the shop for hours waiting for him to get ready some work; thus it frequently happens that a man may have been in the shop the whole day and not have earned one penny wages. The worker has always to be at the beck and call of the foreman, and scarcely gets a job that does not cost him an hour or more time getting his instructions from him.

Good workshops are the exception; many of them are in a very unhealthy condition, badly lighted, ventilated, and dirty.

Out Workers.—A tailor who works at home or in other places than the workshop provided by the employer, is in some respects a little better off than the indoor man. For instance, he has much more freedom as to hours of labour, and if he has no work he is not compelled to sit in the workshop waiting to be called, and almost afraid to go out for fear some one else gets his work; he is also allowed by most firms to use the machine at his work, and even in firms that do not allow machine work he can do a good deal that escapes detection; but in the present condition of the trade, the greatest advantage of all is that he has the power of making profit out of his own family, or the labour of an outsider whom he may engage to assist him. He can also—and it is very extensively done—work for two or more shops in the busy season, and getting a share of the work in the slack from all, he is never so hard up as the indoor man. The disadvantages are, however, very great. He has to pay for workshop room, light and firing; or if he

---

* It ought to be said that in tailoring the "*hour*" does not mean *sixty minutes*, but is the recognized allowance of time for a certain stint of work, which a quick workman will complete in considerably less time.

works at home, his house is always dirty, and in fact he surrenders all home comforts. He never gets more, but often less, money for his work than the indoor man; many employers compel him to supply thread, silk, and twist, needed for his work, and some compel him to purchase the same from them at an enhanced price, and not infrequently he has to buy his work by tipping the foreman, either directly or indirectly. The temptation to work extra hours is very strong; indeed, at times it is a necessity. It is no unusual thing for an outworker to get a job at night and be told that he must have it in by 10 o'clock next morning, which means working all night. Sundays are very extensively drawn upon to make up for any little extra pressure put upon them by the busy seasons, and many a time does a Christian employer give out work on the Saturday afternoon and require it to be returned completed the first thing on Monday morning, which is equal to commanding the worker to do it on the Sunday.

All outworkers employ labour of some kind; it may only be an errand girl, a member of his own family, but he very soon instructs her how to sew and fell, then machine, and so on until she becomes a full-blown tailoress, almost equal to himself as regards the amount of sewing she can do. Some go even further than one girl and employ several; many also employ one or two men, who through drink or other causes, have got too low down to go into a respectable shop to work. Thus the outdoor system is really nothing more than a kind of respectable sweating system.

I can scarcely tell how this outdoor working began, but it would seem to be coeval with the introduction and use of machinery; one thing is certain, that side by side with the cheapening of machines and the extension of the weekly payment system there is an ever-increasing number of outworkers. Doubtless the drinking and gambling customs prevalent in some shops, as also their unhealthy condition, with the meddlesome interference of a tyrannical

foreman, had something to do with it; but the ever-
increasing difficulty of getting a good living indoors,
with the knowledge that he can take an hour now and
again and make up for it at night or on the Sundays, as
also the fact that a profit can be made out of the employment of female labour, helps greatly to make a man an
outdoor worker.

The effect of outdoor work on the trade generally is
bad.   With the aid of the outworker, many firms are
springing into existence who are competing against and
crushing out the old-fashioned employers who treated their
workmen as human beings.   The men, never meeting or
scarcely seeing each other, do not and cannot know what
rate of pay each is getting; hence in many shops one man
is paid 2s less for making a coat than another man, working for the same firm.   Of course the general tendency is to
cut down prices to the lowest minimum accepted by the
cheapest worker.   This tendency is so marked that in many
firms they are now paying on some jobs about one half less
than they were two or three years ago; indeed, some of the
first-class firms have a regular supply of garments made by
the Jew sweaters, as in the busy time they cannot get the
West End tailors to work at the low price they have
reduced them to.   The Jews have, in fact, been regularly
established in the West End through the cutting down
tactics that outworking has enabled employers to pursue.

The tailors' organization is very weak, having only about
2600 members out of an estimated possible membership
of ten thousand in London.   The union has not been
able since the year 1866 to take any active steps to raise
the price or shorten the hours of labour; they are
working to-day on a log drawn up by masters and men in
that year; but instead of this statement being acknow-
ledged by at least two-thirds of the West End employers,
as it was then, scarcely a fourth of the firms now pay the
prices therein laid down.

Many blame the foreign tailors in London for the low position they are in, and undoubtedly there are a great many foreigners working at the trade, very few of whom belong to the tailors' union ; but they are not as a rule to be found in the low-paid shops, although they do as a body show a decided preference for outworking.

The ladies' tailoring, which is a distinct branch of the trade, or has only sprung into existence within these past ten or twelve years, is supposed to be the best paid of all the branches, and it is significant that in this section the foreigners largely predominate.

Female competition has done much to keep the trade down; in fact, women have almost entirely wrested one branch of the trade—waistcoat making—out of the hands of the men, whilst trouser making is fast going the same road, although, as in coat making, they usually require a man to do the pressing.

The general tendency of the trade is in two distinct and opposite directions—the first is towards the highly organized and specialized factory system; this to-day has not reached further than to the clothing of the working and middle classes; the second is towards the old home industries of the eighteenth century. Between the two the modern West End tailor is being fast ground out of existence. He may stop, and possibly crush out, the home working by greater regulations as to hours of work and stricter sanitary inspection, but nothing, so far as I can see, will prevent the application of the factory system of production to the tailoring trade as a whole.

(3.)—WEST END TAILORING—WOMEN'S WORK.

Nowhere can the difficult problem of home work be better studied than amongst the tailoresses in the Soho, St. James's, and St. Giles's districts. Advantages and dis-

advantages seem almost equally balanced. Home work is
here the rule, if under that term we include work in the
workshop or living room of a tailor who has taken work out
from the shop, and not merely work in the home of the
tailoress herself. This being the case, we find that the
conditions of labour vary with each individual family. It
may seem at first sight of little importance whether a
woman works in her father's workshop at her own home, or
with one or two other women at someone else's workshop;
but the position of the woman may be very different in the
two cases. In the latter she is paid a fixed rate of wages ;
she must work continuously at times fixed by her employer,
and is subject to a strict supervision. But she meets her
employer on equal terms, can make her bargain with him,
and leave him if she likes, and although frequently obliged
to work overtime, can make it unprofitable to insist on it
unnecessarily by exacting some extra pay. If she works
for her husband, no price is agreed upon for her work ;
the proceeds are paid to her husband, and, were it necessary,
it would be difficult for her to determine or to claim
her equitable share of them. A daughter works under
somewhat similar conditions, but is generally allowed
pocket money, a privilege not always accorded to the wife,
who cannot at any moment give notice, and look for work
elsewhere as her daughter can. If the head of the family
is sober and steady, and fond of his wife and children, all
the advantages of family co-operation at home become
apparent. The wife is then only expected to help her
husband in her leisure time, when she has comfortably
performed all her household duties. In ordinary and slack
times she does very little work for him ; and in the busy
seasons she enables him to get his work sent to shop in
time without employing extra hands, and without excessive
'overtime. The daughters work fairly long hours, but are
not over-strained, and are free to take little holidays now
and again, and to rest when they feel tired. They are not

obliged to compete for employment with other women, and are free from the nervous fear of loss of employment. Their position relative to that of other women is as the position of an eldest daughter who teaches her brothers and sisters in her father's house is to that of a daily governess. But, as the daily governess is frequently better off than the daughter who teaches her brothers and sisters, so the tailoress at home may frequently be in a far worse plight than the one who goes out to work. The wife may have to work at every odd moment; she and her daughters may have to toil far into the night, and may be driven and bullied as no one but a husband and father could venture to drive or bully; and she may have the reward of seeing her husband drunk on the money of which she has had no opportunity of intercepting a share.

The desire to call their earnings their own is probably one of the reasons why so many girls work for other tailors in preference to working for their father; and only from these girls, and from widows and married women who are obliged to go out to work, can we arrive at any idea of the wages of women in the trade. It is absolutely impossible to estimate the separate value of the husband's work and the wife's work when all that we know is that the man was helped by his wife. This help may be of the slightest and most unskilled kind, or it may be the making of the garment throughout, with the exception of fitting and pressing; it may have been given for two hours a day or for twelve or thirteen. A tailor who has not been so fortunate, from a pecuniary point of view, as to secure a tailoress for his wife, and whose daughters either go to service or go out to work elsewhere, has to employ women, and his own earnings can be ascertained. All these circumstances combined make generalizations as to the effect of home work on wages almost impossible.

Analyzing the cases in which the wages of women in full

work have been given to me, I find a few instances in which
they are stated to be as high as 20s a week. The first is a
widow with five children, a waistcoat hand, whose husband,
a chair frame maker, had done no work for five years
previous to his death. She gave her earnings as 20s in
full work and 10s a week in slack time; her daughter,
age nineteen, was earning 10s a week at another workshop
as trouser finisher, and her son was an apprentice at the
same shop as his sister, earning 5s a week.

The next is a married woman whose husband, a dyer, had
been ill for eighteen months. He belonged to the Hearts
of Oak Society, and received an allowance from it, and with
this and the wife's earnings the family had been supported.
The eldest of the three children, aged fourteen, was learning
tailoring from her mother.

The third is a deserted wife with two children. She earned
20s in full work, but in the slack time in winter had only
earned 5s to 8s a week. During that time she had received
food and clothing and other assistance from her mother, and
when in full work again was paying back some of her debt.

The fourth is a girl of eighteen, who was helped by her
mother, sixty years of age. She supported her mother,
whose help was very small.

In all these instances there was obviously a reason for
putting forth all their energies and doing their utmost, and
there is little doubt that full work with the tailoresses must
always be accepted as including overtime. The ordinary
rate earned by a strong, industrious girl, after she has gone
through her apprenticeship and worked a year or so as an
improver, is from 15s to 18s a week, without over-pressure,
when fairly busy. Even in the details given by applicants
for assistance from the Charity Organization Society, 10s
is the lowest rate given, and 12s to 15s is a common one.
To be strictly accurate, I should mention that within a
period of two years, two tailoresses in the St. James's and
Soho district stated that their wages in full work were less

than 10*s*. One was an old woman, sixty-five years of age, the other was a woman of extremely bad character, and a confirmed drunkard. Of those who earned as little as 10*s* when in full work, one was a girl, *eighteen* years of age, who had a child eight months old, and whose husband, a silver-smith, had only had odd jobs for the last ten months; another was a woman who called herself a widow, and drank; another was a single woman in bad health; the fourth was a girl of sixteen, and the fifth was an old woman of sixty-six. In the two remaining instances, there were no special reasons to explain the lowness of the rate stated.

Skill in this trade is to a great extent hereditary; and it is noteworthy that the daughter of a tailor rarely takes to dressmaking. Her work must be good and trustworthy, and many a dressmaker would prove quite incompetent to do it. But on the other hand there seems to be among the tailoresses a repugnance to undertake any work requiring mental exertion; and dressmaking demands thought and attention, owing partly to the constant change in fashion. Waistcoat-making might be almost entirely in the hands of women were it not for the reluctance of the tailoresses to incur what they call "responsibility." Very few can make the whole garment, and they are nearly always content to leave the "fitting" to men. One garment, however, is sometimes made throughout by women—cassocks. The demand for cassocks is, I am told, on the increase, and women can make them throughout because they need not fit.

A natural result of this home work system is that nearly all the members of a tailor's family learn tailoring; and another consequence is frequent intermarriages between tailors and tailoresses. To marry a tailoress is to a tailor the same thing as marrying an heiress; and the tailoress runs the same risk as the heiress; she is only too frequently married in order to be exploited. She sometimes has to earn her living and do the housework for nothing as well. Again, the family in busy seasons may be collectively extremely well off; in slack seasons they may all be out of work together. In such cases, however, they have no excuse for pleading poverty, as too many of them do when out of work; their earnings, in good times, being quite sufficient to enable them to save for the bad season. But prosperity is frequently too much for them, and, coming as it does for only about four months in the year, tempts them to indulge extravagantly in amusements. Living so close to the theatres they are unable to resist the temptation to go whenever they can, instead of at the rare intervals at which they could afford this luxury if they earned an average regular wage.

If the life of a tailor's wife is at times an endless drudgery, there is no doubt that in one respect she is better off than the wives of the majority of artisans. Widowhood does not bring with it such poverty and wretchedness as it often does in the case of women who are left to support their children, and who have not worked at any trade since their marriage. The widow of a carman, or porter, or labourer has often no resource but to go out as charwoman or to take in plain needlework. The tailoress, unless she has a very large family, can manage to keep herself and her children without appealing to charity or the parish for relief.

[*Note to Edition of* 1892-3.—Little, if any, change has to be recorded in the East End tailoring trade. The Trade Union organized immediately after the Dock Strike in 1889, comprising machinists, basters, and pressers, has practically collapsed, owing mainly to internal divisions among the members, many of whom, wholly ignorant of English language, customs, or ideas, have demanded a strike, or, at least, some tangible benefit for their pence, before they have been a month clear on the books. Thus a section of the organization were ever ready to discharge a

committee who refused to take action, another set were
as ready to throw out the committee that *did* take action,
while all sections united to tear to pieces anyone in office
who might be on the losing side in a dispute. Thus, when
the officials of the Union declared a general strike in 1891,
only a small number of those concerned obeyed the order,
and when the strike was lost, for all practical purposes the
Union had ceased to exist. Several efforts have since been
made to reorganize this section of the trade, but with very
little success.

During the early part of 1892 the West End tailors'
committee approached the County Council with the object
of securing the payment of fair wages to those employed
upon the clothing contracts for the Council, and, at the
request of that body, called a conference of the various
organized trades so employed. This conference drew up a
special "Log" for the clothing contracts, but owing to the
differences and divisions amongst the workers themselves,
it was never presented to even one firm usually engaged in
contract work. Result: no Trades Union rate of pay for
the Council contracts.

In the West End, early in 1891, the tailors employed by
the best firms sent a circular to their employers requesting
the concession of healthy workshops, a uniform time
Log for London, and the abolition of partnerships.*
Failing to receive satisfactory replies to these demands, a
strike was ordered by the London District Committee.
Immediately this step was taken the employers began to
give way, and ultimately conceded the three points
demanded by the men. The Log was, of course, the central
point, and has increased the prices paid by the best City
and West End firms for making garments from 10 to 50
per cent. Though many employers evade paying the full
Log price, the general result has been a substantial

* As described in notes on Coatmaking.

increase on the previous rates of pay. As to the provision of healthy workshops, it would be safe to say that not half-a-dozen employers have attempted to keep their pledge upon this point; and it must also be admitted that the Union does not seem inclined to press the matter very urgently. This may be accounted for by the fact that the greater portion of the work is made by men and women in their own homes, who would in all probability refuse to go into workshops if offered to them, unless under strong pressure. It does not suit the employers to use this compulsion, and the Union is not strong enough to do so effectively. It remains to be seen whether there is power enough behind the recent orders of the late and present Home Secretaries to enforce the healthy workshop on the workers and employers in the tailoring trade. Generally speaking, the West End tailor seems to be losing ground; three out of every four employed in the trade will, if questioned, unhesitatingly give it as their opinion that trade is more irregular than ever, and, in spite of the Log, the yearly income smaller. If asked the reason, the indoor worker says it is all the fault of the outdoor hands, while the outdoor worker—with perhaps a keener perception—gives it as his firm belief that the trade is being entirely eaten up by the Jews. Certain it is that the Jews have now got a firm foothold in the West End tailoring trade, and, it is greatly to be feared, with no good results to the Gentile worker.]

CHAPTER VI.

THE FURNITURE TRADE.

1.—INTRODUCTION.

THE following pages are an attempt to describe the general conditions of the more important branches of the Furniture Trade in the East End of London. The statistics available have not been sufficient to enable me to classify correctly, either as regards functions or earnings, the total numbers engaged, and it has thus been found impossible to do more than describe the general features of the group; to indicate the classification of the different branches of which the group is composed; to consider some of the economic points that the description brings into prominence; and finally to consider some of the more important and more immediate causes, or apparent causes, that seem to have brought about the present condition of the trade.

The group is, moreover, of so great a complexity; the trades included in it so numerous; the varieties of articles made, and often solely made, by the individual worker, so great; the scale of earnings and the range of prices lend themselves so little to classification on account of variations in shape, and size, and quality, that in many directions much ground must be left uncovered. Even as regards those branches of the subject which are dealt with, it is felt that nothing more than approximations to truth can be hoped for when generalizations may be attempted.

I am indebted to many for the help they have given me, both to those who are members of the trade and to those who are outside it, especially amongst the latter to Mr.

G. E. Arkell, one of Mr. Booth's secretaries, for valuable help and information, and to Mr. E. W. Brooks, of King's College, Cambridge, for his assistance in collecting evidence.

Numbers.—The total number of men over 20 years of age engaged in this group of trades in Shoreditch, Bethnal Green, Hackney, and the Tower Hamlets, were, according to the 1881 Census returns, 12,030, and according to an estimate based on Mr. Booth's inquiry, made 6 years later, 12,769. In addition, it is estimated that there are about 2,200 youths and boys engaged, and thus the total number (exclusive of women) may be estimated at the present time to amount to about 15,000. The women, according to the 1881 Census, numbered 778.

Of the men, 5,117 are entered by Mr. Booth as "heads of families," and taking five as the average number of persons in a family, we shall then have an approximate total of those working in or dependent on this group of trades of about 36,000. These figures include, however, a certain number of box-makers, shop-fitters, and undertakers, who have been scheduled under the Furniture trade group, but who are not included in the scope of this inquiry. The first of these are enumerated with the turners, and their numbers cannot therefore be accurately estimated. It is probable that about 1,000 should be deducted to allow for these three branches, and there will then be left a total of 35,000.

Area.—The trade is carried on chiefly in Bethnal Green and Shoreditch, and while the former includes the larger number, the latter embraces the chief centre of distribution. Bethnal Green does hardly anything but make. Shoreditch also makes, but it is there that the Curtain Road district —the chief market of the trade—is located.

The following comparative table will best show the distribution of adult workers. The figures indicate the place of abode, and this would in many cases be different from the place of employment. If the latter could also be indicated, the concentration of the trade in Shoreditch and Bethnal Green would probably be still more marked:

	Shoreditch.		Bethnal Green.		Hackney.		Tower Hamlets.		Whole district.	
	Census 1881.	Mr. Booth's Inquiry.	Census 1881.	Mr. Booth's Inquiry.	Census 1881.	Mr. Booth's Inquiry.	Census 1881.	Mr. Booth's Inquiry.	Census 1881.	Mr. Booth's Inquiry.
Cabinet Makers and Upholsterers	2460	2769	2843	3154	1079	1315	1278	1181	7660	8419
French Polishers ...	475	612	290	393	87	135	187	176	1039	1316
Wood Carvers and Gilders	548	606	631	737	227	216	302	247	1766	1948
Wood Turners and Box Makers	264	354	466	440	86	127	221	118	1037	1039
Shop Fitters, &c.* ...	107	56	96	42	125	67	198	82	526	247
Total ...	3912	4339	4328	4766	1604	1860	2186	1804	12030	12769

* For this group the basis of classification differed in the Census and in Mr. Booth's inquiry. The apparent discrepancy of the totals is thus explained.

The Curtain Road is the heart of the East London trade, and the whole neighbourhood pulsates with its movements. In every adjacent street are seen signs of the dominant industry of the district, and the shops of cabinet-makers, french-polishers, upholsterers, turners, and chair-makers (with here and there a timber-yard), are found at every turn. Even the majority of those in the streets are connected with the trade, and on Saturdays the whole district is alive with those who are taking their goods to the wholesale dealers, —who may have ordered them, and who in any case may buy.

"The Road" itself is now almost entirely made up of warehouses, and these establishments are also numerous in Great Eastern Street, the main thoroughfare that crosses the Curtain Road, and in three or four other of the principal adjacent streets. Many of these warehouses are simply show-rooms, some of great size; a few have workshops of different kinds on the upper floors, but for the most part the buildings flanking "The Road" are places of sale and not of manufacture. The various technical processes are carried on in back streets more or less remote, and the important question of the relation between those who make and those who sell must be considered later.

To the west of the Curtain Road the trade spreads over a large part of the parish of St. Luke's (Finsbury), and in Bunhill Row and its neighbourhood there are many large and a few first-class workshops. Chiswell Street and Sun Street roughly mark the southern boundary of the trade, but the greater part of this district, including the whole of that lying within the borough of Finsbury, is not included in this inquiry. With the Finsbury trade, therefore, we are not concerned, except to note that it provides a market for much of the produce of the East End, and gives employment to many of its inhabitants.

In the Tower Hamlets there are, as the foregoing table shows, no large numbers employed, and it is in Bethnal Green that we find at once the largest numbers employed and the largest area covered with the typical East End trade, viz., that carried on in the small workshop. Of the Bethnal Green trade Gossett Street, the western continuation of the Old Bethnal Green Road, may be considered the centre, and in the immediate neighbourhood of this street the atmosphere of the trade pervades the whole area, no less than it does in the streets lying immediately around the Curtain Road. But there are differences : there are no warehouses ; even large workshops are few and far between, and the most conspicuous signs of the chief crafts of the district are the timber-yards and the saw-mills. But in many of the houses, and in nearly every workshop, furniture is being made : there are fewer polishers and upholsterers than there are further west, but chair-makers, cabinet-makers, turners, and carvers abound. It is the region of small makers, whose presence in the trade in such large numbers gives at once the most striking characteristic of the East End furniture trade and furnishes the key to so many of those special problems and special difficulties that this group presents.

Gossett Street is the centre of this district, but the area spreads over a wide field ; beyond the Cambridge Road the density of shops diminishes, but they are still found in considerable numbers, and the Regent's Canal may be taken as the eastern boundary. The area of the trade has been gradually extended in all directions, and, in consequence, a considerable number of shops are found north of the Canal, and in Hackney we find that there are some 1300 makers living. But the Canal may still be taken as roughly marking the northern as well as the eastern boundary line.

Market.—Two outlets for the produce of the East End workshop have been mentioned, viz., the dealers of the City and Finsbury district, and those of the Curtain Road and its district, and it is to the latter of these that most of the furniture made undoubtedly goes. The Curtain Road dealer is, however, a "middleman," and only a very small part of his stock goes directly to the consumer. His market is rather found in the shops of the Tottenham Court Road, of the suburbs, and of the provinces, and he carries on a large export trade. The same markets that are open to the producer through the agency of the dealer are, however, open to him directly, especially if he can give credit, and there are many signs that the dealers of the provinces and of the other parts of London are buying their goods to an increasing extent direct from the makers. The export trade seems to be almost entirely in the hands of the warehousemen, and they still form that section of the trade which is most enterprising and most energetic in carrying on the task of extending the market for East London furniture : it is they who may be said to do most to form that "connection" which every trade may be regarded as needing in its entirety, in the same way that every individual needs it for his own particular business.

General Organization of the Trade.—In attempting to describe the general organization of the trade, it will be found most convenient to be guided as far as possible by the order in production, and to endeavour to trace the material used from the timber-yard to the show-room. Before attempting to do this, however, it will be desirable to state one or two facts relating to the general features of the trade.

Recent controversy has turned a somewhat fierce light upon the group with which we are now concerned, and the residual impression that has been left in the minds of many seems to be a belief that those engaged in the East End furniture trade are made up of wage-earning slaves, of driven and driving "garret masters," and of a class of powerful and wealthy wholesale dealers. And the impression contains some element of truth, albeit partial and misleading, if accepted without careful qualification.

During the past fifteen years or more there has been

a rapid increase in the number of small makers, earning for the most part little themselves, and their employees somewhat less; and making chiefly goods of medium or inferior quality for large wholesale dealers. But in the East End there are still a few makers of considerable size, the produce of whose shops rivals that made in any other part of London, and who pay almost as high wages as any in the West End, in spite of that keenness of competition and the increasing demand for cheap articles which make it harder for first-class firms to hold their own. But still there are representatives of this class in the very centre of the East End, and the quality of work turned out and the character of the shops found there shade down from this superior minority through every grade, until we reach the produce and the tenements of those pariahs of the trade who work with little or no capital; and who only have some specialized and half-taught knowledge of their craft. It is they who, if orders fail, are driven from the need of money, either to meet their own personal expenses or to pay the wages of the one or two men they may employ and to buy material for the next week's work, to go out and sell their goods wherever and whenever they can.

From the East End workshops, therefore, produce goes out of every description, from the richly inlaid cabinet that may be sold for £100, or the carved chair that can be made to pass as rare "antique" workmanship, down to the gipsy tables that the maker sells for 9s a dozen, or the cheap bedroom suites and duchesse tables that are now flooding the market. Remembering, then, that the East End trade is far more complex and representative than it is generally considered to be, we may still single out the following as general tendencies in the trade : (1) the multiplication of " trade shops," mostly of small size, which make for the wholesale dealer, and not for the retailer or for the private customer ; and (2) accompanying the former, partly as cause and partly as effect, the rise of a large class of those whose main business is that of distributing, far and wide, the produce of the workshops. As regards makers, therefore, the tendency is towards a small system of production, often so small as to make the furniture trade in many of its branches almost a domestic industry; while as regards wholesale dealers it is, in spite of their large numbers, in the opposite direction, and tends to concentrate in the hands of a few large houses this branch of the trade.

The only other ways in which the trade seems to follow what is considered the modern tendency, viz., that of a gradual substitution of the large for the small system, be it of distribution or of production, are, to a great extent, the latter system under disguised forms. For the very few large factories in which expensive and elaborate machinery has been set up, and the large "saw-mills" in which the turning and small sawing are chiefly done, are, for the most part, either places where the work is largely executed by "piece-masters," with one or more working under them and paid by them, or by those who are actually sub-tenants of the proprietor, working on their own account.

In spite then of what has been written as to the variety of the East End trade, it still remains true that the typical producer is the man of small means, working with from three to six under him, and with little capital and no machinery; and it is the knowledge of the system of production followed by such men that will give the most insight into the condition of the East End makers. Let us take the case of a chair and couch maker who is making the frames of cheap dining-room suites* "for order" for a wholesale dealer.

If he be, as is assumed, a man of very small capital (though many small men are by no means working thus from hand to mouth), he will probably have to buy

---

* Generally consisting of one couch, two arm-chairs, and six small ditto.

the timber to be made up one week with the earnings of
the week before, and he will procure this material from a
neighbouring small merchant.* The timber required will
be bought in planks ready for "marking out," and when
this has been done, the wood will have to be taken to a
sawyer, who will probably be working on his own account
in a neighbouring saw-mill. If there be any turning or
fret-cutting needed, these processes will again be executed
by different workers and probably in the same mill. The
maker will now have the whole of the material again in
his hands, but if there be any carving to be done, the parts
to be so worked must go into the hands of the carver, who
is also, very likely, especially in those branches of the trade
in which there is little carving introduced, to be an outside
worker. The "maker," in spite of the help he thus gets
from others, has much to do himself in planing, shaping,
dowelling, glueing, cleaning-up, and glass-papering. These
parts of the work will be carried out according to the size
of the order and according to the habit of the workshop;
sometimes, and most often, one man making right out, at
others, two working on what is called the "hand-in-hand"
system, and at others the same piece of furniture passing
in the making through several pairs of hands. The frames
are now ready, not for the consumer, but for the wholesale
dealer. They go to him "in the white," that is, with the
polishing and upholstering still to be done. If we followed
them we should probably find that they were kept in that
unfinished state in the warehouse of the dealer until
ordered, and were then sent either into his own workshop,
or more probably into the workshop of a contractor, to be
polished and upholstered.

Mutatis mutandis, the history of the production of other

* A week's credit is often given by the small timber merchants, and sometimes a month's. It is rarely longer, but varies according to business
character, and some small makers can get considerable credit even when orders
are not coming in, but when they are known to be making "for stock."

articles made by the same class of maker would be similar. Division of labour would always come into operation, although the number of processes employed and the extent of the subdivision would necessarily vary, as would also the proportion of the work that would have to be done outside the shop. But in the vast majority of cases the sawing, the turning, and the fret-cutting would be done outside, as would also the polishing, and, when required, the upholstering, and frequently the carving.

The foregoing indicates that the furniture trade forms a somewhat highly organized group, but no mention has yet been made of many of the branches into which it may be divided. Under the heading of "cabinet making" in the roughly made census classification of trades, no less than forty-one branches are enumerated, and although it will be unnecessary to use for the purposes of description so minute a classification as this, a more complete one must be at least indicated than has yet been done. Veneer cutters and dealers, designers and draughtsmen, marquetry cutters and inlayers, and engravers, with many others, are among the distinct branches of the trade. But for the purposes of this inquiry it is specially necessary to emphasize the fact that almost every chief division of the trade, such as cabinet making, turning, &c., is capable of repeated analysis and subdivision. It is impossible, for instance, to tell what a man may be able to do who calls himself a cabinet maker, for one frequent consequence of the localization in a small area of a great industry, when carried on under modern conditions, is found in this group in the inefficiency of the worker, and the incompleteness of his industrial education. It requires effort, and it requires time, to get an all-round trade equipment, and if a market makes it possible, and even easy, quickly to earn some sort of livelihood at making hall-stands or gipsy tables, the temptation is great (and the temptation that comes from inertness is often strengthened by the pressure that comes from the need either of self-support or of supporting others) to stop at this or some other equally partial knowledge, and to run in one narrow industrial groove through life. There are thousands doing this in the East End to-day, and thus it comes about that we have as a leading characteristic of the furniture trade, not simply the presence of very large numbers of small masters and of men working on their own account, but also a highly and excessively specialized use made of the skill that they do possess. We find men who call themselves cabinet makers making only one, or it may be two or three articles, and this fact, coupled with that of a small system of production, may be said to be the leading characteristic of the whole district. Having seen how highly organized is the group, and how very much subdivided is the labour employed, and remembering always how great a variety of standard of production it presents, the attempt must be made to describe the position in the group of some of its leading branches.

II.—The Branches of the Trade.

Timber Merchants.—The timber merchants may be roughly divided into two classes: (1) the large dealers, who buy direct from the importers and supply the larger manufacturers and the smaller timber dealers; and (2) these smaller dealers themselves. It is, as might be expected, the latter class that supply the majority of East End makers, and their presence in large numbers is the normal accompaniment of a large market of buyers, who can only purchase in small quantities, and whose credit is small. Many of the makers of the East End need a small timber dealer close by, who may perhaps be induced to give them credit, and who will in any case sell to them in very small quantities, in the same way that the housewife with small means and irregular income is obliged to patronize the small "general shop" in her own street. The small timber merchant is one of the many classes that make up the organization of a trade that is perhaps too admirably adapted to suit the convenience of the small maker.

The timber merchant often not only supplies the maker with his material, but cuts it up for him, and we thus come to the sawyer, who, as has been already indicated, is important not only on account of the demand that there is for his services, but also from the way in which he also facilitates a small system of production. We may for the most part neglect the designer and the draughtsman, and the veneer cutter and dealer, who represent indeed important sections of the trade, but whose numbers are not large and whose position in the trade does not call for any special description.

Sawyers and Turners.—There are three descriptions of mills at which "the trade" can have their wood sawn. The timber merchant himself, if he has no machinery, and the large maker send much of their timber to be cut up at one of the three or four large saw-mills in the East End, which are the only ones that have a complete plant of machinery, and where alone all kinds of cutting can be done from sawing a log into three-inch planks down to preparing the knife-cut veneers of which sixty will go to the inch. It is these mills that are used by most of the veneer dealers (of whom there are now about twenty in the East End) as well as by timber merchants and makers. The vertical saws that are used for plank-sawing, by which a log may be cut in one process into as many as fifty sections, are also set up by many of the timber merchants themselves, and also by the proprietors of those "saw-mills" in which steam-power and bench-room are often let out to various classes of workers. This vertical sawing is therefore in the hands of large or of fairly large capitalists, but the "band sawing" and the small circular sawing is carried on by a much wider class; it is they who form a large part of the tenants of those saw-mills in which steam-power is let out, and it is they who, as a matter of course, execute the small orders of the small makers around them. They do not cut into planks, but they cut into the various sections and shapes that the maker requires. The band saw, which is as the name suggests band-shaped, revolving like the leathern connecting gear of machinery, is used to cut patterns of all kinds and the circular saw for straight sections. In both cases the wood, resting on the table in the centre of which is the revolving saw, is pressed against the tool and carefully guided by the sawyer, and the sawing is done with astonishing rapidity, not less when a pattern has to be followed, and the wood constantly readjusted so as to trace the marking on it, than when straight sections have to be cut. The fret sawing is largely done by a corresponding class of small sub-tenants.

Economically the turner occupies an exactly analogous position to that of the band sawyer, although from the nature of his craft he is more often a maker of articles finished and ready for the market, and thus, as a class, is less dependent for a livelihood on the employment that he gets from the makers. But most of the turners are simply the auxiliaries of the latter class.

The turners and the sawyers make up by far the greater part of the tenants of the saw-mills, in which steam-power and bench-room are let out. There are about twenty mills of this kind in the East End of London, in which it is the prevailing custom to let bench-room, and, occasionally, the necessary plant, either to men working on their own account or to smaller masters.

At one of the largest of these mills there are some thirty men employed by the proprietor in his own business of timber merchant and cutter to the trade, and in his work-shops there are about 150 all told, who, either as his own immediate tenants or as the employees of his tenants, carry on their crafts under a single roof. Many work alone, while others have as many as four or five men, and very occasionally even a larger number, working under them. The building is partitioned off into small shops of varying size, and in these roughly divided compartments the tenants carry on their trades. With one or two exceptions they simply hire the room, the rent of which with steam-power varies in amount from 6s to 10s a week. If a lathe be hired, as well as steam-power and room, 4s per week is charged per lathe. All the tenants are English, and most of them are turners, but the turnery is of every description, from the turning of draughtsmen and the little wooden spindles covered to make ladies' embroidery, up to parts of ordinary furniture, and, at the time of our visit, to the high altitude of the wooden head-piece of a church spire. The larger number were working for the small makers of the district in which the mill is situated, who send their timber, marked for cutting or with directions for turning, pay their cash, and take it away to complete the making of the article of which it forms a part.

The demand for room in these large saw-mills is not as keen as it was ten or twelve years ago, and this is explained, not because the labour of those who occupy them is less in demand, but because the number of large saw-mills has been steadily increasing, as has also the number of shops in which a small capitalist can put up his own machinery. Of these smaller shops it is estimated by one of the proprietors of a large saw-mill that there are now about 100 in the East End. In the larger shops the numbers working in them vary from about 35 to 150; while of the smaller, the greater number contain from 6 to 12. The smaller shops are sometimes conducted under the immediate control of the occupier, but the practice of letting off parts of them is also common.

Sawyers, those who cut the wood to the marked pattern, turners to the trade, and fret-cutters, make up the great proportion of those working in these shops, be they large or small, but the trades carried on in them are very various, and moulders, glass bevellers, folding-chair makers, and towel-horse makers may be mentioned as instances, while the sawing, turning, and fret-cutting, are done for almost every branch of the furniture trade. When makers of any kind are found working as tenants in these mills, the article made is generally one in which the greater part of the work can be done by machinery, and in which the fitting, if there be any, and the putting together are short and simple processes.

The increasing number of saw-mills greatly facilitates the subdivision of labour that is found in the furniture trade of the East End. It is easy to send out of the workshop the part on which machinery can be used, and when this can be done but very little capital is necessary for those who wish to set up as makers; a pound's worth of tools and a second pound in cash starts many "cabinet-makers" on the career of independent worker, and double that amount will often convert him into an employer. On the other hand, the capital required to set up as a sawyer or a fret cutter or a turner in one of these mills is small, and if a man can hire a turning lathe the amount required becomes quite insignificant. This being so, a young turner who is perhaps earning his pound a week as a journeyman will be tempted at the earliest opportunity to start for himself even though he cannot with his increased responsibility earn more than 25s a week. A large proprietor has informed me that it is chiefly from competition acting in this way that the earnings of turners have fallen.

CABINET-MAKERS.—The most important division of the trade is that grouped under the comprehensive term "cabinet-making." No single basis of classification of the cabinet-makers gives a clear division : whether size of shop, quality of work, the kind of article made, or the market supplied be taken as the basis, all are found useful, but all overlapping. I propose to take the first of these. It will be convenient to exclude the wholesale dealers, who are often described, and who nearly always describe themselves, as makers, from the present section ; they are not infrequently the proprietors of workshops, and it is true that they occasionally have makers' shops under their own immediate control, and somewhat more often do the polishing and upholstering, but the rule is for them not to *make*, but to sell, and, as has been said, their first function is to create and extend a market. Chair and couch makers also, as forming a distinct branch of the trade, must have separate but very brief consideration.

Factories.—Of the cabinet-makers, then, of all kinds, including in this term makers of cabinets, bedroom furniture, office furniture, tables, book-cases, overmantels, whatnots, fancy work, &c., &c., we find first a very few, not more than three or four, large factories, with elaborate machinery, where from about 50 to 190 men are employed. Their output is large, and the quality of the work varies from the cheapest (although not perhaps the most roughly made) to good. Their market is found not so much with the wholesale trade in East London as with the large dealers in the Tottenham Court Road, in the provinces, or in the colonies. One at least of the largest of these makers exports considerable quantities of furniture to Australia, where he has representatives ; and he has also travellers in England. This class at the present time forms but an insignificant portion of the trade ; it contains, however, the sole representatives of the large system of production.

Larger Workshops.—In a second class come the shops of medium size in which from 15 to 25 men are generally employed. It is in this group that the best East End furniture is made, but the number of first-class shops is very small. Many good firms have had to give up altogether in recent years, while others have had to make an inferior class of goods, and the consequence is, that those who can weather the storm of a prevailing demand for cheapness are very few in number. One first-class journeyman has given me the names of only four firms that he reckons as "good" in the whole of the Bethnal Green district; and another man, whose knowledge of the trade is wide, reckons the whole of the really good makers in the East End, chair-makers included, at about 20 ; and it is probable that this is an approximately correct total.

There are not more than five or six firms in the whole district that buy original designs; a few others would execute, and in the best way, the new designs sent them by their customers; but in the great bulk of the trade repetition, and the making up of fresh patterns which are simply slight variations on those already in the market, are the ruling practices. It takes time to be original, and to do really new work, and there is no time to spare in the furniture trade in East London. No doubt the necessary skill is often available, but the hurry is too great, and the popular demand for cheapness, cheap things " at any cost," too strong, to give much opportunity for the exercise of artistic talent, or to allow much really good and careful work to be produced.

The majority of the few good shops that do exist work for " the trade " in London and the provinces, but not, as a rule, for the wholesale dealers.

There are a considerably larger number of shops of about the same size in which inferior work is made ; many of these have a " special line," in the same way that the smaller men have, such as bedroom furniture, or dining tables. Their market is found to a much greater extent among the wholesale dealers of the East End, but their goods are also sent largely to retailers, both London and provincial. Of shops of this size and character there are

probably about 35 or 40, thus giving an approximate total
for the whole district of 60, in which an average of about
20 are employed.

The Small Makers.—Thirdly, come the small shops with
from four to eight men generally working in them. The
work in the two preceding classes is chiefly carried on in
separately built workshops or factories ; in this third class
it is also often carried on in small workshops either built
behind the house, or away from it; in the latter case, forming very often one portion of a block of buildings which is
divided into workshops and let off to separate tenants. But
more often it is carried on in the homes themselves. As a
general rule the larger shops turn out the better work. But
even among the small men excellent work is done, in the
same way that it has been seen that large shops often turn
out cheap and inferior goods. But with the small shops we
may act on the principle of *de minimis non curatur,* and
divide them into those in which goods of medium quality are
made and those in which the quality is inferior, and from
the former standard the products will shade down through
all the intervening grades until we reach the rubbish of the
market—furniture that is knocked together with nails where
dovetailing should be used, is made of timber that is
unseasoned, and in which, in short, the ideal of "scamping"
is realized.

Estimates already given of the numbers of factories and
medium-sized workshops would give a total of about 1500
cabinet-makers employed in them ; and thus, according to
the table given on page 159, we should have nearly 7000
makers of all kinds, and of upholsterers, still to be
accounted for. The total number of upholsterers has not
been estimated, but it may be safely put down as about
equal to that of the polishers, or 1300, and this would be a
very liberal estimate. Cabinet-makers of all kinds, together
with chair and couch makers, working in small shops or
working alone (and of the latter class there are a consider-

able number) would thus be about 5700 or about 80 per cent. of the whole number. If we take the unit of the workshop at 5, we shall have a total of nearly 1140 places, be they shops or rooms, in which the small making is carried on. The roughly kept official lists of workshops in the furniture trades in the East End include about 1250 names, but in this list many classes, such as dealers, polishers, turners, &c., besides the larger makers and some names of those who are no longer in the trade, are included, while they are excluded from the preceding estimate. On the other hand, many small shops would not find their way on to the inspectors' lists on account of their smallness and rapid establishment and disappearance. It is probable therefore that the above estimate of 1140 rooms or shops in which manufacture on a small scale goes on is approximately correct. Figures are not available for separating the chair and couch makers from the cabinet-makers, but the latter class comprises the very large majority of the trade.

The market of the small maker will naturally be found chiefly at the nearest centre, and that, as has been said, is the Curtain Road and its district. Small men sell there, not only because their produce is adapted to this market, and not only because it is most accessible and therefore requires the least expenditure of time and money for the carriage of their goods, but also because it is the only large market where they can be sure of getting cash, either at the week's end, or when the goods are taken in. Shops further West, and the provincial trade, for the most part take credit, and this the small maker can rarely afford to give. The great majority therefore make for "the Road;" generally for order, and very often for two or three shops only. If orders run short, the more stable men work "for stock" and wait until the orders come in, or are found.

Hawking.—But large numbers cannot thus afford to wait, and then the trouble begins. During the few weeks after Christmas, for instance, which is the dull season in a trade which does not, however, vary much throughout the year, the ranks of those who habitually "hawk" their goods are recruited by numbers of those whose capital and whose credit alike force them to realize on their stock. Much has been heard of late of this system of "hawking," and we find its proximate cause in the large number of small makers in active competition with each other. It is not a system created by a class of dealers (who, however, often profit by it), but is the result of certain conditions found in this group of trades. It is not, as would seem to be sometimes supposed, something almost arranged by a malignant and grasping association of middlemen, but the accompaniment and normal outcome of a method of production which very small capitalists, whose own skill and that of whose workers is excessively specialized, to a great extent create. But although the practice of hawking is common, and although it may become a still graver source of disorganization than it is at present, reducing a larger body of workers in this trade to a position that is more analogous to that of the seller of penny novelties in the streets than to that of members of a skilled industry, its prevalence must not be exaggerated. It is true that articles of nearly every description are now hawked, sometimes of fair quality made by men who know their trade,* but as a rule it is poor albeit often very showy work that is sold under these poor conditions. Makers of any standing, even small men, never sell in this way, but work, as has been said, either for order, or for their own stock if orders temporarily fail.

Independent Workers.—Fourthly, the cabinet-makers working alone must be mentioned. They do not compose a large class, and make as a rule the smaller articles that can be easily manipulated by the solitary worker. Most will employ others when orders are plentiful. There are some excellent workmen in this as in other branches working alone, who

* In the dull Christmas week of last year, a solid mahogany bedroom suite, priced at £12, was " hawked," but not sold, as the highest offer was £7.

depend for their livelihood entirely on orders, whereas others as habitually sell "on the hawk." The largest proportion of independent workers however in the furniture trades is found among the turners, carvers, fret-cutters, and sawyers. Among the actual makers relatively they are not numerous.

To begin quite alone, either in the home, or by hiring a bench in a workshop, is however a frequent practice, and it is one of the drawbacks of the trade that men can so easily do this, and after having helped to "degrade" the market for a time, fall back again into the ranks of the wage-earners that it would have been better if they had never left. For others, this step is the starting point of a permanent change in position, that may or may not turn out to be improvement. It would be misleading however to leave the impression that all who start on their own account do so quite voluntarily; industrial conditions are often too powerful to allow of free action, and it is these conditions that often inexorably determine the position that a man shall fill. A large class therefore "start for themselves" because they cannot get employment, and to start thus, even though sale by hawking or sale by auction is a man's only resource, becomes in these circumstances a natural and even a necessary thing to do. But although the ranks of those "making on their own account" are constantly being recruited from this cause, those coerced thus are rarely the better members of the trade. Many small makers are undoubtedly, even though they do begin on a capital of £1, steady, industrious men who mean "to get on in the world;" but large numbers are the unthrifty and the irregular. Smart, unsteady men who dislike the regularity of the workshop often start making in this way; with many it would be the aim to start independently as soon as a little money had been got together; and many do it under the least commendable of all conditions, viz., when they have got to know the connection of their employer, and, having learnt not only his customers but his prices, will offer their goods at the price that they know will just undersell him.

The increased temptation that comes to the wage-earner to try and make his own market if his wages are small, bringing as it does the chance of a comparatively great success, must not, however, be forgotten. Every maker of to-day, be he large or small, will tell you that one of the greatest sources of disorganization in the trade is the very large number of small shops. But many of those so complaining were themselves wage earners a few years back, and the wage earner of to-day does but yield, from more or less honourable motives, and with the exercise of more or less freedom, to the same inducements that have acted on others in the past.

The better class of wage-earners, however, view this multiplication of small shops and of solitary workers with keen regret, and, believing as they do in the value of association and of the voluntary organization that association makes possible, recognize in the "garret-master," and in the ease with which others may become such, one of the greatest obstacles that they have to face. They hold that no man is justified in employing others who is dependent for the money to pay the wages of his men on what is realized on the produce of the current week,* and this is what so many do; the cheque from the dealer goes straight to someone who will cash it, be it a banker, the veneer merchant, the timber dealer, or, as is often the case, the publican who has constituted himself a kind of banker for the small maker, and the cash obtained is constantly used to meet part of the expenses of production of the past week, and for the purchase of material for that which is coming.

This practice of cashing cheques in public-houses that expect a kind of discount in the purchase of a small quantity of "something," generally spirits, is common;

---

* A first-class all-round cabinet-maker has carefully estimated the amount of capital on which he would be willing to start for himself (as he says, "decently,") at about £200. A fellow workman, who wanted the foregoing to join in partnership, had reckoned the minimum at £70.

but it is important, not so much as a great grievance that involves a considerable deduction from a man's earnings as a sign of the conditions under which a great part of the trade is carried on.

CHAIR-MAKERS.—The second important division of makers is that of the chair-makers. As has been stated, there are no separate figures available for those in this branch of the trade, but this is of less importance, for although, as a craft, it forms a branch quite distinct from those included under the head of cabinet-makers, economically its conditions are for the most part similar.

The most important divisions of the trade are into the makers of "suites," dining or drawing room, and of bedroom and other chairs which are simply repeated, such as hall chairs and folding chairs. "Repeats," with little or no variation, be it of single chairs or of suites, still make up the greater part of trade; but the variety of designs made up in the same shop is much greater in the higher branches of the trade. As already indicated, there are a few first-class makers, whose work is excellent, both as regards making, carving and inlaying, and from whom it is possible to get executed original designs of great beauty, requiring the best and most artistic skill of the worker. And it is one of the few special points that must be noted in reference to this trade that the total number of good shops, small though it is, has increased during the last twenty years.

The furniture trade as a whole in the East End has steadily extended, but while the better firms of general cabinet-makers have been often extinguished, those of the chair-makers, relatively to the total numbers engaged in this branch, have more often held their own. This is explained by the more recent migration of the better class of chair trade to the East End, and by the change in the fashion of drawing-room furniture, the older "suite" having very largely given way to "occasional" or odd chairs, and the latter being more often than the suite of good workmanship and executed in a greater variety of styles and shapes.

The migration of the better class of trade has been from the south of London, especially the Kennington district, to the East End, and I am told that while there are now some six or seven shops which regularly turn out very good work, twenty years ago there was only one.

The migration eastwards has been accompanied, moreover, by the rapid growth of provincial centres of production that compete more keenly than in the making of other parts of furniture, with the commoner East End trade. Of these centres High Wycombe and the district round is the most important. Increased keenness of outside competition in the trade generally is illustrated by the fact that while in 1830 there were only two chair manufacturers in High Wycombe the inspector now estimates the output of chairs at 1800 dozen per week. The considerable quantity of Austrian bent-wood furniture imported during recent years has been another source of competition in this trade.

While however, relatively, there is a larger production of better-class chairs than of general furniture, and while the outside competition of cheap producers is more marked, the general features of the East End chair trade are similar to those of the other branches of the group: a small system of production; great specialization of skill; the very infrequent possession by the maker of the machinery used; and, in general, the production of cheap goods, or those of medium quality.

LOOKING-GLASS FRAME MAKERS. — We find the same features here: dealers, and "trade shops" making for them; and of the latter an increasingly large number of a small size. The craft is different, but economic analysis shows us exactly the same industrial organization. There are several dealers whose trade is solely in frames, but the large general warehouses also supply them. The chief parts of the trade are the making and the gilding, or, when not gilded, the polishing. Gilders frequently have orders from the dealers for frames ready for the market, and in that case buy them from the makers and then do the gilding. Glass bevelling is a separate subsidiary industry often carried on in the saw-mills which have been already described. The wholesale dealer himself, however, most often supplies the glass and has it fitted, and in some of the largest warehouses as many as two or three men are employed almost solely for this work. It would however include the fitting required for those pieces of furniture, such as overmantels, toilet tables, and wardrobes, which have glass in them, as well as for the separate mirrors. The looking-glass frame trade, it may be noted, is severely handicapped by the extensive manufacture of toilet tables which are furnished with glasses, and which displace the old swing mirrors, and by the present large demand for overmantels; but looking-glass makers and dealers are now beginning to include the latter in their own branch of the trade.

CARVERS.—The position of the carvers in the trade has been already indicated; they form one of the most important subsidiary classes, and except on quite small articles, never work directly for the consumer or the dealer. The skill of the carver is not specialized in any very marked way. The most important division is that of the cabinet and general carver, and the chair carver, but the technical differences between them are not great, and a good chair carver, for instance, could soon adapt himself to other kinds of work. Classification would, therefore, if attempted, have to be based almost entirely on skill and ability, and not on the lines in which the skill and ability are employed.

The demand for the carvers' work has been prejudicially affected during recent years by the extensive substitution of curved and other shaped machine mouldings, and fret saw work for hand carving; by the greater use of the steam turning-lathe, and by the fashion during recent years for inlaid work. There are, however, signs at the present time of a revival of the demand for carved work. There are very few master carvers in the East End, the carvers' shop with a considerable number of workers in it, being found almost exclusively in the West. A considerable number, however, work as "piece-masters," who, employed by others, themselves employ one or two to help them to execute the work they undertake. But, as a rule, carvers are either journeymen working on piece or time work, or are independent workers, with a boy sometimes to do the glass-papering, working either in their own homes, or at a bench hired in a workshop.

In the chair trade the amount of carving required is larger than in any other branches, except a small part of the best cabinet work, and in a good shop there would be as many as three carvers to every four workers, and in the smaller shops, where only four or five men are working, one or two are generally carvers. On the other hand, much of the work (for instance, that on bedroom suites and dining tables), does not, as a rule, introduce much carving, and this part of the work would then often be done by an outside man. In the larger shops, other than chair makers, carvers are employed in the proportion of about one carver to ten makers.

FRENCH POLISHERS.—The polishers form an additional subsidiary group, dependent for their employment entirely on one or another section of the furniture trade. There are two main divisions of the trade: (1) the polisher of large surfaces, such as those of tables, sideboards, &c.; and (2) of small surfaces, the latter including all upholstered goods. It is frequent for the upholsterer also to have his polishing room.

The polishers—and doubtless, if figures were available, it would be found true also of upholsterers—are, as the general table shows, chiefly located in Shoreditch, and this is explained by the fact that the dealers are their chief employers. Some of the dealers have their own polishing shops; but most often their work is sent to a shop outside. In both cases the work is contracted for by a master polisher, who, whether he rents a shop, or whether he works in the room provided for him by the dealer, is himself the employer of his workmen. Most of the polishers to "the trade" in "the Road," however, rent their own shops, and work generally for only two or three of the warehousemen. If they work in a room which is rented by the latter, they not only engage the labour, but find all the materials that are used.

Master polishers may be thus divided into (1) the stationary tenant master, and (2) the more or less nomadic piece master; and often the latter, working with a gang which will vary in size according to the season and the demand, works continuously on the premises of the same firm for many years. The numbers employed vary according to the amount of work contracted for, but rarely exceed twelve. There are also many polishers working alone, either in their own houses or in the shops of those who employ them.

The position of the journeymen has been already indicated; they are, for the most part the employees of the contractors. The craft is easily learnt, and there are many in it who follow it as a secondary trade, turning to other means of getting a livelihood when work is slack. But although entry to the trade is easy, the rates of remuneration are not so low as in many branches of the furniture trade, and this may be probably explained by (1) the fact that no polisher can make anything for sale, and is thus unable to use the deteriorating market of the chance buyer—he must be employed and cannot hawk; and (2) it is particularly easy in this trade for a man to work according to his pay. It is the recognized custom for the contractor to polish according to his price, and when a price is agreed on, directions are given accordingly to the workmen. Even if this were not done the latter would not fail to follow the custom, if the amount paid them was lower than the rate to which they considered the market price entitled them. No journeyman polisher earns high wages, but, on the other hand, when he has once mastered his trade (and this does not take very long, three months as learner, and perhaps two years as "improver," are enough), they are, relatively, never very low. We thus find that in this trade, in which the practice of sub-contracting is most common, the average earnings of the journeymen per hour are least variable, and best maintained at the Society rate of 7d per hour.

The seasons, however, cause greater variation in this trade than in others of the group. As has been seen, most of the furniture that forms the stock in the warehouses is "in the white," just the frame or carcase unpolished, and the chairs, &c., except of the commonest kinds, are not upholstered. It is in the spring and summer and during the few weeks preceding Christmas that "the Road" is busiest, and it is then that the press of work comes on the polisher. The maker, on the other hand, is much more uniformly employed, since he has to supply during the slacker seasons the large "stock" which is then accumulated, and this greater equalization of demand, it may be noted, is one of the advantages that the presence of the warehouses helps to secure.

UPHOLSTERERS.—The french polisher acts as an auxiliary to most branches of the furniture trade; the upholsterer on the other hand may be regarded as the auxiliary of the chair and couch maker alone; work on chairs and couches, with settees and music-stools, making up the greater part of his trade, as the result of a differentiation that is becoming more general throughout London, and is almost complete in the East End.

As in the case of the polisher, the dealer is his chief employer, and in consequence the upholstering is to a great extent concentrated in Shoreditch, where the dealers are mostly found. Much of the work is executed under very similar conditions to the polishing. Room is frequently found in which the work is done, and the work is also sometimes put out to an outside contractor. When the work is done on the premises of the dealer it is generally of the better quality, it being easy to "scamp" work in this trade, and obviously easy to introduce inferior materials under the cover.*

The work is generally contracted for in the same way as in the polishing trade; the journeymen are sometimes paid by the hour, but more frequently by the piece, especially for the commoner work. There is a considerable amount of sub-division, but the chief source of disorganization in the trade seems to be an extensive employment of young labour either as apprentices or "improvers." The total number employed in any one shop is never large, probably never exceeding twenty. The competition in this, as in all other branches, is keen, but the upholsterers appear to be in a better position than any other members of the group. They are not very numerous (about 1200); like the polisher they can rarely, except in the case of cheap goods, hawk their wares; and the necessity of cutting up the material they use makes it easy to waste, and thus necessary that a man should be both trustworthy and intelligent if he is to do his work well.

There are a few upholsterers who are also makers, but as a rule the two branches are entirely separated. The upholsterers frequently do the polishing, however, or get it done, and the frames are then sent to them "in the white." It may be noted here that a considerable quantity of produce is sent away by the dealers neither polished nor

---

* *e.g.* short "pig" hair for the more expensive horse-hair.

upholstered, partly to save the risk of damage in transport,
but sometimes doubtless because the buyer wishes to see
what kind of frames are being supplied him, as well as to
know with what material the covers are stuffed.

It is this difference of quality, both in frames and in
the upholstering, that very largely determines the conditions
under which the latter is done.   The cheaper the goods
supplied, the less important it is to know how the frames
are put together, of what wood they are made, and the
amount and thinness of the veneer; also, the less does it
matter what is used for the "stuffing";* and so also as
regards the quality of the springs and the way they are
fixed.   It follows therefore that the cheap upholstering
work is much more often done in the small shops and by
the small "garret masters" of the East End than that of a
better quality.   These small men generally buy the frames
themselves from a neighbouring maker; often employing a
polisher, or if not, getting the polishing done, and thus
selling their goods ready for the consumer.   Much of this
cheap furniture is useful and durable, and is upholstered
under these conditions by a class of small men who work
habitually "for order," but it is under these conditions also
that we find the commonest goods produced.   Such are
often "hawked," and I have myself been offered upholstered
couches in "the Road."   It is these very common goods
that frequently find their way, not to the wholesale dealers,
but to the "show shops" of the East End and of the
suburbs owned by the men who strew the pavement with
their wares.

WHOLESALE DEALERS.—In spite of the increasing extent
to which retailers and provincial dealers are buying direct
from East End makers, it is still true that by far the greater
proportion of their produce is destined either for the
warehouses or for the immediate supply of the customers

* Alva and flock together are largely used, the flock as the softer material
being placed near the leather or other cover used.

of the East End wholesale dealers. The market that the latter supply,—London, suburban, provincial and export—is that upon which the majority of employers and employed alike depend. This market is made and extended by the wholesale dealers in many ways; especially by providing show-rooms, by sending out representatives, by establishing agencies, by circulating catalogues (sometimes elaborate volumes) and price lists; and, perhaps to these should be added, by giving longer credit than the maker can usually afford. This is the wholesale dealer's chief function—the making of the market; and on its importance it is unnecessary to enlarge. The attendant gain of a greater equalization of demand from makers throughout the year that comes from the creation and the command of a widely diffused market, and from the need of keeping a large stock, has been already mentioned.

It has been also seen that the dealer generally supplies certain parts of furniture needed for its completion, such as the marble tops to washstands, and glass to mirrors of different kinds; and that it is he also who orders, generally by contracting with an outside man, the polishing and the upholstering to be done. Further, he has to "pass" the work he buys, and he takes all responsibility for the quality of the goods he sells. The combined duties of the wholesale dealer are thus seen to be of first-rate importance.

The growth of the wholesale dealer as a distinct class is comparatively recent. Thirty years ago "the Road" was almost entirely made up of workshops, and the differentiation of the dealer and maker has been going on rapidly during the past fifteen years. When we ask why it is that this change has been going on we find the chief answers to be the following. The present system of "trade shops" making for the dealers (1) saves the rent of a workshop; and (2) saves the trouble and responsibility of directing and arranging the rate of the remuneration of labour. Further, a large number of shops, most of them small, and all in

keen competition with each other, are able to supply the
dealer with goods at lower prices than he could produce
them if he had a large workshop or factory and made
them himself. The general condition of the trade—the
abundant supply of labour and its want of organization;
a large market allowing of excessive specialization; the
growth of the "saw mills" and small turning and sawing
shops, and thus the absence of the need for any expensive
plant; and the consequent ease with which men can start
for themselves, all these conditions make the increasing
number of small makers an almost inevitable and a growing
feature of the trade, and the existence of the wholesale
dealer helps to make this feature increasingly pronounced.
It must be admitted therefore of this class, as the proprietor
of one of the large "saw-mills" himself admitted to me of
his own division of the trade, that, although now indispensable, even for the maintenance of the present volume of
trade, its effect on general conditions is in many ways
harmful, because it promotes the unequal and excessive
competition of large numbers of small makers.

Three things must, however, be noted here : (1) that the
dealers are themselves in keen competition with each other;
(2) that the market that they supply is represented for the
most part by men who know their trade, and who would
turn to the maker, still more than they are doing at the
present time, if high prices were charged, and that thus
there is nothing of the nature of a monopoly possessed by the
wholesale dealers of "the Road"; and (3) that many of them
employ, either entirely or with one or two others of the
wholesale shops, many of the men who make for them, and
that there is thus frequently established a permanent and
desirable relation between dealer and maker. The competition among the latter works largely uncontrolled and
even unstimulated from above, and is seen in its most dis-
tressing forms among those who are seeking, often with a
mad fatuity (but sometimes, from the pressure that comes

from actual need), to be "makers," and not "men ;" who, for the most part, are not all-round masters of their trade, but are able to make and to direct the making of one, or it may be two or three articles; and who, as a rule, make the showy cheap goods. But because this class is so large, because the demand for cheap goods is so extensive, and because the cheap and inferior goods can so often be made to look like the more solid and superior, this system of production influences with powerful and deteriorating effect the general condition of the trade. To such small makers, and to all who are prepared or compelled to undersell their fellows, the market of the wholesale dealer opens a too wide portal.

III.—PRICES, PROFITS AND WAGES.

So far we have been chiefly concerned with the general organization of the trade and with its system of production. It is now necessary to consider the question of prices, profits and earnings.

PRICES.—With reference to the former it is impossible to do more than generally to indicate the course of recent tendencies. As regards the prices paid by consumers, the tendency has been undoubtedly downwards, excepting in the case of the best kinds of furniture, during the last fourteen years. Stores and large retailers have probably been the most powerful agencies among distributors in bringing about this decline. The prices of retailers, however, are not our immediate concern, except in so far as they are indications of changes in the level of prices likely to be realized by those who supply them; and everything points in these directions also to a lower level.

When it is asked *why* prices are lower than they were in 1875 for goods of the same quality, the answer is, not that this is due to any great diminution in the expenses of production owing to greater cheapness of material used, or to the introduction of new machinery, but to the force of a prevailing competition, and to the changes in the organization of the trade by which this force is manifested.

Machinery.—The effect of machinery in cheapening production during the past twenty years seems to have been slight. The economy brought about by the introduction of the band and the circular saw has been followed by no other important mechanical invention. In a few factories, it is true, we find machinery, not only for turning and the different kinds of sawing, but also for planing, moulding, mortising, dowelling, dovetailing, and grooving, but, as has been seen, machinery for these various processes is rarely set up in a market in which workers are so numerous and labour so cheap as in the East End of London. There, the small system prevails, and there are no signs that it will not continue to hold its own against the large system that would have to take its place if all the above processes were ordinarily done by machinery. Except as regards sawing, turning, and moulding, the use of machinery in the East End does not seem to be increasing or important in its effects. It is otherwise in some of the provincial centres of production, *e.g.* Beith, Bath, or Barnstaple, where there is a smaller and less highly organized market, where skill is not so specialized, and where the relative supply of labour is smaller.

Cost of Material.—Neither is there any great diminution in the prices of the material used. Some woods, for instance, mahogany and the common kinds of walnut are cheaper, but neither in the woods used for veneers, nor in the cheaper kinds, including deal, has there been any general fall causing a great diminution of the expenses of production, from increased cheapness of the commodity that enters most largely into them.

Cheap Goods.—Change of fashion and change of quality of goods made have been powerful influences in bringing *cheap furniture* into the market; but it is clear that a lower level of prices, if due only to these causes, might have been accompanied by higher prices of materials, higher wages, and higher profits. This has, of course, not been the case, but the question as to whether a lower level of prices rules for the *same* goods now than ruled fourteen years ago is to be kept carefully distinct from the other question, as to whether there is a production of a much greater quantity of goods, which are cheaper because less work and less material are put into them. And this has been conspicuously the case.

The fundamental cause of this enormously increased supply of cheap goods of endless variety is the character of the popular demand, and it has been possible to meet this, not only because of the industrial conditions under which the trade is carried on, but also from the even too fertile readiness of resource frequently shown by those who supply. The following will illustrate this :—

A few years ago mahogany bedroom furniture was in demand. Good solid work in this material would have Spanish mahogany veneer (the best kind) on a solid Honduras mahogany (the cheapest kind.) But many makers, following closely the fashion, uniformly veneer on deal, and by degrees, the public learning slowly in these matters, and by experience alone, mahogany went out of fashion, largely from the amount of deceptive furniture thus put in the market. Rosewood came in, and this wood, which is not only too expensive, but also too brittle to be made in the solid, should also be veneered on mahogany. The same process followed ; rosewood was veneered more frequently on the soft and cheaper deal, and rosewood went out of fashion. It is now the turn of walnut (which, with birch, is being now largely made and sold) to get into disrepute with a public that pays but little but has to suffer much.*

* Good seasoned deal well selected and without knots makes a good basis for most furniture. It is bruised more easily than the hard woods, but is durable, and if well veneered looks well. But the thin knife-cut veneers are

A change of fashion that deserves mention from the considerable effect it has had on the trade, is the extensive substitution of wardrobes for chests of drawers. The cheap bedroom suite trade, that is, the production of wardrobes, toilet tables, and washstands, has become, largely in consequence of this substitution, an important and well-defined branch.

Cheap production is, however, often accompanied by increased showiness of appearance, and wardrobes, for instance, which have the material thinned down in the doors and wherever else it is possible; which are without any inner fittings, such as a box or shoe drawer; the insides of which are left rough, with a fixed instead of a sliding pegrail, and a piece nailed on to the back of the door behind the mirror, if there be one, instead of a panel: such a wardrobe may yet, by veneering, bevelling, beading, by ornate pediments, and by other means be made to present a far more showy appearance than its more useful and durable companion. We have thus two main causes for the lower level of prices that prevails in almost all branches of the trade: (1) the universally increased keenness of competition; and (2) largely the effect of the former, the greater production of commodities in which cheaper or less material is used, and on which less labour is spent. It is the former of these causes that necessarily affects profits and wages. The latter only affects them conditionally and indirectly, and it does so in the East End furniture trade, because cheap production is there accompanied by an increasing specialization of skill, and by greater facilities for enabling a man to enter the trade as an employer. This being so, the power of the first cause, viz., the increased severity of competition, to affect profits and earnings is indirectly increased.

PROFITS.—Generalizations as to the average rate of

often put on unseasoned and knotty deal, and it is furniture thus made up that tries the patience of the incautious purchaser.

profits prevailing in any trade can rarely, if ever, be based on a sufficiency of numerical data. Conclusions may, however, often be based on general determining causes, and the condition of the East End furniture trade justifies, I think, the conclusions that the members of no section of the trade are earning high rates. The amount necessarily varies, from the bare livelihood of many of the solitary workers and small employers, to the considerable income of the large wholesale dealer and exporter, but relatively to the amount of capital invested and power of industrial initiative shown, there are no signs that dealers and the larger makers are able, except in possibly a very few cases, at the present time to make excessive profits.

The opinions of one class in a trade are rarely biassed in the direction of under-estimating the profits of another class, and it is the tendency for most minds to do the reverse. But in this group of trades it is the exception to find anyone who thinks that the members of any other class, much less those of his own, are in a very prosperous condition. This is so, even with most opinions held as to the profits of the wholesale dealer. It is the common admission among makers that the range of prices charged in "the Road" has fallen considerably of late, largely through the tendencies on the part of many of their customers to skip those who, in spite of their varied duties, may be best regarded as middlemen, and to go straight to the makers; and I have on several occasions found it believed among makers that one of the largest dealers prices his goods, when sold wholesale, at a uniform gross profit of 7½ per cent. on the price, less 2½ per cent. discount, at which they were bought in. It is certain that a maker can often, if he happens for any purpose to want his commodities back again, repurchase at an advance of 5 per cent. A considerable maker has averaged profits as follows :—His own 12½ per cent. to 15 per cent., retailers 25 per cent., and

wholesale dealers "often not more than 10 per cent." I
have been told by one of the wholesale and export dealers,
in whose opinion the export trade was by far the most
valuable to them, that 10 per cent. was the gross profit
generally made when cash was obtained, and from 15 per
cent. to 20 per cent. when credit was given. The credit is
often for three months (with a three months' bill often
taken at the end of that time), but is sometimes longer.

The following extracts from our evidence refer chiefly to
the small makers and bear out the general statement that
the keenness of competition prohibits excessive profits :

1. Maker of mahogany furniture, chiefly chests of
drawers ; employs 5 men ; earns* about £2. 5*s* per week.

2. Deal worker (chests of drawers, &c.), 2 or 3 employed ;
earns about 35*s* per week.

3. Maker of cheap toilet tables ; employs 2 men ; a single
man : works himself only about 8 hours a day ; estimates
own labour at 18*s*, and average earnings at 33*s* per week.

4. Maker of dining-room suites ; employs about 12 men ;
his chief employer, a wholesale dealer of the Curtain Road,
reckoned his earnings at less than 50*s* per week.

Of cabinet makers working alone the following may be
taken :

5. Maker of davenports ; sells for £3. 10*s*; cost of
material, &c., 30*s* ; they take one man about a fortnight to
make, but work very irregular, and £1 reckoned considerably
above his earnings per week.

6. Maker of cheap bookcases, &c. ; works at home, for
order. Estimates average at 18*s* per week.

7. Maker of fancy boxes ; works at home ; reckons average
24*s* per week.

Of individual articles the following :

8. Dining table, mahogany ; price of one of the larger
makers to wholesale dealer £4, profit 15*s*.

9. Sideboards, price to dealer £4; expenses of production :

* It is impossible to use any exact analysis of profits and earnings, see p. 198.

material, &c., 35*s*; labour (one week) 30*s*, leaving profit of 15*s*.

10. Gipsy tables; wholesale price 9*s* per dozen "in the white," profit ¾*d* per table or 9*d* per dozen. These tables of foreign make, imported in sections and put together by girls, are said to be in the market at 7*s* 6*d* per dozen.

The following figures give with greater exactitude the expenses of production (including rent of workshop, but excluding labour); the gross receipts and the profits of a small maker, working with two young relatives almost solely for order for the trade and making chiefly wardrobes of fair quality.

	Cost of Material.	Rent of Workshop.	Gross Receipts.	Profits, (including Remuneration of Labour).
1884.	£.	£.	£.	£.
January-June	79	5	180	96
July-December	79	5	166	82
1885.				
January-June	97	5	201	99
July-November (21 weeks)	66. 16*s*	4. 4*s*	152	81

Principal Items of the Expenses of Production.

	Timber (including some Veneer).	Veneer.	Brass work.	Glue.	Sawing.	Carriage.	Rent of Workshop.
1884	£ *s. d.*	£ *s. d.*	£ *s. d.*	£ *s. d.*	£ *s. d.*	£ *s. d.*	£ *s. d.*
July-December.	50 13 8	15 9 5	7 14 7	1 9 6	4 1	1 8 9	5 0 0
1885.							
January- June.	52 4 9½	12 2 9	9 12 2	1 8 10	3 10	1 16 5	5 0 0

[No carving was introduced into the work in 1884-5. It is at the present time to a slight extent, and is done by two men, father and son, who hire bench-room in a neighbouring workshop, and who work for "the trade" as already described. No machine mouldings are bought, those used being cut by hand.]

The elements of the expenses of production of a mahogany wardrobe,* maker's average price £8. 10s, have been carefully calculated for me as follows :—

	£	s.	d.
Mahogany (Honduras) for exterior ends, doors and panels of face, &c.	1	13	10
Deal, for inside ends, tops and bottoms, frame backs, &c.		16	10
Veneer (Spanish mahogany)		14	0
Brass work		10	0
Glue, glass paper, brads and screws		3	0
	3	**17**	**8**

The total cost of material would, however, not be less than £4. An average man would take nearly 3 weeks to make, working 56 hours a week, and his remuneration would thus be somewhat over 30s per week.†

The foregoing table of profits gives a total of £358 for 99 weeks during 1884-5, or an average for 3 people, aged about 50, 18, and 16, of £3. 12s 4d per week, including the remuneration for their labour. In spite of the increased earning power of the two younger men the three estimate their total earnings at the present time at about £3 per week. During 1870-3 the eldest of the three, working on piece-work as a journeyman, earned on the average about £2 a week, and it was the exceptionally busy and prosperous time of

---

* "Six foot, short tray."

† On this estimate the maker has written as follows :—"I have taken this job, as it is a good representative one; they are now (Jan. 1889) made in walnut of different patterns (but on the whole there is somewhat the same price prevailing), mahogany being out of date. . . . The price of these goods for the last three years has not been at all a fixed one : at depressed periods more makers go round to the dealers, asking for orders, consequently the dealer has more people to inquire of, telling each one as he comes that he is able to get it for a certain sum off the man who has called before."

He goes on to say that a walnut wardrobe has just been made by him, similar in pattern to the mahogany one, "for £4 less" than one would have been made seven years ago, but adds, that although the price was then so low, the beginning of the year being the slackest season, "perhaps before, or in the Spring, they may fetch as high a price as ever."

that period that made him start for himself. Although the above figures show that his present earnings as a small maker are correspondingly small, his position is a satisfactory one compared with that of the majority around him. His credit is good with those who supply him with material; on only one occasion since he started has he allowed his goods to be "hawked," and then did not sell on account of the low prices offered; he is one of those that can afford to wait during the slack season after Christmas for busier times; and one who, although the competition of goods somewhat similar in appearance to his own, but made up with commoner deal, and more of it, and with thinner veneers, presses heavily on him, still makes furniture of a very fair quality—not by any means the best, but far removed from the commonest kind.

It is impossible to state in figures the average profits of different classes, and the foregoing extracts have been given rather to illustrate this impossibility than to lead to the attempt. Profits range from the zero of the numerous class whose members "go broke," and from the bare margin of the large numbers who manage to struggle on, through all grades of material well-being, until we reach the minority of the "well-to-do." But classification is almost impossible. Most of the small makers of the East End may however be safely described as being in a position remotely analogous to that of foremen of departments in a large workshop, but with greater responsibility, with earnings less regular, and with their yearly average frequently lower.*

* The average profits of a master polisher are, I am told, secured if a journeyman is being paid 7d an hour, and earns at the rate of 1s an hour as gross income for his employer. Out of the remaining 5d materials, rent, and other expenses can be paid, and leave an average profit. The cost of materials seems to be about 2½d in each 1s. A steady man employing two others will probably earn, including the remuneration for his own labour, about £2. 7s 6d a week if work is fairly regular, which it rarely is in this trade. The following are some figures given me by an upholsterer

WAGES.—Wages start in amount from the same low level
as that to which the earnings of the small or solitary
maker often sink, but although as regards amount there
is thus no difference at the bottom of the scale, it has
been convenient to group together as earners of "profits"
all who are not working inside the workshop of an employer under his direct supervision.   But no clear line
of demarcation can be drawn.   The "profits" of the small
maker, for instance, would nearly always include the remuneration for his own manual labour, although wages cannot
be said to be paid to him.   On the other hand the "piece
master" working in a shop with one or more under him
may be regarded either as a wage earner on piece-work, in
his relation to his own employer, or as an earner of profits,
in respect to those who work under his personal direction.
But still it is convenient to use the old division of the wage
earner and the earner of profits, remembering that there
are many cases when a man must be regarded as acting in
a double capacity.

Most wages are paid by the piece, excepting in the case
of the polishers.   Wages are sometimes paid by time, but

working in a small way (buying in the frames from a neighbouring maker)
on the better "ordered" class of cheap goods :—

Dining-room "suites" of nine pieces (six chairs, two arm-chairs and
a couch).

Quality.	Price to dealer.	Expenses of production (including own labour at 8d per hour).	Profit.
	£ s. d.	£ s. d.	£ s. d.
3	6 5 0	5 18 0	7 0
2	6 15 0	6 5 0	10 0
1	8 0 0	7 10 0	10 0

One other upholsterer, one polisher and a boy are employed.   One of each
of the above suites would be a fair week's work.   His total earnings may thus
be reckoned as follows :—Own labour (56 hours a week at 8d), £1. 17s 4d ;
profit (as above), £1. 7s ; total, £3. 4s 4d ; but a considerable deduction must
be made from this for slack time ; average earnings are probably about £2. 10s.
The average of many of this class, but making still cheaper goods, and without any business connection, and thus obliged to hawk their goods, would be
considerably lower.

the former practice is by far the more common. Nominal
time-work is moreover often "time-task" work, the
amount of work expected in a given length of time being
both known and demanded.

Piece-work, it is hardly necessary to say, is hardly
ever working to a scale. Elaborate lists have been
prepared in the past, but are now very rarely used—the
keen competition, the increased cheapness of most of the
furniture made, and the greater variety of designs and of
articles made up having led to this almost complete disuse
of the old scales. The piece-work of to-day is thus rather
"lump-work," as it is called, that is, work taken at a price
for the whole "job," and not reckoned up by an analysis
of its parts and reference to a recognized scale.

The ways in which a price for the job is fixed, in the
cases in which there is no recognized rate, and no
tradition of the workshop to determine it, are numerous.
In very few shops in the East End is there now a "shop
committee," that is a committee of the men who speak in a
representative capacity for those working there, and whose
final decision is absolute for all. In the absence or
inapplicability of a scale, such a system, if frankly
recognized by the employer and loyally and moderately
carried out by the men, may be regarded an the best.
But from this point the mode of fixing remuneration
shades down through every degree of combination,
from that found in the better shops, where although
not organized as above it is still fairly complete, to
complete disintegration. In some cases men are
allowed a definite time during which they consult with
their shopmates; at other times this would not be allowed,
or if allowed, the absence of combination in the shop would
make it useless. In many cases the "take it or leave
it" plan is followed: work is offered at a price and
refusal will often mean loss of employment. A lower
price once paid in a shop becomes, as a rule, the accepted

price for the future. The pressure from above, be it of
consumer or retailer or wholesale dealer, as well as the
competition of makers with makers and of men with men,
and the inefficiency of much of the labour in the market,
is tending to force the speed with which work is done, to
lower the quality of the work, and to some extent to force
down wages. But the best men, if they can get work
adapted to their skill and standard, can still earn as good
wages as ever, and even unsteady clever men can still
command their market.

Turners, &c.—In turning, as in other branches, wages vary
greatly. A skilled turner who can do the more difficult parts
of the work, such as the spiral or " polygonal" turning as
well as the more mechanical kinds of work, and who can
thus adapt himself to various tasks, can get fair wages.
An exceptional man can however not expect more than
40*s*, and average men earn from 30*s* to 33*s* per week. It is
probably not often that turners working alone on their own
account can earn more than the first-mentioned sum.
Journeymen sawyers are generally paid by the week at the
rate of from 9*d* to 10*d* per hour. Those working independently
form a much smaller body than the turners; their plant is
more expensive; and as journeymen their wages are higher.
They may as a class, I think, together with the fret-cutters,
be said to be in a somewhat better position than the turners.

Cabinet-makers.—The time wage recognized by the
Alliance Cabinet-Makers' Association, since the 10 per cent.
advance obtained in 1872, is from 8*d* to 9*d* per hour,
varying according to the class of shop. But the
proportion of East End workers who earn these rates is
small. A very few exceptional men on time wages
earn 11*d* and 10*d*, but even 8*d* is still far above the
average for the East End. Our evidence shows rates
ranging from 11*d* down to 4*d* per hour, the latter being
the rate for a very few who are paid time wage, but
representing the rate of earnings of a considerable number

who are on so-called "piece-work." In one shop where
about twelve are employed, one is paid 7*d*, two 6*d*, two
5½*d*; four or five 5*d*, and one ortwo 4*d* per hour; but it is
the exception to find that in a shop paying these rates the
men are employed by the hour. The general average for
the whole district I place at about 6*d* per hour.

Weekly earnings scheduled vary from averages of about
£2. 5*s* down to 15*s*. There are probably a very few *bond
fide* wage-earners whose weekly "draw" exceeds the higher
amount; but, on the other hand, there are but few that
earn as much. In one shop where a good class of furniture
is uniformly made the average is about 34*s*. In another
case, where it is an exceptional thing for a man and boy
working together to make £2. 18*s*, the average wages are
about 30*s*. In another, where small cheap tables are made,
the average is 22*s*, and one small maker has averaged the
earnings of his men at about 18*s*.

The following are some individual cases:* (1) a good
all-round cabinet-maker, weekly averages, 1884, £2. 2*s* 1*d*;
1885, £1. 18*s* 9*d*; 1886, £1. 16*s* 10*d*; 1887, £1. 18*s* 3*d*;
1888, £1. 18*s*. During this period the maximum "draw"
in one week was £3. (2) Average weekly wages, 1887,
£1. 12*s* 6*d*; 1888, £1. 11*s* 2*d*.

As instances of the low-priced "piece-work," the following may be mentioned: deal washstands, 7*d*; average men
can make about seven per day. Deal chests of drawers,
3*s* 6*d*; about four can be made in three days. Black walnut
wardrobe, for making, £7. 10*s*; time for one man about
five weeks at nine hours a day.

Average earnings, however, throughout the year depend
on the regularity of work, but the difference of average
on account of the seasons has been seen to be not great.

* The following are the weekly average wages of five men working in a good
shop for the most part on scale piece-work in 1872: (1) £1. 3*s*; (2) £1. 17*s* 2*d*;
(3) £1. 18*s* 3*d*; (4) £1. 19*s* 7*d*; (5) £2. 1*s* 8*d*. In August of this year the last
rise (10 per cent.) was obtained. Before 1865, when a previous 10 per cent.
had been gained, the "Alliance" rate was 6*d* per hour, *cf.* p. 200.

Before Christmas there is often considerable pressure, and for a few weeks after considerable slackness, but work does not vary very greatly.

There is a much greater variation in the number of hours worked per day. Regulation workshop hours vary from 52 to 56 hours in some of the best shops, up to 60 hours per week, but the greatest variation is that determined by the character of the individual workman. The prevalence of piece work, and a small system of production (small shops being as a rule less under regulation than large ones) leave both masters and men free, except in busy times, to work when they please, and extreme irregularity is the frequent result. The practice of "keeping Mondays" is less common now than in the past, and it is generally admitted that in this respect there has been a marked improvement. But the irregular division of work through the week is still very great in many shops. On Monday, even though it be not "taken," very little work is often done and each successive day is allowed to have a greater share of work allotted to it, until on Thursday and Friday the pressure becomes great and harmful. In many shops it is the practice to work late on these two evenings, and in busy times it is not an unusual thing for men to work until midnight, and sometimes I am told even through the night. The harmful effect of this irregularity on morale and physique and on the organization of the trade is great, but it is probable that the average number of hours made through the week is not greatly altered by it, and the general remark may be hazarded that the working week throughout the year is fairly uniform as regards length, varying from 52 to 60 hours (although occasionally longer), and that it is also fairly constant.

The average wages of cabinet-makers may, I think, be safely put as follows:—Exceptional men, £2. 7s 6d; very good all-round men, £2; average, £1. 12s to £1. 15s; inferior, £1 to £1. 5s; and "chaps," i.e., those working under a piece master : boys, 10*s* to 12*s*; and men, 18*s* to 20*s*.

In the first two classes there are very few, probably not one per cent., in the East End. It should be noted that among the makers of the common goods, earnings vary greatly ; cheap furniture is often knocked together quickly by smart men whose weekly "draw" is often equal to that of the better worker. But these are the exceptions and not the rule.

Chair-makers.—The wages of chair-makers correspond with those of the cabinet-makers ; we find the same great variation, and although there would be relatively a somewhat larger number earning higher rates than in the cabinet-making, the averages would not be approximately affected and the same may, I think, be said to prevail for both. The highest weekly average given in the evidence is 44*s*, and the lowest (a man employed to do the papering-up, and working on time rate) 12*s*, an amount in some cases paid also to learners. Time wages, as in the cabinet-making, are the exception. Those who know their trade can here, as in the other trades, generally earn good money ; specialization, too, as elsewhere is in the article made rather than in the subdivision of the single article : a man as an exception may make, for instance, the " seat-frames for cane chairs," but the rule is for one man to make some special kind of chair, such as dining-room, folding, or fancy, and to tend to specialize in the kind of wood worked on, and to become for instance a maker "used to rosewood work," rather than still further to degenerate into the maker of backs or rails, or any of the other parts of which chairs are made up. There is, however, much less scope for excessive specialization of skill than in cabinet-making. But in the latter also, the character of the specialization is the same.

Carvers.—The Society rates for carvers are somewhat higher than for makers, being 10*d* instead of 9*d*. It does not, however, seem that there is any great difference in the East

End as regards the maximum earned, although the average
for journeymen carvers is undoubtedly higher, the rate rarely
falling below 7*d* per hour. The number of journeymen,
however, except in the chair trade, is small. In this trade
it is true one carver is required for about every three
makers, and in some branches of the trade a much higher
proportion. But a small minority only of the makers of the
East End are chair-makers, and the small cabinet-makers
almost always, and the chair-makers sometimes, get their
carving done outside. We thus find that most of the
carvers of the East End are outside independent workers,
hiring a bench in a workshop or working at home.

The evidence shows rates per hour varying from 1*s* (in
one case only) to 7*d*, and per week from £2. 18*s* to £1. 10*s*.
It has been estimated that there are not more than about
thirty carvers in the East End whose yearly average is at
the rate of over £2 per week. The average for the majority
probably does not exceed 32*s*, and it is between these two
amounts that the weekly earnings of the outside workers
would also seem for the most part to range.

Polishers.—The wages of the polishers, as has been
indicated, vary less per hour, but more according to the
season than those in the other branches. The Society rate
of 7*d* is very often earned, but all rates are paid, down to
4*d* for improvers and young hands. For those who know
their trade 6*d* or even 6½*d* may be taken as the average.

The seasonal variation is great, however, and one man
working at 7*d* per hour, who has been in the employment of
the same contracting polisher for eighteen years, averages
the number of hours he worked per week at 42, 24 being a
very slack week and 52 representing nearly his maximum.
He thus averages his weekly wages, although the rate per
hour is 7*d*,* at only 25*s*, but when slack he sometimes works
a little privately, and this would have to be added to make up
his total earnings. A contractor, employing, in partnership

* £1. 12*s* 8*d* for a week of 56 hours.

with another, several hands and paying 6*d* per hour, estimates the average earnings at the same weekly total of 25*s*. Another, paying 8*d* to his foreman, 6*d* and 7*d* to full workers, 4*d* to improvers and 10*s* to 12*s* per week to boys, and working, if busy, 60 hours per week, thinks the best men only average 21*s* per week. The maximum weekly earnings may be put down at 35*s*, and the weekly average throughout the year may probably be safely estimated at about 23*s* for full workers.

Upholsterers.—The wages of upholsterers correspond very nearly with those of the carvers. In the furniture trade generally the earning power of journeymen, as indicated by the rates of the various trade societies, ranges as follows:—(1) carvers; (2) upholsterers; (3) cabinet-makers and chair-makers; and (4) polishers, the earnings of the first two being about the same; slightly lower for the two classes composing No. 3; and for the last class showing the considerable drop already mentioned. Although there is hardly an upholsterer in the East End who is a trades unionist, their position as indicated by the societies is found to hold good there, the *average*, however, appearing to be if anything somewhat higher for the upholsterers than for carvers. In the West End, a very good upholsterer can, it is said, sometimes earn £4 a week, but even there this is an unusually high rate. In the East End, the evidence does not show anything higher than £2. 6*s* 6*d* for a single week, and £2. 5*s* as an average weekly wage for the year, and although there are doubtless a few who may be earning regularly somewhat more than this, it is clear that the earnings of the majority of the East End upholsterers are considerably lower. For upholstering the commonest suites, sold to the dealer by the upholsterer for £4. 10*s* and under (the price often sinking considerably below this amount), 12*s* and 11*s* are paid, and occasionally a somewhat lower sum. Men can do about three such suites per week. This would make the weekly earnings 36*s* or 33*s* per week, if work were regular. 30*s* may, I think, be said to be the low-water mark of a single full week's wage.

A small maker has put the average wages of upholsterers at 38s per week, saying that they can earn this comparatively high rate because they "hang together better" than the cabinet-makers, and that skill and responsibility are more uniformly demanded from them. Another employer, who holds that the "trade is good enough if people only stick to it," also gives 38s as the average, but it seems that this more nearly gives the weekly wage of a fair worker on the common goods than the average for the year, and the latter may, I think, be more safely placed at 33s or 34s.

Female labour.—The question of female labour is of very minor importance in this group of trades. The 1881 census returns* give a total of 204 under 20 and 778 of all ages working in the East End district. Of these 572 are enumerated as living in Shoreditch, Bethnal Green, and Whitechapel. The only occupations scheduled are : "Cabinet makers and upholstereresses," 530, and "French polishers," 248. The former number would be almost all upholsteresses, a few women, possibly, who help home-workers in the "papering up" or the gluing, returning themselves as "cabinet-makers," but certainly only in a very small number of cases. Most of the women then are either upholsteresses or polishers ; there are also a very few female gilders working chiefly on looking-glass frames and small fancy articles.

The upholsteresses do almost exclusively those parts of the work in which sewing is required. The cutting out of the covers is still generally done by the men and regarded as their work, and the "stuffing" is always. In the former of these processes there is, however, a somewhat increased competition on the part of the women with the men, and the best female workers learn this part of the work.

The weekly wages for an exceptional upholsteress are 20s ;

---

* The figures of the census for female employments are not to be relied on. Many employed women do not return their occupations.

the weekly pay recognized by the Upholsteresses' Society,* 15*s*; and a frequent rate in the East End, about 12*s*. Those who earn less than this would be simply seamstresses, knowing how to sew, but ignorant of the technique of the upholstering work.

The women polishers work almost exclusively on the smaller articles, at times on light furniture, but for the most part on small fancy cabinet work. Although the numbers employed seem to be increasing, their competition with men is but slight, the work they do and can do being well defined. The evidence shows one case of 15*s* per week being paid, but this is considerably above the average. It appears that a woman generally earns about half as much as a man, and that she generally takes half as long again to do the work. If this be so, she can more than hold her own in those branches of the trade into which she can enter, but, as has been stated, these branches are few in number.

Nominal and Real Wages.—"Nominal" wages alone have been referred to in the preceding paragraphs, but it is clear that the extensive fall in prices that has taken place during recent years must have considerably increased the "real" wages of a man who nominally earns at the present time the same amount that he earned, say, fifteen years ago. In some of the better paid branches of the work, where rates have been maintained, the position of the wage earner may therefore be said to have improved. But this is rarely admitted, and there are two explanations of the refusal to allow what would seem to be incontestable in view of the diminished expenses of living. First, it seems that the standard of comfort of the better class of journeymen has been raised: they often dress better, live better, and have better homes than formerly, and the gain that comes from increased cheapness of food,

* Now numbering only about one hundred members, of whom none are known to work in the East End.

&c., is often lost, and desirably lost, in the greater variety of the wants of themselves and of their families. And, secondly, it seems that in this as in so many other trades the hurry and the drive have increased, and many men, even though they may be better off, long to-day for the greater quiet of the past. For them it has gone, and although for some of the cleverer men greater pressure may induce a greater regularity and steadiness that is wholesome for them, for others, who are not only clever workmen but steady men, present conditions are harmful, the pressure of their trade narrowing their lives and destroying that love of the craft which is needed for the production of true work. Extended wants and greater pressure thus make it easy to understand how it is that the small number of men who may still be earning their £2 per week regularly, will not readily see that this may represent as much as the £2. 10s of, say, fifteen years back.

IV.—INFLUENCES.

Industrial conditions are but the signs of underlying forces, and economic inquiry is essentially a problem of causation. It is necessary, therefore, briefly to consider what seem to be some of the more important proximate causes that have led to the present condition of this group of trades. The more fundamental ones must be left untouched : they would take us too far afield, for it would be necessary to traverse, as best one could, much of the realms of politics, psychology, and ethics, to say nothing of political economy, in order to explain fully the industrial condition of the poorest worker in Bethnal Green to-day.

Before considering the special causes of marked importance that stand out in close relationship with the furniture trade group, it will be convenient to consider the extent to which Jewish and foreign labour* enter into it. As distinct

* There is no foreign competition which makes itself widely felt: the bent wood furniture; some common kinds of furniture in sections; and a

causes these two elements seem to be imaginary rather
than real, but constant reference is made to them in the
evidence, and it has become indeed a habit with many to
look to them for the solutions of many of the disturbing
phenomena of several of the East London trades.

It seems, however, that neither of them can rightly be
regarded as original sources of disturbance. For the
majority of the Jews and the foreigners enter into the
trade in precisely the same way that Englishmen do. In
this group of trades, the former cannot be said to set in
motion, in any important way, a fresh chain of causes that
are powerful either for harm or for good, but must be
regarded as being subject to the same wider and more
fundamental influences that are already at work and which
tend to affect all alike, whatever their creed or race
may be.

Jews.—The number of Jews in the furniture trade
is not large, but is increasing. No exact figures are
available and estimates vary from 350 to 1000.
The Hebrew Cabinet - makers' Association, which is
growing and fairly vigorous, contains more than 200
members, a proportion to the total numbers employed
that compares favourably, even if the higher of the
above estimates be taken, with that found in any other
branch of the furniture trade in the East End. It is
improbable, however, that there are as many as 1000. This
number was given to me by one who has had considerable
opportunities of judging, and who has now, after further
consideration, considerably reduced his estimate. Whereas
a Jew, who at first put the total at 350 and promised to
supply me with a list of every shop in which they worked,
and the numbers that were employed, has found the task a

certain quantity of the "antique" carved furniture (chairs, &c.), are imported, but the great bulk of the trade is carried on without any pressure
from outside. An exception is found in the fancy cabinet box-work ; in this
branch of the trade the Continental competition appears to be keen.

more difficult one than he imagined and had to increase his
estimate.   I think that the approximate total may be safely
put at the mean between 350 and 1000, or at under 700.*

Jews generally work in Jewish shops.   Of these there are
several of medium size, in which no work is done on Saturday, and which are open on Sunday, generally from about
8 A.M. till dark.   In these and in the shops of the Jewish
small maker most of the journeymen are found.   The
small makers are numerous, but there is no evidence to show
that there is a disproportionately large number of them in
the Jewish section of the trade.

The great majority of the Jews in the trade are cabinet-
makers, and the class of goods they make is chiefly of a
medium quality.   Bedroom suites, pedestal tables, and
duchesse tables are the kinds of furniture most often made.
There seems to have been a marked influx of Jewish labour
into the first-mentioned branch of the trade during recent
years, and a diminution of the numbers making duchesse
tables—the first article it may be noted that was largely
made by Jews in the East End, and the one in which the
possibilities of cheap production are being perhaps most
nearly realized at the present time.

There are a certain number of Jewish carvers and upholsterers and a very small number of chair-makers and
polishers, but cabinet-makers of the class described form by
far the largest proportion.†

---

* The following figures throw a sidelight on this point.   Numbers relieved
by the Jewish Board of Guardians :—

	1885		1886		1887
Tailors	647	...	939	...	692
Cabinet-makers	25	...	34	...	27

The better position of the cabinet-makers partly explains their comparatively
small total, but the chief explanation is undoubtedly to be found in their
smaller numbers.

† Jewish lads have been apprenticed as follows by the Jewish Board of
Guardians :—1884-8 : Cabinet-making, 24 ; chair and couch-frame making,
7 ; bentwood furniture making, 1 ; overmantel making, 2 ; carving, 8 ; marquetry inlaying, 3 ; French-polishing, 8 ; upholstering, 23 : total 76.   The
numbers for each year were : 1884, 18 ; 1885, 9 ; 1886, 12 ; 1887, 12 ;
1888, 25.

As regards wages, the average of the better workmen would seem never to reach that of the better class of Gentile labour, but there is no evidence to show that the Jew often works for that low pittance, not even reaching to a bare subsistence rate, so often quoted as though it was his customary wage. New comers, the "greeners" of the trade, work, it is true, for a nominal wage during what corresponds to a term of apprenticeship, and the minimum earned by these, of 6s or 8s a week, is lower than the wage of any Englishman. But the "greeners" are few in number, and speedily improve their position. On the other hand the Jewish cabinet-maker appears never to earn as much as the skilled Englishman, the highest level reached seeming to be about 36s per week.* The average weekly earnings through the year, nevertheless, appear to correspond pretty much with that of the Englishman, and the proportion of Jewish workmen who have joined their trade society goes far to prove the fair average that large numbers of them earn. The hours of work appear to be somewhat longer, 8 A.M. to 9 P.M. being a time to which some of the better Jewish shops are frequently kept open. The short Friday that many of them make, the loss of Saturday, and the short Sunday would, however, not leave the average hours per week much higher. The abnormally long hours per day, and the seven days per week during which Jews and foreigners are frequently stated to work, appear to be the exaggerations of prejudice, with little or no more truth with reference to them, than to a very small minority of the poorer English makers.

Foreign Gentile Labour.—The Jew is frequently also a foreigner, and it is impossible to give separate figures of

---

* One man who has been in England 13 years and worked in several shops, is now earning for a time 36s a week, and earned an average of £1. 8s 2d per week during 1886. He admits that wages have not diminished, but urges the common complaint that the old days when a man could earn present rates with less "drive" have passed away.

the latter who are not Jews. There are a considerable number of them in the trade, however, both as employers and as journeymen. It is from Germany that both classes chiefly come, and the latter are possessed of every grade of skill. The foreigner works chiefly in the fancy branches of the trade—card tables, work tables, cabinet boxes, &c. Like the Englishman in the East End, those who do very good work are the exception, but these exceptions are found, and I know of a German and a Pole (a Gentile), whose work has been described to me by good English journeymen as being of as great an excellence as that of any Englishmen they knew. In fact, as an English trades unionist remarked, "There is not much to choose between the Englishman and the foreigner."

The foreigner, whether as Jew or Gentile, has not entered the trade in sufficiently large numbers to be a serious source of difficulty, and there is evidence that he has frequently acted as a needed stimulus to the English journeyman rather than as a source of disturbance. Neither has he brought with him a standard of living and of working which is economically degrading. The vexed and intricate question of foreign immigration has become, generally, somewhat more prominent during recent years, and with the increasing ease with which labour can migrate from one country to another, tends to become still more so in the future. But with its prominence the difficulty of dealing with it, or even of knowing that it should be dealt with at all, seems to increase. In the furniture trade, however, it has not become, nor does it, I think, show any sign of becoming, one of practical and pressing importance. "The foreigner" is indeed a convenient stick with which to strike out the solution of industrial difficulties, but the cudgel that should be more often used is one very difficult to wield, and is for the most part grown in the home woods.*

* Through the courtesy of the Registrar General, I am able to give the following figures taken from unpublished returns obtained for the 1881

Conclusion.—The features of special importance are, then, not found in any effects that Jewish and foreign labour have upon the trade. They are seen rather in the absence of apprenticeship, and in the difficulty of ever making apprenticeship thorough; in the want of appropriate technical education, suited, that is, to meet local needs and local conditions; in the excessive specialization and in the inefficiency of so much of the labour; in the multiplication of small shops and the accessibility of an omnivorous, but well-supplied market; in the extension of the system of "hawking"; in the weakness or absence of trade and labour combinations; and in the *morale* of large numbers engaged in the trade. These are influences that are at work within its borders, and acting from without there is the appetite of the consumer for cheap furniture. All these are direct causes, which, if it were possible to measure them, would be found to supply the greater part of the explanation that we seek of existing conditions.

The craving for cheapness—almost the normal condition of the consumer's mind—is often the result of positive inability to pay more than the minimum prices of the market, and cheap production, however it be brought about, and whatever the attendant conditions, has many compensations.

Census. It will be remembered that all foreign Jews are included in the figures given.

Foreigners BORN *in the different Countries of Europe, engaged in the Furniture Trade (all branches).*

	Poland.	Germany.	Russia.	Italy.	Other Countries.	Total.
Bethnal Green	17	39	2	12	2	72
Shoreditch	5	49	2	6	8	70
Hackney	—	22	1	2	4	29
Whitechapel	80	24	28	2	13	147
St. George's-in-the-Et.	4	23	5	8	4	44
Stepney	1	15	1	—	7	24
Mile End Old Town ...	5	14	—	1	4	24
Poplar	1	10	1	—	2	14
Totals......	113	196	40	31	44	424

In the furniture trade the competition, of which cheapness is a sign, has brought into the market not only much cheap, but much pretty, and it may be even "artistic" furniture, that people of small incomes are fortunate in being able to buy. But the demand for cheap things is often dangerous and harmful when it is gratified in absolute forgetfulness or ignorance of the conditions under which the commodities are brought into the market. The thoughtlessness and culpable ignorance of the consumer, his frequent forgetfulness of the struggle that men often undergo in order to make and to live on the commodities that are quietly bought in the showroom of the retailer, are old but not worn-out texts.

But, after all, the character of the popular demand is largely determined by individual incomes : competition, in as far as it determines them, determines also the power of purchasing. And it is competition acting within the group that determines the extent to which the popular demand will be met.

In this group of trades, this great force of competition—so essential to industrial welfare; upon the strength of which the economic motives of men still largely depend, and thus, since motives determine activity, the very lives of hundreds of thousands of the people of this country ; this force, so powerful both as an incentive and as a restraining influence as to seem to be almost necessary as a condition of social development, yet shows itself to be a force that must be regulated, and tend to become the competition of associations rather than of individuals, if it is to lead to development and not to degradation.

In any given state of industrial morality the social value of competition is measured by its equality—by the possession of equal power, both mental and material, by both sides to a contract or a bargain, and it is because certain tendencies in the group have been bringing about the opposite effect, and thus been making competition less "perfect," that it has been in many directions harmful.

But competition is only one of many causes, and shows itself moreover in many forms. And, unfortunately, economic causes, except in abstraction, can never be isolated. On the contrary, they act in every-day industrial life with bewildering complexity. It may be possible to indicate some of the more ultimate causes, but it is impossible to measure the effects even of these in the thousand phenomena of industrial life. The stream of causation may be one, but it is composed of currents and eddies the volume and the strength of which cannot be known. There seems, however, to be a causal relationship existing between some of the features of the trade that have been already mentioned that it may be well, in conclusion, to try and indicate.

The way in which a craft is habitually taught and learnt is of fundamental causal importance in nearly every trade, and it is so in this group. It is almost needless to say that apprenticing in it is rare, and the conditions under which the trade is chiefly carried on make it clear, indeed, that even one of its main branches could rarely be learnt well in a single shop. Except in the best kinds of cabinet-making and in upholstering, however, boys are rarely apprenticed at all; the worker "picks up" his trade, often in many shops, frequently moving intentionally from one to another, and gaining something from the experience of each. But the education thus obtained is one of chance: it rarely makes him a thorough workman, or leaves him able to withstand the force of a great market that will tend to force him into some special and narrow line.

Apprenticeship of any kind is therefore rare, and when accompanied by conditions that will ensure the learning of the trade, is still less frequently found. Of technical education, as of apprenticing, there is but little; the cabinet-making classes at the Finsbury Technical College with an average attendance of considerably under 20 during the past four years, and those at the People's Palace with a still smaller attendance, being the most serious attempts at its provision.

In the absence of thorough training, and under the pressure of keen competition acting on a highly centralized market, that excessive specialization of skill that has been noticed easily follows.   It is of a particular kind, however, and differs, for instance, from that found in the larger workshops of the contracting coat-maker in the tailoring trade. In the latter, the subdivision is minute, and the organization required great.   But in the furniture trade, as has been seen, although there are several general subdivisions of the trade, such as sawing, turning, making, carving, polishing, &c., which mark the outlines of the general organization of the trade, and may be compared with the coat and other branches of the tailoring trade, excessive specialization is almost uniformly found, not in the making of parts, but in the making of or working on one, or a very few, out of a large variety of articles, to any of which an all-round man would be able with equal ease to turn his hand.   Since, then, there is no great subdivision of the labour in the "making" of the single article, no elaborate organization of the labour in the single workshop is required.   Since, too, a general knowledge of the trade is unnecessary and there is an open market at hand in which each can take his chance, and since little capital is required, men with small business capacity can easily start for themselves; and the shops of small size multiply in number.

But the wage-earners, who become small masters, and small masters generally, do not easily combine, and so far are they from doing this in the furniture trade in the East End, that it is the excessive keenness of the competition among this very class that now forms one of the most conspicuous features and makes one of the greatest difficulties of the trade, leading as it does to constant underselling and to more frequent resource to the practice of "hawking."

But not only is there no form of combination and but little recognized tradition among makers; there is also very little among the wage-earners.   Of this, again, one great cause is found in the number of small shops, for the separation of the men, and the ease with which the wage-earner of to-day can become the small employer of to-morrow, increases disintegration and makes common action more difficult. The system of "piece-masters," also, and the obsoleteness of the old "scales" for piece-work, coupled with the great supply of inefficient labour, are among the further hindrances to labour organization.

But though the existing Societies are weak,* some of their members are among the best representatives of their trade, for they are men who are not only good craftsmen, but who are also conscious of the importance of maintaining and extending the principle and practice of association. The work that these men are doing, in one or two of the Societies, in the face of great difficulties, and against tendencies that are as powerful as they are antagonistic, is one of the bright spots in this group of trades, for it is one in which action is guided by some recognition of a community of interest, and by concern for the welfare not only of one or a few, and not only of a trade society, but also of those who from ignorance, selfishness, inefficiency, poverty, or from some other cause are still without its borders.

* The following figures show the strength of the different Societies in 1888 :—

	No of members in London.	No. of members in East End.
Alliance Cabinet-Makers' Association ...	764	346†
Progressive (chiefly deal workers).........	130	about 130†
East End Polishers............................	—	about 190†
Hebrew Cabinet-Makers' Society	—	about 200

Of the Perseverance, West End Body, and Union Cabinet-makers' Societies, and of the two Upholsterers' Societies with only a total London membership of about 600 in all, there are no East London branches, and no members known to work in that district.

† A considerable number of these would be employed in the Finsbury and City Districts. It should be noted, however, that the paying members of a society do not, at any given time, indicate its real strength. Many are influenced by it who have never joined, besides others who have been members in the past, and from one cause or another fallen out of the ranks.

[*Note to Edition of* 1892-3.—But little change has taken place in the conditions of the above group of trades since the foregoing pages were written three years ago. The local expansion of the Furniture Trade continues, and is characterized by the same general features : by keen competition, acting in some directions with harmful force ; by the small relative amount of genuine factory employment ; and by the consequent maintenance of the small system of production. The Report of the Sweating Committee, with the agitation that followed it and drove a certain amount of trade from the small work-shop to the factory, has had no lasting effect, and the small and, in many aspects, almost domestic character of much of the trade continues, although not relatively to an increasing extent.

The Trades Unions, although numerically somewhat stronger, exercise as yet no strong regulating force over the bulk of the East London trade, but their moral effect is probably somewhat greater in 1893 than it was in 1889.

Machinery for carving has been introduced by a few of the largest firms, but it is still in its infant and almost experimental stage, and has as yet no effect on the general condition of the trade. The position of the hand carvers, even of those who do the roughest work, therefore remains for the present unaffected.

There is thus little change to report, and the picture of three years ago remains generally true of the Furniture trades of East London to-day.]

E. A.

CHAPTER VII.

TOBACCO WORKERS.

THE commanding position that tobacco holds in the economy of the State is often overlooked. Tea and coffee, foreign spirits and wine, contribute no inconsiderable share to our national resources, but tobacco, for revenue purposes, is twice as important as tea and coffee put together, and almost as important as the whole of the commodities specified. Tobacco, during the past financial year, brought in upwards of nine millions sterling to the revenue. This fact alone would be sufficient to make any investigation of the trade interesting, but the interest is enhanced when we begin to examine the conditions that surround it in East London, and to contrast them with those of the other local industries. So many grievous pictures of the misery and distress prevailing in this neighbourhood are presented, from time to time, to the public eye, that the discovery of a labour market where fairly good wages are obtained is at once a source of pleasure and surprise.

Our attention is arrested at the outset by the fact that all the work of the trade is carried on in factories, subject to frequent supervision by the inspectors of the Home Department and by the officers of Excise. Each manufacturer, again, has to obtain an annual license from the Inland Revenue Office, the minimum fee for such license being £5. 5s, and the maximum over £30, in proportion to the amount of leaf on his premises. Moreover, inasmuch as the excise regulations prohibit the transfer of small quantities of leaf, a certain definite amount of capital, ranging probably from £50 to £100, is necessary to start a factory for cigar-making. Much more even than this amount would be requisite in order to manufacture tobacco or snuff, by reason of the heavy and expensive machinery employed in those branches.

The trade being fenced around with these safeguards, leaves no opening for those small domestic workshops which present such a difficult problem in the cheap tailoring and boot-making industries. Nor so far as tobacco, cigars, and snuff are concerned, is there any home work in them whatever, although it exists, to a limited degree, in the cigarette department.

The foregoing conditions, coupled with the fact that the number of operatives is small in proportion to the output of the trade, owing to the large use of machinery for certain processes, have brought about an amount of organization amongst the workers that is quite exceptional. Hereafter, when we examine in detail the subdivisions of labour, we shall recognize to what an extent this organization prevails. True it is, that for the moment, by reason of a considerable influx of female hands, a slight derangement has been produced in the cigar labour market, but there is every prospect that, before long, the women workers in London will—imitating the example set them by their sisters in Nottingham and Leicester—form a union for their own protection, and wheel into line with the men.

As regards wages, speaking generally, and reserving particulars · for future consideration, they are fairly good and are distinctly above the average of the other local industries. But it must be borne in mind that a very large part of the labour employed is " skilled," and requires a term of apprenticeship and a degree of excellence that would always command adequate remuneration.

The particular districts with which we are now dealing, namely, those of East London and Hackney, contain 76 factories for the manufacture of tobacco in one form or another. Of these 76 factories, 17 produce tobacco and snuff, either alone or in combination with cigar work; 10

manufacture cigarettes, and 49 cigars only. In all London there are about 180 factories in this trade, and in the whole of England, including the metropolis, there are about 430, the chief provincial centres being Liverpool, Nottingham, Leicester, Sheffield, Leeds, and Manchester. These figures demonstrate that, so far as the number of factories is concerned, East London occupies a conspicuous position. It is true that, of the factories there, many are of very humble dimensions, but others again are on a large scale, and are well appointed throughout, though few, if any, equal the proportions of the largest provincial concerns.

As regards the workers engaged in various departments of this industry within our selected districts, we shall probably be fairly accurate in estimating them at close upon four thousand. Nor must we omit from consideration the large body of retail dealers who are interested in the sale of tobacco in its various forms. The returns placed at the disposal of the writer by the courtesy of the Inland Revenue Office show that, in 1887-8, the number of such dealers in East London and Hackney who took out a license to trade during the whole year was 4913, whilst 390 obtained a license for only a portion of the year. The returns in question also indicate that during the past three years there has been very little variation in the number of licenses granted each year to the manufacturers and dealers in this locality.

Before closing these general remarks it may be of interest to note that this trade, so far as the masters in East London are concerned, is almost entirely in the hands of the Jewish community. Formerly the cigar department only was adopted by Hebrew manufacturers, whilst tobacco and snuff were produced by Gentile firms, but at the present day this distinction does not hold good.

We now proceed to examine in detail the different branches of our industry, and inasmuch as the majority of factories in East London are devoted to cigar work, we propose to deal in the first place with that subject.

CIGAR FACTORIES.—The cigars produced in English factories are known as British cigars, and vary considerably in price and quality. Those made by the best firms, when hand-worked and of the choicer kind of leaf, are infinitely superior to some of the lower grades among imported Havanas. Competent observers are of opinion that, at the present time, there is a fair field open to our home manufacturers, and that the operation of the "Merchandise Marks Act," will give an impetus to the trade. Previous to this enactment many sham Havanas were imported into England from the Continent; such cigars being ordered from Belgium and other places by retail dealers in this country. But although this spurious rivalry may be checked, yet our home-made cigar has many other competitors, amongst which the Mexican now ranks as the most important. This article has recently been introduced on a very large scale and is sold at threepence, that being about the retail price also of the best British cigar, though the latter, when only of medium quality, can be purchased at a much less formidable figure. In order, however, to hold his own against outside competition, the English manufacturer ought undoubtedly to make a better class of cigar. Now, with the exception of about a dozen houses in East London, the whole of the trade there attempts to do everything as cheaply as possible, careless both of the nature of their leaf and of the character of their work. With a view to cutting down the expenses of labour, they have introduced a large number of women and girls, the majority of whom are engaged in the inferior process of making cigars by "mould." "Mould-work" may be briefly defined to be that system by which the core or central mass of the cigar—technically termed the "bunch" —is shaped by means of pressure in a mould instead of by the manipulation of the workman. An expert can always

distinguish mould-work from hand-work, and he will moreover tell you that a cigar made by the former method is
less pleasant to smoke than one made throughout by hand.
This fact is probably due to the "bunch" becoming
clogged by reason of its insertion in the mould, so that it
loses flavour and often fails to draw freely after the outer
cover or wrapper has been rolled around it. In Germany
mould-work has been discarded for some time, and many
lads and girls are apprenticed to hand-work business;
both men and women are employed there, and they use
better leaf than we do in cigar manufacture. By reason
doubtless of the superior article that they produce the
Germans have developed a large export trade in cigars
with our Australian colonies. But here it must be con-
fessed, that the exclusion of our native houses from this
lucrative market, is not so much due to the quality of their
produce as to the inadequate "drawback" received upon
export. Indeed, the best authorities strongly maintain
that the amount of "drawback" at present allowed is
absolutely prohibitive of any export trade whatever in
British cigars. Setting aside, however, the question of
opening out a profitable foreign trade, there is ample room,
under present conditions, for anticipating an increase in
home consumption, provided that a better article is offered
to the public. The retail dealer seems to be the chief
stumbling-block in the path of the conscientious manufacturer. The dealer has his little weakness in the shape
of a desire to make too large a profit, and, by beating
down wholesale prices, he often gets an enormous return
upon the stock that he purchased from the factory. Now,
if manufacturers would only show the same amount of
cohesion and organization in making terms with retailers
that the men display in their relations towards their
masters, they would derive much advantage for themselves
and also confer a benefit upon the "innocent purchaser."

When we come to inspect the inner life of a cigar factory

our attention is first attracted by the class of operatives
known as "liquorers" and "strippers." They may be
ranked together because in very many houses the "liquorer"
works also as "stripper."

"Liquoring" is the preliminary process to which the leaf
is subjected and consists in sprinkling it with pure water by
means of a spray, or rose, or wisp, or occasionally by simple
immersion in a tank : the object being to render the leaves
soft and pliant, so that they may be safely handled by the
"stripper." In most cases the "liquorer" is the foreman
and gives the stuff to the "stripper." In a large firm a
foreman "liquorer" gets 35s, and in a small firm 25s a
week.

The business of the "stripper" is to strip the leaf by
taking out its mid-rib; this is an operation that requires
some dexterity, and is effected by a slight incision which
enables the leaf stalk to be readily pulled out without causing any abrasion to the surface of the leaf. An ordinary
"stripper" is paid at the rate of 23s to 25s a week. The
work is well adapted for female hands, and in provincial
factories they are largely employed in this department. In
London, on the contrary, there seem to be not more than
thirty women engaged as "strippers."

The "strippers" have a union which embraces the
"liquorers" also, and is called, "The Strippers' Mutual
Association." All the members are English, their union
was founded about forty years ago and consists of seventy-
seven men; there are also about thirty non-unionist men
working in London. Jews do not take to this branch of
business, and there are only six Jewish "strippers."

The leaf, being duly stripped, is given to the "cigar-
maker" in order that it may be fashioned into that familiar
form which is so seductive to some members of the community and so odious to others. In point of numbers this is
the most important branch of the trade, and a noteworthy
fact in connection with it is the prominent position that

female labour has recently assumed in the department.
The number of male cigar-makers in East London and
Hackney may probably be reckoned as about 800—that
figure embracing both members of unions and non-unionists
—whilst the total of women and girls cannot be much under
1100 operatives. Without in any way wishing to disparage
the working capacity of the latter, it can hardly be denied
that the best quality of work is at present produced by men.
Undoubtedly, there are cases where women are employed
also to fabricate an article of high standard, but, as a rule,
they are engaged upon the commoner class of cigar, where
the "mould" usurps the more efficient labour of the hand.
To watch a clever operator manipulating his leaf is an
exceedingly attractive sight. There he sits at a long table,
divided into little compartments; beside him his fillers for
the core or bunch of the cigar—such fillers being usually
portions of less valuable leaf—in addition to this he has his
"wrappers," a sharp knife, a pan of some glutinous substance to finish off the point of the cigar, and a measure for
regulating its bulk and length. Taking deftly a sufficient
portion of the fillers, and arranging them with care, so that
there may be no unevenness to interfere with the drawing
properties of the cigar, the workman, if employed upon
handwork, after rolling up the "bunch" in an inner cover,
until it assumes the shape desired, proceeds to enclose it in
the outside wrapper. This wrapper he has already, by two
dexterous strokes of his knife, cut from the stripped leaf
beside him, and he runs it round from the thick end to the
point with incredible rapidity. In "mould-work" the
central portion of the cigar is placed in a mould and
subjected to pressure for twenty-four hours to give it form,
and the wrapper is then affixed.

The wages are very unequal and are regulated by the
quality of the work. The better the material the more
highly paid is the labour expended, the converse of this
statement also holding good. Piece-work prevails and

prices range from 1s to 5s per 100 cigars. A man engaged upon cigars of the best quality can turn out 150 a day; and 250, if making a cheap article. Men earn from £1 to £2 a week, the week consisting in this, as in other branches of the tobacco trade, of five full working days—from 9 A.M. to 7 P.M., with an hour for dinner—and half a day on Saturday. Exceptional instances occur where men are paid at the rate of only 15s a week, but the trade is at present brisk, and there is a good demand for male hands, few, if any, society men having been out of work for some time past.

There are two unions in existence, the earliest of which in point of date is the " Cigar-Makers' Mutual Association." This society was one of the pioneers in organizing labour; it dates from 1835 and is conducted on liberal and enlightened principles. As an example of these characteristics it may be mentioned that, not only are the foreign workmen in London admitted to membership, but also very substantial pecuniary assistance was rendered by it some years ago to those of their trade who were on strike at Amsterdam. Frequent communications moreover take place between this union and the workers both on the Continent and America, and, in its attempt to introduce an international element, its position among other English societies appears to be almost unique. The number of members now on its books is about 850. The younger organization is styled the " Provident Cigar-Makers' Trade Society," is an offshoot from the parent body above mentioned, and contains 200 members.

Women cigar-makers get from 15 to 40 per cent. less wages than men. Speaking generally, they are set to do a lower class of work, and the majority of them are apprentices. Even when full workers and able to make cigars of high quality they are remunerated at a much lower rate than the men. Some of them, however, when very quick with their fingers, get as much as £1 a week and even more, but the average weekly earnings range from 15s to 18s. At present they have no union in London, but there is a movement on foot to establish one. Some organization is imperative in the interests of both male and female operatives, since a section of masters aims at beating down women's wages with a view to lowering those of the men also.

In the cigar-making industry there is a regular term of apprenticeship of five years' duration. Amongst men workers there are now very few apprentices but, on the other hand, there are a large number of girl learners who begin their course of training at thirteen years of age. Those who have the reputation of being good masters pay

$s.$	$d.$				
2	6	a week for the 1st year of apprenticeship.
3	6	,,	2nd	,,	,,
4	6	,,	3rd	,,	,,
5	6	,,	4th	,,	,,
6	6	,,	5th	,,	,,

and half what is earned above that sum. In such a case the amount of earnings depends entirely upon the ability and zeal of the worker. A clever hard-working learner, for instance, in her third year of apprenticeship, stated that she made 10s a week; a slower and somewhat lazy girl in the same stage of probation, only got 5s for a similar period. Those who are considered to be "bad" masters pay no fixed sum per week to learners, and moreover dismiss them at the end of their term and take on fresh probationers. This is obviously a highly economical method of running a cigar factory, provided that any purchaser can be found for the class of work produced.

As regards the question of nationality it would appear that most of the hands, both male and female, are English, a minority of one-third of the men and one-half of the women being probably of the Jewish religion and of foreign extraction. Concerning the physique and intelligence of the men employed in this branch, it should be reckoned as above the average. With reference to the health of the women, however, there is a conflict of opinion, some authorities considering that the work is distinctly deleterious to it, whilst others are by no means convinced that such is the case.

The last class of operatives that remains for consideration are the "sorters" and "bundlers." Their duty is to separate the cigars according to the various colours of the leaf, and to make them up in packets for storage. This is a nice clean process; requires a quick eye and experience; and seems to be eminently adapted for female labour. There is some piece-work in this section, but it is principally paid by time at the rate of 25s to 28s a week. The "bundlers" are half Jews and half Gentiles, and there are as many women employed as there are men. They have a union called the "Sorters' and Bundlers' Society," comprising 90 or 100 members, in addition to which there are about 40 or 50 non-unionists in the trade.

TOBACCO FACTORIES.—Let us now pass on to consider the manufacture of tobacco as distinguished from that of cigars, cigarettes, and snuff. This is also a considerable industry in East London, but fewer hands are employed in it by reason of the extensive use of machinery. Certain regions of the United States, such as Kentucky, Maryland, Virginia, and Ohio, send large quantities of leaf to our islands, but at the present time there are many other sources of supply. Indeed, upon entering a warehouse where tobacco is stored, the visitor is amazed to find how many quarters of the globe minister to the smoker's pleasant vices. Japan makes her contribution in the shape of a leaf with an exceptionally small stalk : the northern part of Syria provides the famous Latakia, which, in spite of its excellent properties, is by no means pleasing to the eye in its raw unmanufactured state; China furnishes a light-coloured product more attractive to see than to taste and chiefly used to give colour to certain smoking mixtures; whilst America sends bale upon bale of her renowned yellow Virginia, from which some of the most favourite smoking tobaccos are prepared.

The first process in this department is to take the leaf out of the bales and blend it in the required proportions. This is no haphazard performance, but is done with the utmost care by means of accurately adjusted measurement, and the foreman of the "liquoring" and "stripping" department usually superintends the operation. In some firms a practice prevails of steaming the leaf before it is blended in order to open it out thoroughly and free it from the pressure of the bales. The "liquoring" and "stripping" in this branch differs very little from that obtaining in cigar manufacture, and the wages received are about the same. The number of strippers, however, employed by tobacco firms is comparatively few, because much of the leaf is sent over from abroad already stripped, especially in the case of American tobacco, where there is a regular business in exporting "stripped" leaf. In the case of the well-known "Bird's-eye" commodity, the tobacco is cut up midrib and all, and thus the peculiar appearance is given to this article. Many leaves, again, from their very nature render "stripping" unnecessary.

After the blenders and liquorers have done their work the leaf is, in the case of "cut-tobacco," handed over to the machine-men. The machines employed are of two kinds, the swan-necked for the coarser, and the H-machine for the finer qualities of leaf. Men engaged in this work are usually paid at the rate of 34*s* to 36*s* a week; many firms, however, pay their cutters by piece-work, the wages running from 3*d* to 6*d* per pound of tobacco, according to the nature of the leaf worked at. There are no women in this department and the operatives are all English; they also have a union which embraces the "stovers" and the "spinners" whose duties are next treated of.

The tobacco when cut is passed on to the "stovers," and is subjected by them to the following processes. In the first place they put it on a steam-pan to separate the fibres; then they place it on a fire-pan in order to make the

material fit for keeping and improve its smoking quality;
subsequently they deposit it in a " cooler," where a current
of cold air is passed through it with a view to driving off the
moisture ; and finally they spread it out on trays to dry the
article still more completely and enable it to be packed
away for use. The present regulations regarding the
amount of moisture allowed in tobacco renders the most
minute precautions necessary in order to avoid any infrac-
tion of the law.   Stovers are well paid, obtaining the same
rate of wages as tobacco-cutters.

In addition to cut-tobacco there are two other modes of
preparing the leaf for smoking, in each of which a different
class of operative is employed.

The first of these methods is by the production of " roll "
or " spun " tobacco.

Here the leaf, after being liquored, is spun by aid of
machinery into a rope or roll—the thickness of such roll
being regulated according to desire—and subsequently
coiled into cylinders of various sizes.   These cylinders are
then bound up tightly with canvas and cords, are exposed to
moist heat for about twenty-four hours and are subjected to
heavy machine pressure for a month or six weeks.   The
final process is to bake them, and at the end of this operation they present the appearance of a mineral rather than of
a vegetable product.   However, they appeal forcibly to the
critical taste of a large class of consumers, and are esteemed
all the more highly by the purchaser in proportion as they
are hard, black, and shiny in substance.   One of the most
famous of these spun articles is called " Irish roll," and is
composed of strong materials such as Virginia or Missouri
tobacco.   There is a tradition in the trade that only Irish-
men can prepare this particular commodity, and they are as
a consequence employed much in the manufacture of it.   In
Scotland the " bogey " roll is said to be preferred, a small
edition of the Irish article, but like it in most other
respects.

In spinning tobacco, women and girls are used by many firms for the lighter work, making rolls up to two pounds in weight or thereabouts. The girl "spinners" at each machine have generally a forewoman over them. She gets paid by piece-work, never gets less than 12s a week, and usually considerably more. The girls under her get from 8s to 10s a week when full workers, and 4s to 6s a week when learners. The men "spinners" make rolls up to thirty pounds in weight, and the operation of coiling the spun tobacco into cylinders involves a high degree of skilled labour ; they get from 30s to 40s a week.

Having treated of "cut" and "spun" tobacco, a few words are necessary regarding the last method of preparing the leaf for smoking, namely, the manufacture of " cake " or " plug."

In making " cake " or " plug " tobacco, portions of broken leaf of different kinds, called " fillers," are usually enclosed in an outer cover or envelope of large whole leaves of a bright quality. The material is then placed in moulds and subjected to heavy pressure by machinery, and in this way solid cakes or plugs of a regular pattern are turned out. Labour in this branch is paid on the same scale as in the " roll " department.

Snuff Factories.—The manufacture of snuff comes in a natural sequence after that of tobacco, inasmuch as the ingredients of it consist, to a large extent, of the leavings, in the shape of shreds and stalks that have resulted from the methods last treated of. It is not proposed, however, to enter into any detail regarding the various complicated processes that distinguish this branch of trade, because the amount of snuff manufactured in East London is comparatively small, and the number of workers engaged quite insignificant.

It will be sufficient to indicate briefly that the following is the system of fabrication that usually prevails :—If it is desired to make a snuff of finest quality, dark Virginia or Amersfoot leaf is selected, but, for ordinary samples, various broken leaves and midribs are in the first place damped and subsequently allowed to go through a process of fermentation, the heat, at this stage, being regulated with great attention. The material is then ground in a large conical mill; carefully sifted and reground, if necessary, after which it is packed in open boxes in order to undergo further fermentation, and turned over, from time to time, until it becomes uniform in appearance and quality. In the case of some snuffs, the material is fired or toasted before it enters the mill, and the atmosphere of the mill-house then becomes charged with minute pungent particles, and is extremely trying to sensitive olfactory nerves. The snuff-grinders, however, do not appear to be much affected by it, although they occasionally adopt, as a precaution, a light mask or veil when the air is very thick with tobacco dust. The workers in this department are all men, and are well paid, getting from 30s to 40s a week.

CIGARETTE FACTORIES.—The only branch of the tobacco trade that now remains for consideration is the manufacture of cigarettes in our selected districts.

Male cigarette makers in London are nearly all foreigners and most of them Jews, but, curiously enough, there are comparatively few cigarette workers in East London, although that locality embraces a large part of the Jewish and foreign population of the metropolis. There seem to be about ten or twelve factories only in East London and Hackney, employing, in all, less than 150 cigarette makers, whilst in other parts of the capital there are at least fifty firms manufacturing cigarettes. The finest quality of tobacco employed in this branch of trade arrives from Turkey, and is usually sent in smaller bales than the coarser varieties. It consists of young tender leaf, which even after being compressed for export, still retains a wonderful degree of succulence, and presents a fresh and engaging appearance that is quite irresistible. At this early stage the leaves seldom require either "liquoring" or "stripping," their central vein or midrib being devoid of any woody texture, and their whole surface being sufficiently soft to render manipulation easy. Should the weather, however, be exceptionally dry, the services of the liquorer may be needed, and in such a case the process is performed by a light spray, or occasionally by a jet of pure water emitted from the mouth. In cigarette manufacture particular attention is paid to the blending and sorting of the leaf before it is handed to the cutter, and the foreman carefully weighs out the different proportions and then gives the material to the sorters, who pick it over leaf by leaf and mix the ingredients together. A curious method of blending is sometimes adopted, in which the leaf is collected in the arms and then skilfully tossed into the air in such a way as to produce a complete amalgamation of the different samples selected. Liquorers and sorters are paid on the same scale in this branch as in the other departments already treated of.

The business of the cutter now begins, and it differs considerably from that of his comrades in the tobacco trade, because, in all the best class of cigarette business, the cutting is done by hand. Experts maintain that it is a mistake to cut fine Turkish tobacco with a machine, and accordingly the practice prevails of using a chopper that works on a swivel and calls into play a high degree of skilled labour. The cutters are always men, and a good cutter will earn from £2 to £3 a week. Some of the smaller cigarette firms only engage the services of a cutter from time to time, as they need him. In such a case he is paid by piece-work at the rate of from threepence to sixpence per pound of tobacco. A first-class worker can cut fifty pounds of leaf per diem; an average hand gets through thirty to forty pounds in the same period. Most hand-cutters are of foreign origin, and belong to the same union as cigarette makers, whose trade society will be subsequently referred to.

The cut tobacco is weighed out and given to the "cigarette makers." The men working in this branch of business are nearly all foreigners, and principally Russians, Dutch, Greeks, and Germans. As in the cigar trade so also in the cigarette department the best work is done by the hand without the aid of machinery. Female labour has made an extensive inroad upon this market also, and the result has been a diminution in the rate of wages. The majority, however, of the women and girls employed are English-born, whilst their male competitors are mostly foreign immigrants. To roll well even an ordinary cigarette is a much more difficult task than would appear at first sight, and in order to manufacture the commodity now in fashion—the cigarette with a very narrow "lap"—long practice and great dexterity are essential. All the best work is, at present, done by men, the women working largely at what is termed "push-work." "Push-work" bears somewhat the same relation to hand-work in cigarettes as mould-work bears to hand-work in the cigar industry, and simply means that process in which the paper wrapper is first constructed and the tobacco subsequently inserted. This is obviously a much simpler way of making a cigarette than the method of rolling and finishing off by hand, but the result of the two systems of manufacture does not admit of comparison. As regards wages, piece-work is the established rule in this section, and men are now paid at the rate of from 2s 6d to 3s 6d per thousand cigarettes. An average workman can make 1000 best quality cigarettes in a day and 1600 of inferior quality.

Women are paid from 1s 3d to 2s 3d per thousand, and a clever worker earns 15s a week : there are many instances, however, where a girl working hard throughout the week only gets her 6s at the end of it. The comparatively new system of selling cigarettes by weight at 6d per ounce or often at as low a figure as 4s 6d per pound, has had an evil effect upon the labour market, such a price rendering it necessary to employ the cheapest form of labour in order that even a small profit may accrue. Again, the fact that home-work is possible in cigarette making and is practised to some extent places this branch on a different footing from the other departments of the tobacco trade, and is undoubtedly prejudicial to the maintenance of a high wage-standard.

As to apprenticeship, there would appear to be no fixed period, though, nominally, it is from three to five years in duration, and learners get from 2s to 4s a week during their time of probation.

The "cigarette makers" have a society styled "The Cigarette and Tobacco Cutters' Union," which embraces 240 members, of whom twenty-three are women. All of this body are foreigners. The English girls and women engaged in the industry have as yet no organization, and, looking at the low rate of wages that many of them receive, it is extremely desirable that they should take steps to remedy this defect.

There is an interesting little establishment in Houndsditch called "The Cigarette Makers' and Tobacco Cutters' Co-operative Manufacturing Society," where the principle of co-operation, in the interest of producer and consumer alike, seems to be working satisfactorily.

The cigarette trade presents certain general features that are noteworthy. Fashion and fancy exercise a powerful influence upon it. For example, at the present time, Egyptian cigarettes made with a very narrow "lap" are all in "favour." The wrapper again must now be of what is called Egyptian or Danube paper, otherwise the purchaser will not be satisfied, whereas quite recently rice paper with a wide "lap" was in vogue. It is not proposed here to enter into the competing merits of these different types, but it may be well to point out that the so-called Egyptian cigarettes are all made of Turkish tobacco, and that there would appear to be no good reason for preferring those

made at Cairo to an article made of the same leaf
in London. Indeed, the Cairo manufacturer has to pay
so much away in export duties, import duties, and freight,
that it is really hard to see where his profit comes in,
provided that he makes use of the choicest Turkish tobacco.

Concerning cigarette-paper it is curious to note that
both the Egyptian and the rice variety are of foreign
origin, the former being manufactured in Austria, the
latter in France. Either of these commodities could be
equally well made in this country, and might certainly
form the staple of a very profitable industry.

Having thus glanced at the various branches of the
tobacco trade, let us consider what inferences may be
drawn or what lesson may be learnt from the foregoing
investigation. The most obvious inference that arises is,
that—given certain conditions of labour—there is nothing
to prevent fair wages ruling in East London more than in
any other locality. The prevalent notion, that everything
in that quarter must necessarily be black and depressed,
will at any rate receive no countenance from the facts
above set forth. As to what the conditions of labour are
that have led to its being more fairly remunerated in
the tobacco than in the other local trades, so far as this
is the case, they are conceived to be as follow :

In the first place we observe that the labourers are well
organized, being grouped, it is believed, in a more complete
series of trade-union societies than obtains in any other
industry. The number of these bodies, again, may
doubtless be attributed to the prevalence of the factory
system, which renders the task of the organizer comparatively easy, the material being ready to hand and
not hidden away in obscure dens or petty workshops.
Moreover, we may note, by way of parenthesis, that the
duties of the Government inspectors, in looking after the
well-being of the operatives, can be much more efficiently
performed under such circumstances.

If we ask why the factory system prevails, the answer is that its adoption is due to the excise regulations that have already been mentioned; to the absence of very small capitalists in the trade; and to the extensive use of machinery in the various processes of manufacture.

In the second place, it should be borne in mind that tobacco is, to some extent, a protected industry. What effect that protection has upon the wages of the workers it would be hard to determine, but doubtless weight should be given to this incident in any comparison drawn between this and other labour-markets. Moreover the skilled nature of much of the work in the trade: the comparatively small body of workers engaged therein: and the fact that tobacco is in truth an *article de luxe* and not of necessity, are points that must not be overlooked.

We have then trades unionism coupled with Government supervision as the prominent factors that account for the satisfactory rate of wages that prevails.

It is hardly necessary to state that it would be fallacious to argue, from the conditions of this trade, that other industries in East London should be assimilated to it. The factory system, which works well in the case of tobacco, might inflict grievous distress if adopted in the tailoring or boot-making business, where much home-work exists and where the number of hands employed is considerably greater. Nor must it be forgotten that English tobacco factories compete with the same system on the Continent and elsewhere, and not with small shops or with home-work, otherwise the result might be less satisfactory. Each trade, in fine, must be examined in connection with its immediate surroundings.

In conclusion the writer desires to place on record the courtesy that, with very few exceptions, he has met with from both manufacturers and operatives in East London and Hackney during the course of the above investigation.

[*Note to Edition of* 1892-3.—Since the above paper was written the importance of tobacco in relation to State finance has steadily increased. During the past financial year it produced a net revenue of £9,965,220. 17*s* 5*d,* whilst the licence duties paid by tobacco dealers amounted to £78,508. 15*s* 1*d,* and those paid by tobacco manufacturers to £7,019. 5*s.* Thus an aggregate of over ten millions is contributed from this source alone to our national resources.

Within the last two or three years the men's unions in the "Cigar-making" branch of the trade have amalgamated, and now form one society styled "The Cigar-makers' Mutual Association," comprising about 1250 members. Within the same period the "Women Cigar-makers' Protective Union" has sprung into active life, with a membership of nearly 700, including Englishwomen and foreigners.]

S. N. F.

CHAPTER VIII.

SILK MANUFACTURE.

GENERAL REVIEW OF THE TRADE.

No industry in East London is more interesting in itself nor has a more curious history than that of silk manufacture. The art was introduced into England so far back as 1585 by natives of Flanders and Brabant, who had fled from their country during its invasion by the Duke of Parma. Some of these established themselves at Canterbury and appear to have prospered well. But it was not till 1685 that the celebrated Spitalfields industry was established. The Revocation of the Edict of Nantes caused a large number of industrious weavers to leave France, and these, coming to London, settled in Spitalfields, where they founded a trade which flourished rapidly and spread over the district, until almost the whole population of Christchurch (Spitalfields), Mile End New Town, and St. Matthew (Bethnal Green), became dependent on the silk trade. At first all the processes necessary to the carrying on of the trade were gone through in England; mulberry trees were planted in large numbers for rearing the silkworm, and the silk throwsters of London were a very important body.

But the climate of England proved unfavourable to the cultivation of the silkworm at a profit, and after many attempts it was gradually abandoned, and it became the practice to rely on other countries—China, France, and Italy—for the supply of raw silk, whilst the process of silk throwing died out in London and became confined, so far as this country was concerned, to certain places in the north of England. Accordingly, at the beginning of the present century, we find that the silk industry had become greatly crippled in consequence of the war with France, which led to serious stoppage in the supply of the raw material, and also, owing to the impoverished state of the country, to a greatly decreased demand for silk goods. From 1812 to 1816 there was the greatest distress in Spitalfields, but with a period of peace the industry speedily revived, and in 1824 it is said to have been in a very prosperous state, there being about 20,000 looms at work in the district, giving direct employment to more than 50,000 persons, and wages all round averaging from 15s to 16s for plain goods, and from 20s to 25s for figured goods. Up to this point the silk trade may be said to have been, from the time of its introduction into this country, more or less under the fostering care of the Government, which passed various enactments for its special benefit, and had for more than half a century previous absolutely prohibited the importation of certain kinds of silk goods. The results of this policy (not by any means confined to the silk trade) were not always satisfactory, as we read of several periods of distress during the protected period, with strikes and disturbances amongst the operatives.

But in 1824 the attitude of the Government towards native industry was changed. Mr. Huskisson commenced his experiments in the direction of Free Trade, and the ports were opened to various classes of foreign goods, amongst them being silk productions, which were admitted at a duty of 30 per cent. The effect of this alteration, if statements made in Parliament in 1832 are to be relied on, was most disastrous to the silk trade.

On the 21st February in that year Alderman Venables presented to the House of Commons a petition from the silk manufacturers of the metropolis, calling attention to the wretched state of the industry owing to the importation of foreign goods. On the same day Alderman Waithman handed in a similar petition from the operative silk weavers of Spitalfields, signed by 9000 heads of families. These documents gave a very gloomy picture of the trade, stating that 10,000 looms had been superseded and 30,000 persons thrown out of work, and that wages had fallen to 8s a week. Similar distress was reported at Macclesfield, Manchester, Coventry, and other centres of the silk trade. The outcome of the agitation was the appointment of a select committee "To examine into the present state of the silk trade, and inquire what effects had been produced by the changes in the laws relating to the silk trade since 1824, and whether any legislative measure could be devised compatible with the general interests of the country which would have the effect of promoting it; at the same time to prevent smuggling in silk manufacture; and to report thereon to the House."

The instruction relative to smuggling was put in at the wish of some members who asserted that this nefarious practice was carried on so largely in the silk trade as to be mainly responsible for the distress. The Committee sat for five months and received a mass of evidence, which was duly published in a blue book. Its labours only terminated with the session, and the members separated with the evident idea of resuming their inquiries in the following session. Curiously enough, however, the Committee was not reappointed, and consequently its work was never completed nor any report nor recommendations made to the House. For the next few years our legislators were not troubled with complaints in connection with this trade, and reading between the lines, one can very well see that during this time foreign competition found its level. The opening of the ports caused a certain proportion of French-made goods to be introduced into this country, either by smuggling or legitimately. These goods were almost entirely of the best class, and therefore the effect of their competition was particularly felt in Spitalfields, which had long been the centre of the best trade. A number of

Spitalfields operatives migrated to Manchester and other parts where inferior goods were made, and by charitable agency the temporary distress was alleviated.

Then came the introduction of machinery and its application to the commoner descriptions of goods, leading to loud complaints, and probably a good deal of genuine distress, in the North of England; but Spitalfields, continuing to make the richest of broad silks, remained unaffected by this later innovation. Machinery was not then, and never yet has been found, equal to the delicate manipulation and constant care required in the manufacture of the best work.

But changes soon occurred to arouse the apprehensions of the Spitalfields operatives. In 1846 Sir R. Peel brought in his proposals for a general tariff reduction, including the lowering of the duty on silk goods from 30 per cent. to 15 per cent. The weavers found able champions in both Houses of Parliament, and there was a big fight over the proposed reduction, but it was carried, as also was an alteration in the method of levying the duty. Instead of an *ad valorem* duty of 15 per cent., it was now decided to make the impost one of 5s per lb. weight all round. This was probably done owing to the constant variation and fluctuation in the value of the articles; but it was not without its disadvantages. Taken on heavy goods which consume a large amount of silk without much labour, this duty produced the required 15 per cent., but on light fancy articles on which more highly skilled workmanship and ingenuity were expended and less silk used, the duty sometimes fell as low as 3 or 4 per cent. The natural consequence of this alteration was a considerable increase in the importation of fancy silk goods, to the particular detriment of Spitalfields, which, as we have seen, excelled in this description of work.

But notwithstanding these drawbacks the weavers of East London appear to have held their own very fairly until 1860. In that year an event occurred to which is attributed the subsequent decline of the trade as an English industry. This was the passing of the French treaty, or, in other words, the adoption by this country of Free Trade. However satisfactory may have been the result of this policy as regards the trade of the country generally (a question that is, as a matter of course, not entered upon here), it is certain that in relation to the particular industry under notice the effect was singularly unfortunate, and this was aggravated by the circumstances attending the sanction of the measure. The treaty was agreed to suddenly, and so far as silk was concerned took immediate effect. In anticipation of this event a number of dealers had bought up a quantity of silk goods on the Continent and had them ready to put into the English markets so soon as the measure became law. These goods, which were largely adulterated, flooded the markets, and the English manufacturers, who had been preparing for the season, found themselves with a large stock of goods on hand, and little chance of getting rid of them. Several of the manufacturers were ruined at once, and others only struggled on for a short time.

For the next ten years the decline in the trade in Spital-fields was rapid, but it received a check in 1870, when the war between France and Germany, by stopping the supply of silk articles from those countries, led to a great demand for English goods, and even induced one or two firms in England to try the hazardous experiment of starting as manufacturers. This period is looked back upon by many of the operatives as the one bright spot in their industrial lives, for they were then able so to avail themselves of the extra demand as to obtain an increase in the price of some of their work, and the fact that they have ever since been able to maintain this advance would seem to show that the silk trade had by 1870 passed through its more acute crisis. But at best the check was but a temporary one in a gradual decline. As one of the manufacturers remarked to me, it has only been by originality of design and superiority of workmanship that it has been possible to keep the remnants of the trade together. Anything that can be made by the mile goes to the Continental worker, who will accept a wage which to an Englishman appears utterly inadequate.

But it's an ill wind that blows no good, and one effect of this fierce competition has been an improvement in the workmanship of Spitalfields. All authorities are agreed that finer specimens of weaving were never produced than those which now leave the looms. In damasks for hangings and furniture, &c., probably the cream of the trade is in the hands of one or two London firms, whilst the quality of the necktie silks may be judged from the fact that half-a-guinea in Bond Street and 12 francs in Paris is frequently — nay, usually — paid for a tie of Spitalfields manufacture.* Unfortunately, however, for the Spitalfields trade, the prevailing desire for cheapness, and the art with which inferior silks are adulterated—rendering it very difficult for any but an expert to tell a genuine rich silk from one heavily weighted with dye†—have made the demand for best goods very limited; whilst at the same time, in order to keep up a

---

* An interesting example of the skill of the Spitalfields operative is furnished by a story which is current in the locality. In 1870, when the promulgation of the celebrated decree of papal infallibility had been resolved upon, it was deemed necessary that the Pope should wear at the attendant ceremony a new vestment, woven entirely in one piece. Italy, France, and other European countries were vainly searched for a weaver capable of executing this work, and at last the order came to England, where in Spitalfields was found the only man able to make the garment, and he, by a strange irony of fate, one of the erstwhile persecuted Huguenot race.

† Silk naturally loses considerably in weight in dyeing, owing to extraction of the gum from the fibre. A pound of raw silk sent to the dyers would if not tampered with, only weigh from 12 to 14 oz. when returned. A common practice with the inferior silks is to so weight the fabric with mineral dye as to make it appear to be a rich heavy material. The weight may be increased to double or even treble by this process.

trade amongst connoisseurs, it is necessary constantly to change the patterns and increase the quality or quantity of the workmanship, which means increased expenditure of money or labour without corresponding increase in profit or wages.

To conclude a rather lengthy but perhaps not unnecessary review of the general condition past and present of the silk industry of Spitalfields, it may be fairly said that, if its downward march has not been altogether arrested, its pace has, at least of late, been checked through the enterprise of one or two manufacturers, combined with the increase of skill engendered by the operation of that law which has for its outcome the "survival of the fittest."

The apprenticeship system has been long unknown, and, with the exception of a few weavers who may be teaching a son or daughter, no one is learning the trade. Consequently there seems prospect of the trade dying out for want of workers rather than from want of work.*

No doubt if more attention were directed to home productions much might be done to save this interesting industry from extinction; but if the end must come, it will now at least be almost painless.

A Weaver's Home.

As the bulk of the work of silk manufacture is done in the home of the operative it may be not uninteresting,

---

* This is strikingly shown by comparing the ages of males engaged in silk manufacture with those working in other trades as given in the 1881 Census :—

Per-centages :

	Under 20	20-25	25-45	45-65	over 65	Total
Silk Manufacture ...	4·7	4·1	18·0	41·8	31·4	100
Other Trades	16·8	14·5	44·7	20·5	3·5	100

From these figures it will be seen that about 70 per cent. of the persons engaged in the silk industry are past middle life, as against some 23 per cent of other trades.

before proceeding to a general description of the working
of the trade, to give a brief sketch of a typical weaver's
home.   It is one of those old-fashioned two-story houses so
common in Bethnal Green—two rooms on the ground floor
with perhaps a kitchen in the rear ; and upstairs, one large
room running the length and breadth of the house.   The
door is opened to the visitor by the weaver's wife, who,
learning that he desires to see the weaving, courteously
ushers him into a small room on the right of the passage
whilst she goes to inform her husband.   The visitor is in
the parlour, which it is evident from its appearance is only
used for " company " or on other special occasions.   The
horsehair sofa and chairs which, judging from their style,
must be at least half-a-century old, and yet look but little
the worse for wear, are ranged against the walls with the
utmost precision, and the antimacassar thrown over the
head of the sofa reposes at a most correct angle.   There
is one window looking on to the pavement in front of which
curtains are hung so as to protect the inmates from the
inquisitive gaze of the passer-by, whilst in the centre is a
stand on which is an ornament of wax flowers under a
glass shade.   The small round table in the middle of the
room, covered with a dark cloth, holds two or three books
of a semi-religious character and a small album.   Over the
fire-place a fancifully cut border of pink paper protects
the frame of a fair-sized oval mirror, at the sides of which
are some framed cartes de visite ; on the mantelpiece a
couple of cheap ornaments, brass candlesticks, snuffers, &c.,
and on the walls two or three faded pictures in oils, and a
print of the celebrated weavers' flag.   This flag, which was
the property of the Weavers' Company, contained various
groupings and devices, and was considered a marvel of the
weavers' art.   It was mysteriously stolen many years ago,
and its loss is still spoken of with regret by the older
operatives.   On receiving an invitation to step upstairs, the
visitor cautiously ascends the old steep wooden stairs at the

end of the passage and stooping to avoid bumping his head against the low ceiling finds himself in a large but not very lofty room ; on the right hand a window extends the whole length of the apartment, commencing about 2 feet from the ground and continuing to the ceiling, and on the same side close to this window are arranged two looms, one rather larger than the other. On the opposite side of the room, in the part furthest from the door, a large four-post bedstead shows that the room is used for sleeping as well as working, and near the foot stands a quill-wheel for winding the silk on to the quills. The larger loom is worked by the weaver himself ; the other one by his grown-up daughter.*

The frame work of the loom is the property of the operative, but the machinery (*i.e.* harness, jacquard, &c.) is found by the employer. The jacquard is a very remarkable machine, it being possible to form any conceivable pattern with it.

Process of Manufacture.

Passing now to an examination of the working of the trade, it may first be noted that no raw silk is now produced in England, nor has been so produced for a long time past. The thrown silk is imported by the London manufacturer in skeins, chiefly from China and France, but the best sorts in smaller quantities from Spain and Italy. It is first sent to the dyer to be dyed (and perhaps weighted) to order. On being returned to the warehouse it is wound on bobbins by means of a treadle machine, and stored ready for use. The silk threads are divided into two kinds, which it is most important to keep distinct. These are called " organzine " and " tram," and consist of single threads twisted or doubled according to the kind of work for which they are to be used. The " organzine " is used to

---

* The above will suffice as a typical example, but I have often seen three or four looms in a room, this depending on the number of the weaver's assistants, who are nearly always members of his own family.

form the warp or longitudinal threads of fabrics; the
"tram" forms the weft or shoot—*i.e.*, the part thrown in
with the shuttle by the weaver.   The preliminary operations
of winding and warping, as they are called, are performed
by females, whose wages average about 10*s* to 12*s* per week.

The silk is measured out as required, and given to the
weaver, who may be working in his own home or in the
factory—usually the former.

The work done in East London includes neckties, scarves,
and handkerchiefs, umbrellas and sunshades, damasks for
furniture, velvet, serges for linings, sieves and galloons.
Of these the furniture work, although made by hand, is
largely done in manufacturers' workshops, the looms being
too large or too high for the ordinary weaver's room; and
umbrella silks and serges are mostly made in factories by
steam power.   The other work is all made in the weaver's
own home.

Neckties and Scarves.—We will assume that the weaver
is working on silk for neckties or scarves, this forming the
bulk of the work now done in Spitalfields.

On receiving the silk, with directions as to pattern, &c.,
from the foreman at the warehouse, he takes the organzine
to the cane spreader, who spreads it to the width required
for the work.   If the machinery of the loom is new or has
been altered, it is necessary to employ a harness maker and
enterer, who makes a new harness and then passes the ends
of the silk through the leashes of the harness and the dents
(or interstices) in the reed (which is like a very fine steel
comb, varying from 40 to 160 dents to the inch) and then
secures it.   This entering is done by women and is a long
process.   But if, as is generally the case, the loom is in
regular use, a small length of the silk threads used for the
previous job has been left in the loom to allow of the ends
of the new silk being joined to them.   This is done by
twisting the ends of the two threads together, each thread
being passed alternately over or under cane rods, placed in

in the centre of the bed of the loom, which has thus the effect of keeping every thread distinct. In the palmy days of the industry this twisting was a separate branch of the work, but now it is usually done by the weaver himself, though sometimes a man is employed to do it. Whilst the organzine has been undergoing these processes the tram (or a portion of it) has been wound on quills, usually by the weaver's wife. These quills are small reed pipes and are fixed by means of steel pins in the wooden shuttle with which the weaver throws in the threads, the number of shuttles used varying according to the number of colours required to form the pattern. The weaver having completed his task or, if it is required for immediate use, having finished a portion sufficient to be cut off, it is taken to the warehouse, and examined, and if satisfactory is then sent to a dresser or finisher, who imparts to it the necessary lustre. The tie work is of two kinds, that required for plain scarves which are to be tied by the wearer, these being woven usually in widths of three, with a division between each width, and needing only to be divided when finished; and that required for "cut ups"—that is, for the many shaped fancy ties now so much in vogue. The silk for the latter is made in an ordinary piece, about two feet wide, and is cut up to the sizes required at the warehouse. For this material the finishing is especially necessary, as if it were not for the stoutness thus imparted the stuff would curl up as cut and become unmanageable. After the cutter has done his work, the material is given out to women to be made up into ties. These women usually employ other women or girls, who work either in their own homes or in the workroom of the employer.

The work may be either plain or figured silk or satin. The plain work is the easier and lighter to weave, as it does not require the heavy jacquard machinery, the simple pattern being formed in the groundwork. This is usually done by women. The figured work, in which the jacquard plays so important a part, is called by the operatives "tissue," "half tissue," &c., according to whether the figure is spread all over the material or only occurs at intervals. To form this tissue it is necessary to throw extra shuttles, in addition to those required to make the groundwork.

Wages are calculated on the following basis :—For plain goods $1\frac{1}{4}d$ per thousand threads is paid; reckoning the warp to contain 8,000 threads, this would be $10d$ per yard. By the use of a richer harness and closer reed more threads may be got into the width, and the price might go up as high as $1s$ $6d$ to $2s$ a yard, but this involves a proportionate additional amount of labour. Taking, therefore, this $10d$ work as a fair average, a steady operative, working not less than 60 hours, might do about 24 yards a week, or equal to £1. Taking a yearly average, one fourth must be deducted from this for lost time, there being often a good deal of waiting between the jobs, so that the weekly average for a year would be about $15s$.

For figured goods, $1\frac{1}{2}d$ per thousand is paid for groundwork, and $4d$ per yard for working the loom, making the sum $1s$ $4d$ a yard. This is added to by payments for the extra shuttles needed for the "tissue," which may bring up the price per yard to $2s$ $6d$, $2s$ $8d$, $3s$, or $3s$ $6d$. Taking the $2s$ $8d$ as average work, a man might perhaps do 13 yards in a full week. This would be equal to $34s$ $8d$; deducting, again, a fourth for lost time, the total is reduced to $26s$ per week for the year. Subtracting from these earnings the rent of room, cost of fire and light, and other incidental expenses, I am led to believe that the net average earnings of operatives in necktie, scarf, and similar work, would be through the year about $22s$ for men, and $12s$ for women. As many of the latter are married women and have their household duties to attend to, their actual earnings would of course be considerably less. On the other hand, the wages stated for the man are based on the assumption that he is working single-handed, but, as a matter of fact, he is nearly always assisted by his wife, who often works a loom of her own, and when she does not do this does the quill winding, picking, &c., for the man. Taking all the information I have been able to obtain on the point, I am inclined to set down the net average earnings of a man and wife working in this way roughly at 30s a week—rather under than over.

Dress Goods, Velvets, and Serges.—The quantity of material made for dresses is so exceedingly small as not to be worth taking into account. The quantity of velvet made is not much larger—such as is made being used for collars of best-class coats. Prices for weaving range from about 3s 6d to 5s 9d a yard, the latter being exceedingly rich. To make velvet, two distinct warps are required, the raised warp, from which the pile is made, being called the " pole," and the other the " ground "—used, that is, to form the groundwork. Thin grooved strips of wire are inserted by the weaver as he works between the two sets of threads, and then cut out again, thus forming the pile. To show the improved quality of the work, it may be stated that 48 to 52 wires to the inch used to be considered rich work; now 60 and even 65 to the inch are required. The work is hard and requires great skill and care to prevent a flaw or a soil in the pile. Amongst the tools used by the velvet weaver is a trevat into which is fitted a very sharp blade, with which he cuts out the wires; and one or two highly polished razors with which he occasionally shaves with delicate touch the surface of the pile. A man with whom I conversed told me he could by working hard make a yard of velvet at 5s 3d in a day. He had fairly regular work, being employed by a very good firm, but judging by his statements, I should not put his nett average at more than from 25s to 27s a week, and he is a very good hand. Serge (for lining garments) is made to a considerable extent by women, partly in factories by steam power and partly at the homes of the operatives. The prices paid for the hand-work are usually from 7*d* to 9*d* a yard, and exceptionally go as high as 1*s*. A fairly quick worker can make about five yards of the common work in a day, but there is quite the average amount of waiting and slack time. In the factory the wages of the girls vary from 8*s* to 10*s* a week.

Umbrella Silk.—Here we have work largely performed by women. Probably more than half the workers are females. The commoner work is done in the factory by steam power, the looms being attended to entirely by girls, a few men being employed as twisters, examiners, rubbers, &c. The girls are on piece-work, and good hands can make from 13*s* to 14*s* in a full week of 56 hours. They have, however, a certain amount of waiting and slack time, and wages for experienced hands do not average more than 10*s* a week through the year. No apprenticeship is required, this part of the trade being learned in a comparatively short time. The best class of umbrella silk work is domestic, and is done by men, prices varying from 6*d* to 11*d* a yard. The earnings of these men are probably a little below those of the tie weavers, but their work seems to be rather more regular.

Furniture Silk.—This is the most highly skilled and best paid branch of weaving. The work is also much heavier, being sometimes 5 ft. or more wide and requiring the use of several shuttles. It is consequently very hard work, and takes a fairly strong man to do it. This is also largely factory work, but a part is done at home. The work turned out by the London firms is exceedingly rich and artistic, no pains or expense being spared to obtain the most original designs and skilled workmanship. The development of this branch is, I believe, of comparatively recent date, and it is now the most flourishing department of the English silk trade. The best mechanics are said to be able to earn from 50*s* to 70*s* a week when work is good, but they have their wives or other female relatives to do the winding and picking for them. Probably from 35s to £2 a week is the average of the operatives. Much of the richest work goes to America.

SOCIAL STATUS.

As a class, the weavers are capable and industrious people, equal to any of our skilled mechanics, and they still retain the simple, kindly disposition and natural good taste characteristic of the French Huguenot. Trades Unionism is not unknown among them, but their society is not now a strong one, and only numbers 70 members although it has had a much larger number of members on its books, and claims to have been instrumental in keeping up wages. It has a reserve fund of £100, but devotes its ordinary income, after payment of expenses, to the formation of a burial fund. The subscription is 1d a week.

In the French Protestant Hospital, Hackney, the aged weavers who have broken down in the struggle for existence find a pleasant and comfortable refuge in which to spend the declining years of their life. The nucleus of the foundation of the institution was a bequest of £1000 by a French Protestant refugee for the purpose; this was augmented by other gifts, and in 1718 a building was erected in the parish of St. Luke's, not far from the City Road, and received a Royal Charter of incorporation under the title of "The Hospital for poor French Protestants and their descendants residing in Great Britain." In this building the charity carried on its useful work for a great many years, first as a rendezvous and temporary home for the poor refugees, and later as an asylum for the distressed and aged amongst them; in the meantime London had gradually crept up to the site of the hospital, and the value of the land belonging to it became so largely increased, that by judiciously letting it on building leases, a sufficient sum was in time obtained to erect a new hospital, and the outcome is the present handsome building, standing in its own well-kept grounds, which adorns the north side of Victoria Park. This building, which was erected in 1866, is replete with every comfort and convenience for the inmates and staff, and contains a beautiful chapel where morning and evening service is held daily. The present 60 inmates (40 women and 20 men) were nearly all formerly connected with the silk trade, mainly as weavers or weaveresses. They are all well over 60 years of age, the average being probably 78-80. At the suggestion of the Charity Commissioners an effort is now being made to extend the benefits of the institution to persons of a higher social grade, such as aged French Protestant governesses, and others of a similar class. The hospital is admirably managed by a board of directors, who are themselves either representatives of or have descended from French Protestant refugee families: the clearest proof of similar descent is required from all applicants for admission to the institution.

NUMBERS ENGAGED IN THE SILK TRADE.
Number of Firms.

Preparers (including dyers, designers, &c.)	Manufacturers.	Dressers or Finishers.	Total.
6	28	4	38

Number of Operatives.

	Males.	Females.	Total.
Dyers	70	10	80
Designers, Card-cutters, Harness-makers, Reed-makers, Enterers, &c.	18	16	34
Winders and Warpers	—	240	240
Weavers	680	580	1260
Dressers and Finishers	55	5	60
	823	851	1674

The number of looms in use is about 900. The above figures are based on careful estimates of the numbers employed by each firm. The total set down for winders and warpers appears large in proportion to the other operatives, but this is owing to the fact that some firms only have their winding and warping done in London, the weaving being done in the country. In addition to the above there are the wives or children, who merely assist the weaver by performing such minor operations as winding the quills, picking, &c.

CHAPTER IX.

WOMEN'S WORK.

THE results of the investigation into women's work in East London which follow will be seen to bear especially on the condition of the women. The special account of the industries, which precedes the general view of home work and factory work, cannot claim to be in any sense an account of the trade but rather of the work done and the wages received by women in East London employed in the trade. The information has been obtained from women working at their own homes, from factory girls and from employers. The aid of the latter was not asked until facts had been collected from the former about their wages and their treatment. The extent to which I have received assistance from employers is roughly indicated in the account of the industries. The statements of the women and girls with regard to wages tallied very closely with those of the employers; but of course with regard to management and supervision the information given by workwomen on the one hand and by employers on the other was one-sided, complementary, however, rather than contradictory. For information about the wages of the City work-girls, many of whom live in the East End, the student should refer to Mr. Lakeman's valuable Report upon the Social Condition of Factory and Workshop Female Operatives in the Central Metropolitan District. Mr. Lakeman's suggestive remarks on home work have thrown considerable light on the points to be studied in examining the conditions of the home industries. The notes collected independently from workers in different parts of East London and kindly

lent to me by the Secretary of the London Bible and
Domestic Female Mission have been most useful in indicating directions in which inquiry should be made. From
the managers of homes for girls, superintendents of clubs
and evening classes and others I have received most
interesting accounts of the lives and habits of the factory
girls, and have been afforded opportunities of making the
acquaintance of large numbers of the girls themselves. I
am most indebted to Mr. Geo. E. Arkell, from whose notes
a brief abstract has been made with regard to the women
employed in making trousers, vests, and juvenile suits, and
who collected nearly all the facts given about the fur trade.

It will be observed that I have passed over millinery,
dressmaking, and mantle making. A very large number
of women are milliners and dressmakers. Many of these
are employed in supplying local wants; and the condition
of the rest can only be adequately treated in connection
with the condition of women similarly employed in other
parts of London.

Trousers, Vests, and Juvenile Suits.—Most of this work
is done by women and girls. As to *trousers,* the best work
is done by skilled tailors, but they (in East London) usually
work at home, and are assisted by their wives or daughters.
In the organized workshops, where some common as well as
good work is done, the pressers are usually men, but the
machinists as well as finishers are for the most part women.
Workrooms under female management, employing only
women, usually take the commoner work, and, frequently
putting out the finishing, are a half-way house to the distributing contractor who has no workshop, only a room in
which to stock the work, give it out both for machining and
finishing, and press it when returned. The condition of
the women in the organized workshops, which are most of
them concentrated in Whitechapel and managed by German
Jews, is better than in other parts of this trade. There is
a certain amount of factory inspection, which tends to limit

the hours of work ; the workshops are better looked after ;
the work is not so irregular, nor is so much time lost in
waiting for it. Both Jewish and Christian women are employed, and pay is fairly good. In the better class of shop,
machinists will make from 2s to 3s a day according to skill
and speed, and finishers from 1s 6d to 2s. As the quality
of the work deteriorates, and with it the pay, fewer Jewesses
are to be found, and at the bottom the work is generally
done by the wives of labouring men, the lower rate of pay
being accompanied by greater irregularity of work. The
workrooms of the female employers and the houses of distributing contractors are to be found scattered in Mile End
Old Town, Poplar, and Stepney; and most thickly near
Burdett Road and Stepney Green. The work is almost
entirely slop, and the workers in both cases are drawn from
the same class of people. Before marriage they go to the
shops, and after marriage, if obliged to earn money, take
the work home. In the lowest rank are, naturally, those
married women who, without any previous training, take it
up under pressure of want. Theirs is the poorest pay and
the most irregular work. Here we find truly "starvation
wages." In the making of *vests* we see the same progress
downwards, from the shops in which male basters, pressers,
and machinists are employed, to those in which women only
are found. As price and quality decline, so women take an
increasing share in the shop work. The medium quality of
work is made almost entirely in the shops (most of which
have been established within the last seven or eight years),
and the tendency is for all except the commonest work to
be done more and more in this way. Home-work, however, lies above as well as below. There are women who,
working at home on good "order" work, earn 20s a week
in the season (Easter to August), and are never quite
without work. They are paid 1s 6d to 2s 6d a vest, while
other women do cheap waistcoats at from 5d to 1s and earn
from 1d to 3d an hour according to the work and their

aptitude. In the shops, girls start as learners at 2s 6d a week, and the pay rises to a maximum of 10s for ordinary or 13s for best hands. Button-hole hands are usually paid 1½d for six holes; a quick worker can make 18 holes in an hour, against 12 for an ordinary hand.

In *juvenile suits* the trade is either carried on in large work shops, in which all parts of the work are done on the premises or in shops in which all the machine work is done while the finishing is given to women working in their own homes. The shops of the former class are few in number but employ a large number of young women, who usually begin as learners and after a period of probation are put on piece-work and earn in the case of good ordinary workers about 10s per week, occasionally in the busy time making 12s or 14s. These shops are usually placed in the midst of a working-class population so that a good supply of workers may be obtained. In Whitechapel there are a few shops in which men are employed, but they do not compete with the other shops, being as a rule engaged on a better class of work.

The shops of the second class are nearly all in Poplar and the outlying districts. The majority are private houses or parts of houses adapted to the requirements of the trade. The workers in the shops are young women, but the finishing is given to home workers, who are usually married women. One man who had advertised for workers said that over 80 women called in one day, and all of these wanted home work, not indoor work. The rates earned by these finishers are about the same as those earned by the trouser finishers.

Shirts.—The unskilled workwoman at the bottom of the social scale finishes trousers; the unskilled workwoman at the top in the same neighbourhood finishes shirts. She is generally elderly if not aged, infirm, penniless, and a widow; she never expected to have to work for a living, and when obliged to do so has recourse to the only work she ever learnt to do. She is nervous and timid and takes work at whatever price it may be offered her; the price after all matters little to her; whether she gets 5*d* a dozen for finishing shirts given her by the first distributor or 3*d* a dozen from a fellow lodger who has taken home shirts, it is equally impossible for her to live on her earnings. If she were young and strong she might be able to earn 2*d* or 2½*d* an hour, and the 10*s* or 12*s* would be sufficient to a woman with the standard of comfort usual in the poorer artisan class. But many of these shirt finishers could not earn more than 8*d* a day, or 4*s* a week, if they could get the work, and many of them would find it very difficult to live on 10*s* or 12*s* a week. These shirt finishers nearly all receive allowances from relatives, friends, and charitable societies, and many of them receive outdoor relief. Their homes are better furnished and much more comfortable than the homes of many of the home workers who consider themselves in fairly good circumstances. To live in such places would be misery to the shirt finishers.

The shirt machinists who take work home belong to various grades in the social scale. If of the same class as the finishers they are younger and possessed of more force of character; the most skilled are generally women who have worked before marriage at shirtmaking or belong to a class in which women are used to work. Many of them have workrooms and employ as assistants young women who would not like to go to fetch work themselves, and who either cannot find work in the large workrooms or prefer to work in what to all appearance is a private house. These women who have workrooms give out the finishing, always paying less for it than they receive themselves, and considering the amount subtracted nothing more than a fair remuneration for expenses and the trouble of bringing the work home. There are so few local branches of first hand distributing firms that the work must either be obtained second hand or almost as much money, if not more, must be spent on tram fare as is retained by the middlewoman.

The machinists employed in the workroom of an East
End branch of a City firm are young women and are said
to earn good wages ; but the ground for that statement is
the fact that they are well dressed, from which the only
certain inference is that their fathers earn good wages.
But as even home workers, machining a poorly paid class of
shirt, can earn 2*d* to 3*d* an hour if at all skilled, it is most
probable that the girls who are engaged to work on the
premises of the wholesale firm or of the contractor, and
who are required to do a better class of work and to
execute orders at short notice, can earn 12*s* and upwards.
But this is only an inference. The girls are young ladies
who do not care to talk about their work, and frequently
do not let their relatives know how they earn their living.
The shirt distributors (*i.e.* the City wholesale houses)
will give no information whatever. The willingness of
employers to give information seems to increase as sub-
contract disappears. It is, therefore, by beginning with
the finishers that I have been able to trace shirts back to
their original sources as represented in the genealogical tables.

I. First City Firm.

Workroom in East End. Distributing Branch   E E.

Woman's workroom. Machinist. Finisher (4).

Finisher (3).

Machinist.   Finisher (2).

Finisher (1).

II. Second City Firm.   III. City Firms.

Distributing Branch in E. E.   Man's workroom.

Machinist.   Man's workroom.

Machinist (7)   Finisher (8).

Finisher (5).   Finisher (6).

Finisher (9).

Shirt (1) was given to the finisher by a machinist who received the work from a woman in whose workroom some shirts were machined but who gave out others ; this woman took the shirts from a distributing local branch of a City firm, which employs a large number of indoor hands at this branch in the East End, but gives out a great deal more than it makes in the workroom.

Shirt (2) was received from the woman's workroom where it had been machined.

Shirt (3) was given to the finisher by a machinist who took it direct from the first distributor ; and shirt (4) was given to the finisher by the same distributor.

The third table is based on the information given me by the master of a workroom, who did not give me an opportunity of discovering the shirts which he gave out to machinists and finishers. I believe that often the pedigree of the shirts done for these City firms, who have no distributing local branches, is the longest of all, but the intermediate steps are missing. The sub-contractor does not know where his shirts go to; the finisher does not know where hers come from. With regard to the rate of pay for which these shirt finishers work, the statements of six of them all doing the same kind of work, and visited separately in their homes, may be contrasted. They were button-holing gussets, making button-holes, and putting on buttons on flannel undershirts at $5d$ a dozen received direct. One of them was a girl who was " allowed to work for pocket money ;" on this work she earned $2d$ an hour, as much as common work of any kind is paid. Another was a widow, over 60, who could do a dozen a day ; she earned $5d$, but from this $2d$ had to be subtracted for tram fare ; "if she went to prayer meeting she had to work till 11 o'clock to do the dozen ; " her children and friends practically supported her. Another widow, also over 60, could do two dozen a day ; she received parish relief. She spent $2d$ on tram fare, and could not carry more than two dozen ;

she had previously made shirts by hand, giving out some of them to other women, "getting about ½*d* a dozen for her trouble." Another was a widow over 60, of a much lower class, who had been a silk weaver, and afterwards had worked in a rope factory; she could do one dozen of these undershirts a day, but did not have to pay tram fare. A fifth was the wife of a dock labourer out of work; on this work she earned 1¼*d* an hour; she was over 50, and had only learnt to make button-holes four years before. A sixth was a widow 78 years old; she could do a dozen a day; a neighbour fetched them for her, and she received parish relief. One shirt finisher when she was able to get work at first hand earned 1½*d* an hour: on the same work, when given to her by a middle-woman, she earned ¾*d* an hour; she also was a widow. One delightful old woman, 77 years of age, began shirtmaking at the early age of 68. She had no work when I saw her, and was living with her daughter, the wife of a dock labourer in work.

Incapacity and sub-contract are two causes of the low wages paid for shirtmaking. A third cause is to be found in the indifference to quality of work on the part of the consumer. This becomes apparent when we contrast the wages of the shirtmakers in the East End (where hardly any but common shirts are made), with those of the collar-makers. Collars are small, and large quantities could easily be taken home; it would seem at first sight that this industry would tend to become a domestic one. The tendency seems to be in the other direction. The work is sometimes given out to a man or woman having a workroom in the East End, but it is not often given out again; it is nearly always done on the premises. Even this practice is not universal, and one large City warehouse at least, has increased the number of its workrooms in order to have all its collars made at the warehouse. The wages of collar makers, even of those who work for the sub-contractor, begin almost where the low-class shirtmakers end, ranging from 11*s* to 17*s* even in the East End. The collars have to be run, turned, and stitched. Every part of the work requires care. Collars are worn to be seen, and here lies the explanation of the comparatively high wages. The work must be done well. And when this is essential the difficulty of enforcing good work is so great, the waste resulting from bad work so costly, that it pays the employer better to have the work done in the warehouse under supervision. As one shirt machinist remarked of her own work, " They don't pay for good work, and they don't get it " in the East End. Both shirts and underclothing requiring good handiwork are made in middle class suburbs of London, in the provinces, and most of all in the North of Ireland ; what the Irish peasant girls are paid I do not know, but it is notorious that the middle class needlewoman is paid less than any decent factory girl in the East End.

Ties.—The sub-contract system prevails in tie-making, and there is therefore no uniformity in the rate of payment. The City firms all employ a number of women in their warehouses, but give out most of their work. The better houses, that is those who do the highest class of work, do not employ the sub-contractor to so great an extent as the firms which sell the cheaper ties. Wherever the work passes through several hands before it reaches the actual maker, the pay diminishes and the work is inferior. The prices paid by the City wholesale houses for what is nominally the same kind of tie, vary according to the position of the firm, one firm perhaps paying twice as much as another. Some City houses give out 100 or 200 dozen ties at once to one man who will perhaps give them out again in smaller numbers to middle women who either have hands to work with them, or give out the parts of the work to be done by women at home. There is one check to the number of times that the work can be subdivided. It is impossible to tell beforehand when to expect a busy season, and when orders do come they have to be executed with great rapidity. The sub-contractors who take work from the wholesale houses in the afternoon, frequently give it to their outdoor hands in the evening, and have to take it back themselves to the warehouses by 9 o'clock in the morning. On the one hand the home worker is thus obliged to sit up all night, and may then perhaps have nothing to do for days together; on the other hand the payment can never sink so low as it is found in the shirtmaking. Nor do the middle-women get more profit than they are entitled to, considering the great uncertainty of the trade, the worry entailed in getting the orders executed in time, and the expenses incurred for rent, gas, firing, and machines if hands are employed in her own work room. These women nearly always do some of the work themselves, generally the fitting, and they have to pay a shop-girl to take the work to and from the City.

It is impossible to decide whether the rate of payment of those who take work from a sub-contractor, is much lower than that of those working directly for the warehouse. There are so many varieties of the same kind of tie, the rates paid by the different City firms vary to so great an extent; the quality of the work is so different that even when rates for nominally the same tie are compared, no conclusions can be drawn. For instance, one woman takes ties direct from the City, and makes them throughout, fronts, knots, bands, and fittings at $8d$ a dozen. Another tie maker was paid $2d$ the dozen pair for fronts, $1\frac{3}{4}d$ the dozen for bands, and $1\frac{1}{2}d$ or $1\frac{1}{4}d$ for knots, making $5\frac{1}{4}d$ or $5d$ for the part she did; the fitting was done by someone else, and the work was given her by a Jewish sub-contractor. Another woman, doing the same work, received it from a middle-woman who took it from the City; she did the bands only at $1\frac{3}{4}d$ the dozen; others did the knots at $1d$ the dozen, and others did the fronts at $1\frac{3}{4}d$ the dozen pair; fitters generally received $2d$ a dozen, but this the middle-woman did herself. Here therefore the price paid by the

middle-woman was $4\frac{1}{2}d$ the dozen without the fitting.
Sometimes one side of the band has to be machined, and
one woman who had no machine paid $\frac{1}{2}d$ a dozen out of the
$1\frac{3}{4}d$ paid to her. Another received $1\frac{1}{2}d$ a dozen for bands
which did not have to be machined. But without a know-
ledge of the prices in each case paid to the various sub-
contractors, and of the quality of work required, it cannot
be positively asserted that a large proportion of the price
paid was intercepted on the road.

With regard to the rate per hour, as usual among home
workers, there is a great variety in the degrees of skill, and
I have found the rate varying from $1\frac{1}{2}d$ to $4d$ an hour. In
this as in other trades where sub-contract prevails, I have
received too little assistance from employers to be able to
give any reliable statement as to the wages of girls in the
warehouses.

Trimmings.—There are several fancy trimmings factories
in Bethnal Green and the neighbourhood, employing comparatively few indoor hands, and having a large number of
outdoor hands on their books. But the number of outdoor
hands is not so great as might be inferred. The trade is
very uncertain and irregular; the employers compete with
each other in cutting down prices, and when one factory
is very slack another may be fairly busy. Many of the
home workers therefore go to several factories and get as
much work as they can from each. They tell me that the
factories pay differently, and they never take work from
the worst paying ones unless the others have none to give.
The number of outdoor hands employed by each factory is
always fluctuating. The majority keep, or try to keep,
a few indoor hands regularly employed, who make the
samples; but when new styles of trimming are being made
up, the employer takes on a larger number of indoor hands
to prevent other employers from imitating them. So that
in the largest factories there is great irregularity, and
many of the outdoor hands cannot get six months' work in

a year from one place. The trade seems to be a dying
one. Germany, as usual, is regarded as the principal and
successful rival of England, France being passed over
because she never competes in low-class work. Besides
manual dexterity, mental activity is requisite for success in
the manufacture of new designs, and mental activity is not
a characteristic of East End working women. Fringe is
out of fashion, and the fringe makers suffer accordingly,
if they have no alternative occupation. Child labour is
exploited in this industry by women who take as much
work as they can get from the various factories, and pay
young persons 2s 6d a week, or perhaps as much as 4s,
5s, or 6s to do simple parts of the work. These women
escape the notice of the factory inspector, and it is to be
feared, when they have enough work, keep the children at
it extremely long hours, beginning perhaps at 8 in the
morning and going on till 9.30, or even sometimes, as I
have heard, till 11 at night. The best work, whether in
the factory or outside, must be made by one person
throughout, and such work as ordinary braid trimming,
which does not lend itself to subdivision, cannot be
advantageously given out by middle women, unless the
girls who take it do not know where it comes from. But
in such work as beaded drops, or corded ornaments, in
which parts can be made separately and put together
afterwards, there is great scope for farming. Children
can be set to bead over the wooden balls or do other parts
of the bead work, and as there is no factory rate for these
parts, the sub-contractor can make her own terms, and the
more sensitive the parents are as to their social position,
the lower the rate at which they will allow their children
to work for " a friend at her own house."

Although employers have told me the wages paid to
their regular hands, they have given me no opportunity of
verifying their statements, and although several home
workers have told me about their work, they are unable to

give any reliable information as to rates of payment because of the variety in their work and its great irregularity.

The rate of payment is lower to outdoor than to indoor hands, but it must be remembered that the indoor hands have to make the samples, and very frequently to show the home workers how to do the new fashions ; the higher rate, therefore, when given, is paid for more difficult work.

Umbrellas.—Umbrellas and parasols are either made in City warehouses or by women at home. The class of maker varies with the class of umbrella. The cheapest and worst kind of umbrella is made by Jewesses in the East End. Several of these Jewesses are married, and the fact that they take this work home shows that they belong to a low social grade, for married Jewesses of the better class do not have to work for money. The umbrellas and parasols that they make are principally for shipping orders. Sticks and frames are made by men. The silk, alpaca, cotton, whatever it may be, is folded into eight thicknesses and cut by men into the eight triangles required for the umbrella. These covers and the frames are then put together in dozens and given out to the home workers; the parts of the cover have to be machined and the cover put on the frame by a finisher. Sometimes the machining is done in the warehouse and the finishing is given out. Generally the very best work and the newest fashioned parasols are all made entirely in the warehouse and the rest given out, sometimes a fixed price being paid for machining and a fixed price for finishing; sometimes a price being paid which includes both, and which leaves the home worker free to employ an assistant on any terms she can make. The City firms do not take learners as a rule; there are so many women in the East End who have an interest in teaching girls the work that any system of taking on learners is found unnecessary and troublesome. The best work given out to be done in the East End are parasols, paid at a rate as high as 1s 3d and 1s 6d each.

The cheapest work that I have heard of is paid at the rate of 9*d* a dozen. One Jewess who was making common sateen umbrellas at this rate, with the help of a finisher, a girl of seventeen, said that it took them two-and-a-half hours to do the dozen, giving about 3½*d* an hour to the two. For cotton zanellas they were paid 1*s* 6*d* the dozen, and it took them three hours to do the dozen, giving 6*d* an hour. In very busy times, which only lasted about six or seven weeks in the year, she could earn £1 and her finisher 12*s*. But after November they had very little work, and time and money were wasted in going to the warehouse for what they did get. Another Jewess, whose sight was bad, was making white calico umbrellas at 1*s* 6*d* a dozen; she and her finisher together could do the dozen in about six hours. A Gentile umbrella maker, who was doing unlined scarlet parasols at 1*s* 6*d* the dozen, with the assistance of her daughter, could do the dozen in three-and-a-half hours.

Higher up in the social scale a better class of work is done. One woman who finished umbrellas and parasols, the machining being done at the warehouse, was paid 2*s* 6*d* the dozen for the cheapest kind of parasols given her; the prices went up as high as 8*s* or 9*s* the dozen for finishing sunshades, which included covering, lining, and edging with lace. She could earn 2*s* a day, more if she worked long hours. There were slack seasons when she only had half work.

All the home workers complain bitterly of the long time that they are kept waiting for work at the City warehouses. The small number who are employed in the warehouses are better off in this respect. The prices too of the lowest class of work have been very much lowered owing to the increasing competition of manufacturers in this branch of the trade, and here again the home workers who do all this cheap work are worse off than the warehouse women, who are employed on better work and who do not suffer from reduced prices to the same extent.

Although several City workgirls live in the East End, it is doubtful whether they are among those who receive the highest pay, and therefore the following details of wages given me by the foreman in a City warehouse cannot be taken as representing wages earned by East Londoners. Table hands, who were finishing parasols and trimming them (for the West End), were paid from 10s to 18s a week as time workers. The machinists on piece work earned from 18s to 20s, but one machinist earned £2 a week, being twice as quick in doing the most difficult work as the others were on the ordinary work. The forewoman had 32s a week.

But according to the statements of City workgirls living in the East End, their wages approach near this level. One girl who worked at silk umbrellas at 3s 6d the dozen, said the lowest kind she ever did were 1s the dozen; of these she could do between three and four dozen a day. She had done parasol work at prices ranging from 2s to 6s the dozen. The highest wages she ever earned in the week was 18s, and she never earned less than 8s if she had work at all. Another City workgirl said she was paid 10d the dozen for machining, and 9d for finishing cashmere umbrellas. She could do the whole in two-and-a-half hours, earning, therefore, about 7½d an hour. She had earned as much as 17s 6d a week, but she usually earned from 16s to 17s in the season. She could not earn so much on the better class of work as on the commoner class mentioned above. A moderately skilled hand would earn about 10s or 12s a week.

Besides these City workwomen and women working at home for the City warehouses, there are small umbrella manufacturers in the East End who supply shops in the neighbourhood; they buy the sticks and frames and get orders; and their family are all employed in the actual umbrella manufacture.

Corsets and Stays.—Steel busks are made and covered in

separate factories. They are cut, shaped and japanned by men and boys. The latter operation, which is very dirty and disagreeable, is performed by girls in one small workshop at least in the East End. Women and girls cover the steels in the factory, and fix clasps and put in eyelet-holes with small machines. The stay-bones used for dress bodices, when covered, are given out to home workers to be fanned. This work is light and easy, and the women who do it are nearly always helped by their children out of school hours. The wages of fourteen home workers in the last week entered in the books were: 7*s* 8*d*, 8*s* 5*d*, 6*s* 1*d*, 4*s* 2*d*, 7*s* 10*d*, 2*s* 6*d*, 8*s* 9*d*, 6*s* 8*d*, 19*s* 7*d* (a woman with several children old enough to help her), 6*s* 8*d*, 6*s*, 9*s*, 14*s* 5*d*, 11*s* 6*d*. Whenever the wages were above 10*s* it might be safely concluded that the woman was helped by one at least of her children. One woman said that she was paid 6*d* a gross, and could do three gross a day, working about nine hours, giving a rate, therefore, of 2*d* an hour. Another told me that she was paid 4*d* a gross, and that it took her one day to do two gross; but she had only done the work for two or three weeks, was always being interrupted, never sat down to work for one hour at a time, and had a child just recovering from the measles. In some cases women take out the work and give it out again, paying ½*d* a dozen less for it, but this is only done to a very slight extent. In a busk factory where children from the age of 13 were employed the percentage receiving above 10*s* was unusually large.

Percentage of Women and Girls Earning—

Under 4*s*	4*s* to 6*s*	6*s* to 8*s*	8*s* to 10*s*	10*s* to 12*s*	12*s* to 15*s*	Over 15*s*
2·94	50	—	2·94	5·9	14·7	23·52

The corsets and stays themselves are principally made in Ipswich, Sudbury, Portsmouth and Bristol, but there are a few factories in the East End; several small staymakers have workshops of their own, employing a few hands besides the members of their family, and a few hundred women do work at home for the factories.

The cloth and linings are cut by men and machined together by girls. In some factories this machining is done inside, but the greater part of this simple work is given out to home workers. The parts, when thus machined, have next to be machined together, and this requires more skill, and if the number of parts in the corset is very large, is perhaps the best paid work of all. The common corset has only about ten to fourteen parts, but in the better corsets there may be fifty or more. When the parts have been put together, and the cords, bones, or steels have been inserted, men called "fitters" cut off the rough edges, and send the corset back to the binding machinist. The binders are skilled women, and have to be well paid. The corsets are then starched and laced tightly on heated metal models, and left until they have assumed the required shape. Children's stays are much simpler to make, consisting of very few parts, and when bound only needing to have bands, buttons, &c. put on, and to be pressed and ironed. Children do the former part of the work, put in eyelets, insert cords, and do other light work. At one stay factory where over sixty girls are employed, and where a great quantity of plain machining is given out, some hands earn 17s and 18s a week; the rest range from 6s to 14s, learners beginning with less than 6s, but able, if at all up to the average, to earn 7s or 8s in a very short time. The outdoor hands earn from 6s to 12s.

No two factories in any of the minor industries can be relied upon to have the same system of engaging and paying learners. Several of the staymakers learn from small staymakers, or from women who take work home, who pay them a small weekly wage. At one factory learners work for nothing the first month, the girl who teaches them getting the benefit of any work they may do; after that they are put on piece work, only earning about 6s or 7s for the first few months. The wages went as high as 18s, 19s and 20s in the last week entered in the wage book.

Percentage of Women and Girls Earning—

4s to 6s	6s to 8s	8s to 10s	10s to 12s	12s to 15s	Above 15s
8·5	23·4	19·2	34	—	14·9

Here all the outdoor hands had worked at the factory before marriage. They were paid the same rate as the indoor hands, but had to provide their own machine. One of them that week earned 17s 2d, but she had two young girls to help her; some earned 9s, one 6s 7d, another 4s 9d, and another 2s 6d, the amount they would take home diminishing as their household duties increased.

Furs.—The fur trade, both in the City and in the East End, is in the hands of Jews with very few exceptions. The furs are bought by merchants and large manufacturing furriers at the large sales held by the Hudson's Bay Company in January and March, and smaller sales are held in January, March, June, October and November. At the January and March fur sales representatives from all countries attend; Russians, Germans, and even Americans, come to buy their own furs. The skins are bought in the raw condition, and then sent to the dressers, who return them to the furriers. The cost varies considerably, owing partly to changes in supply, and very much also to changes of fashion which affect the demand. The City manufacturing furriers have some of the work done at their own warehouses, but most of them, if not all, give out skins to East End chambermasters, and several, besides this, have sewing done by home workers. The more respectable houses pay their cutters weekly wages, and engage and pay their nailers and sewers themselves. Many, however, employ the cutters on piece work; and a few at least allow the cutters themselves to take on and dismiss the sewers.

The chambermasters have skins given them both by the City furriers and by wholesale houses, receiving good or poor skins according to their ability and the confidence that can be placed in them. Several of them buy skins themselves as well, and make up capes and trimmings themselves, which they sell to the wholesale houses.

Besides these chambermasters, who rely principally on orders given them, there are, in the East End, several small furriers who buy pieces or cuttings, the leavings from skins, which are sold to them by chambermasters and others. These pieces are also imported from France and America. Articles made up from pieces of course require the greatest amount of sewing, and being also the least valuable, give the smallest return for labour.

There are a few manufacturing furriers working on skins of their own in the East End as well as in the City. One of these firms has the unenviable distinction of being mentioned by every manufacturer and chambermaster as being the worst sweating firm in the trade, although without the intervention of any sub-contractor. It employs "greeners" as soon as they land, taking advantage of their ignorance of the language and their poverty to induce them to work for very low rates indeed. Although. they employ a large number of hands, they work early and late, as all the world can see from the lights in their factory.

The season does not begin till May or June, and ends in November; and for five or six months in the year there is very little or no work done in most of the workshops. The work, which is disagreeable and unhealthy, has to be done in the hottest part of the year, and is done very often in little workshops in private rooms managed by Jews, often evading inspection altogether.

The workers employed in every furrier's workshop are: (1) cutters, who are nearly always men; (2) sewers, who are nearly always women, and (3) nailers, who are either men or lads. The cutters match the skins and give them to the fur-sewers; when they have done their part of the work, the pelt of the skin is thoroughly well damped with water, and then the skin is nailed down on a board on which the pattern of the article to be made has been chalked. The skin is usually a little smaller than the pattern, and the nailing stretches it to the required size. After being nailed on the board the skin is left to dry until the next day, or if wanted quickly it is dried before the fire, so that it retains its shape. After it is taken off the board the pieces are "evened off," the parts of the skin overlapping the chalked pattern being cut off; if at any part the fur will not stretch to the required extent a piece is sewn on. The parts of the article being made are then sewn together. The lining is generally done elsewhere, frequently being given out by the wholesale house or the furrier to liners, who get the work done by women in their homes.

The prices paid by the wholesale houses have fallen considerably. The City manufacturer has to give "Christmas terms," allowing credit until the end of the Christmas quarter. This the East End manufacturers cannot do. They buy stuff and make it up and take it round to the wholesale buyers and are obliged to sell it at once; they receive payment at once, but discount is deducted. The chambermasters also have from 2½ per cent. to 5 per cent. deducted when they are paid for orders executed. They accept very low prices because of the competition between chambermasters, several of these Jewish masters being willing to work for the smallest profit. The chambermasters complain of each other and of the small furriers working on their own account, who are not rich enough to ask high prices; the small furriers complain of the chambermasters for cutting down prices. The prices paid vary in the different wholesale houses. Rabbit-skin capes are generally quoted as examples by the East End masters; the price paid them

for these has sunk in the last three years from 12s a dozen
to 6s at some houses, 5s at others, and 4s 6d at the worst.
One chambermaster who took these capes at 5s in order to
keep his hands at work in the slack season paid his cutter
1s 9d the dozen, two sewers 1s 9d the dozen, the nailer 8d
a dozen, making 4s 2d in all; 5 per cent. was deducted, so
that he made 7d on the dozen. Another chambermaster on
the same work said he paid his cutter 1s 9d, his sewers 1s 9d,
and the nailer 10d, making 4s 4d altogether; 2½ per cent.
was deducted, leaving him 6½d the dozen. Another master
paid only 7d to the nailer, but 1s 9d to cutters and sewers.
Another master who was making rabbit-skin capes with his
own skins paid his cutter 1s 3d, his sewers 1s 3d, and his
nailer 6d the dozen. He gave the capes out to a liner who
supplied material and had them lined at 6s the dozen. A
fur-sewer who took fur capes home was paid 1s 3d the dozen
and found her own thread; another home worker was paid
the same price. An extremely good hand, working full
factory hours at 1s 9d the dozen, only earned 17s 6d; at 1s 3d
she would have earned 12s 6d, and an ordinary fur sewer,
even at high pressure, at this rate would not earn more than
9s. The cutter in the first case quoted, working full time,
earned 35s.

Some of the small masters working on their own account in the East End only employ hands in the slack
season, when they are in great want of work, paying
them at a lower rate, and selling the goods when the season
begins.

The number of fur sewers supplied by one cutter varies
according to the work; on capes, a cutter would require
about 3 sewers, on muffs not so many, and on trimmings
more. The trimmings of the commonest kind are frequently
given out to be done by home workers, none of whom could
make as much as 9s, even if they could get full work. A
recently introduced fur-sewing machine, which is beginning
to be used by the masters who can afford the £12 in ready

money required for it, will considerably reduce the number
of women required.

With regard to the wages of the women, both City and
East End furriers say that they can earn as much in the
East End working for a chambermaster, on good skins, as
they earn doing better work in the City. One City furrier
determines the price paid for articles by finding the time
in which the forewoman, a medium worker, can do the work,
and paying a rate which would give a sewer of the same
ability $2d$ the hour; best sewers would thus make about
$2\frac{1}{2}d$ an hour and worst $1\frac{1}{2}d$ an hour. The sealskin sewers
are a distinct class, and even they do not get more than
15s or 16s a week in the City. Another City furrier said
his hands averaged from 10s to 12s. A home worker on
sealskin mantles told me that she made $2\frac{1}{2}d$ or $2\frac{3}{4}d$ an hour,
and that the highest she ever earned when at the ware-
house (unless she worked overtime) was 15s 9d. Good
hands in the East End seem also to average about 10s to
12s a week, earning 18s or 19s at the highest occasionally,
and falling below the average rather frequently. But the
inferior hands in the City, and those doing the commonest
work in the East End, never get more than 9s a week.
And these rates are those earned in the season, it must be
remembered. For several months in the year the fur-
sewers have either no work or earn about 3s or 4s a week,
and many of them work in overcrowded, insanitary workshops in the season. Fur-sewing is the worst paid industry
carried on in workshops in the East End, with absolutely no
exception. And as a result a curious fact must be noted
with regard to the women engaged in it. By far the
greater number are Gentile women, many of whom are
elderly. Although nearly all the furriers are Jews, young
Jewesses rarely enter the trade unless they are too poor
and friendless to be supported while learning a trade.
Some of the young fur-sewers in the City, and a few in the
East End, are in comfortable circumstances, and can afford

to stay at home in the winter. But they are in a small minority. Girls must be very poor or incapable to take to fur-sewing for a living, or they are girls who do not like regular work. It is difficult to say whether the immorality of many of these younger fur-sewers is the cause or the effect of their entering so irregular a trade.

Box-making.—Although nearly all the manufacturers describe themselves as plain and fancy box-makers, the majority of them in the East End only make plain boxes. Those factories in which fancy boxes are made have this work done almost entirely on their premises, but every manufacturer who deals in plain boxes gives a part of the work to be done by outdoor hands at home. The card-board is cut out by men with machinery worked by steam power in the larger factories, by hand in the smaller ones; the rest of the work is done by women and girls. Several box-makers only employ cutters on their premises and give out the whole of the work when thus prepared. Skill is required, and a girl does not become a good hand until after about two years' training in the plain work, while a fancy box-maker requires about three years to thoroughly learn her trade. The terms on which learners are taken differ according to the views of each particular employer on the subject. Some employers give 3s a week for three months and give a rise of 6d every three months, putting the girl on piece-work at the end of the second or third year according to agreement. Others give nothing the first three months or a nominal wage of 1s a week, but under-take to really teach the girl every part of the trade and keep her on time-work for two or three years, the learner in the third year earning generally about 7s to 8s. In one factory the learners are put on piece-work at the end of six months, or, if they prefer it, they can arrange to work for another girl who pays 4s and gets the benefit that may accrue through their assistance. The plain box can be made throughout by the girl without any division of labour, and very frequently it is so made, the girl cutting the paper into strips and laying it on the glue-board herself and then putting it on the box, the gluey finger being raised and carefully kept away from the box. In one factory, employing 160 women indoors, about 50 to 60 were learners in their first, second, or third year; about 30 earned from 8s to 10s, another 30 or so earned 10s to 12s, and the rest earned from 12s to 16s. Those who made the cloth boxes for patterns and samples could earn 20s when the work was required, but this was only for a short time in the year. About 25 outdoor hands were employed; these were all married women. In another factory the wages ranged from 7s or 8s earned by improvers to 16s and 18s earned by very good hands, the majority earning from 11s to 13s. Two women making cloth pattern boxes told me that they were paid 20s and 21s a week on time-work. One girl said she averaged about 14s taking the whole year round. Another girl said her average was about 9s or 10s. A packer received 17s. Several of these women looked considerably over twenty.

At another factory which employs a very large number of women and girls on fancy boxes the time required to learn the trade is three years; the same range of wages prevails here. An average worker can get from 12s to 13s and good hands can earn from 13s to 17s or 18s according to capacity. I rarely meet the women who earn as much as 17s or 18s at these places; but girls who earn on an average about 12s or 13s tell me that there are several who earn more than they do themselves.

Those factories which have a large number of indoor hands generally give out work to a comparatively small number of women, who have worked in the factory, and left it shortly after marriage.

They give out the smaller class of work, such as boxes for soap, butter-scotch, wedding-cake. They say that this class of work can only be paid at a rate which would not be remunerative to them if, in addition, they had to provide standing room. They do not pay a different rate to the outdoor hands, because they do not give that class of work to the indoor hands. Box-makers who employ no women indoors do this cheap class of work, and by throwing the whole of the expense of working, space, firing, gas, and glue upon the home-workers, are able to sell at a price much below that at which the employers of indoor hands can afford to sell, unless they have very large orders and great advantages through good machinery.

But even this lower class of work requires skill, and nearly all the married women who make boxes at home have worked at the trade before marriage, and if they could get the work regularly, or if they were willing to give the time to it, could earn fair wages, as East End wages go. Box-makers whom I have visited have told me the prices of their work and the rate at which they could do it if they were not interrupted; the rates of payment thus obtained range from $1\frac{1}{2}d$ to $2\frac{3}{4}d$ an hour. Three women, in different parts of the East End, each making a different kind of box at $2s$ the gross, each calculated that they earned $2d$ an hour; two of them added that a quicker hand could get more.

The following table has been calculated from the wage books of an employer in the East End who employs a larger proportion of outdoor hands than the factories mentioned above. All the indoor hands who earned less than $8s$ were learners; of full workers no one earned less than $9s$ a week. The week chosen was a representative one, and in looking through the wage book it was noticeable that the amount earned by a particular hand varied very little.

Percentage of Women and Girls Earning—

	2s to 4s	4s to 6s	6s to 8s	8s to 10s	10s to 12s	12s to 15s	Over 15s	Comparative numbers employed.
Indoor Workers ...	20	12	12	8	24	24	—	10
Outdoor Workers...	28·2	43·8	15·6	6·2	—	3·1	3·1	26

Match-boxes.—The price paid by the match-box contractors is the same throughout the East End, 2¼*d* the
gross for the small size, and rising with the size.   They
can be made by children of nine or ten years of age.
No previous training is wanted, and match-box making
is the last resource of the destitute or the first occupation of little girls expected to make themselves useful
between school hours.   A child can earn 1*d* an hour;
most of the women who call themselves match-box makers,
assert that they can only earn that amount, and that
they cannot get enough work to keep them occupied
throughout the week.   Many women, I am convinced, only
take the work in order to make an appearance of industry,
and so qualify themselves for charitable assistance.   One
woman who did work hard, was separated from her husband,
and had to support her child.   She earned 1¾*d* an hour.
She was not strong, and worked very long hours, but she
was always well supplied with work, except in the summer,
when she did not have full work.   Before marriage she had
made match-boxes at home and earned from 9*s* to 10*s* a
week, being much quicker then.   Another girl, who worked
at home, with her sister, both of them being unmarried,
said she could earn 2½*d* an hour; she generally earned 8*s*
or 9*s* a week, and her sister earned the same.   She used to
earn more, but she thought she grew slower the longer she
worked.   Another girl, who was a cripple, said she made
about 1½*d* an hour, but her sister earned about 2*d* an hour.
They worked hard and always took back work at the time
promised, even if they had to work very late hours, and
therefore they always received enough match-boxes to keep
them occupied throughout the week.   Industry, not skill,
is the chief requisite, and 1½*d* to 2*d* an hour probably
represents the amount that an average worker could
earn if she worked hard and really wanted to earn her
living.

Brushes.—The numbers of men and women employed
in the brush trade are about equal; certain parts of the

work which used to be done by men only are now being done by women; but on the other hand machines have been invented which do the work generally done by women, and would if used to a great extent diminish the proportion of women to men. There are three departments in the trade, viz. heavy goods, light goods, and fancy goods, the latter class including all brushes which are highly polished, hair and tooth brushes being among the most important. Heavy goods are never given out to be done at home, but are always made at the various works, by men in some cases, by women in others. Men dress the fibre or bristles, bore the holes in the stock into which the fibre is inserted and do every part of the work except the actual drawing of the fibre or bristles into the holes, the trimming of the ends, the gluing and polishing. Light goods, such as boot brushes, scrubbing brushes, stove brushes, and fancy goods are always "drawn" by women, and heavy "drawn" work is done by them. In drawn work half the number of bristles or fibres required to fill the hole in the stock are drawn through a loop of wire, which is then pulled tightly so as to double the hairs and force them into the hole as far as possible. The wire-work at the back is concealed in some cases by gluing backs on the brushes, sometimes by veneer and sometimes (in tooth brushes, for example) by waxing it. The better class of tooth brushes are bored by a process called trepanning; the holes are not drilled right through the ivory, but the drawing is done by means of four longitudinal bores; and after the bristles have been drawn and secured the four holes at the end of the brush are filled with ivory powder, and hardly noticeable.

Much of the heavy class of goods is done by "set" or pitch-work. This pitch-work is the kind referred to as formerly only done by men; now it is done by women to a great extent. The girl takes the quantity of fibre necessary to fill the hole of the stock of the bass broom, deck scrubber, scavenger brush, whatever it may be, dips it into a preparation of pitch, ties it with a thread or "thrum," dips it in the pitch again and twists it into the hole.

This pitch-work in bass (piesava fibre) goods done by girls is paid at 1*d* for forty to sixty knots, no two factories apparently paying the same rate exactly. At this work girls can earn 12*s* to 14*s* a week. At one factory where about forty-five girls are employed on this work, the lowest earned is by learners who have 6*s* a week for a month and are then put on piece-work. One of the hands, who told me this, a girl of seventeen, said she was paid 6*s* a gross for bass brooms and generally earned 9*s* or 10*s* a week, working eight and a-half hours a day; older girls were able to earn more. This factory has not the reputation of paying quite so well as other factories.

Drawn work is paid about 1*d* for 120 knots including the trimming done with shears. The factory which pays the highest rate gives ¾*d* the hundred knots for such work as boot brushes and 1*d* the hundred for scrubbing brushes where the trimming is more difficult. One woman, who had worked at home for this factory for twelve years, said she could do 400 knots an hour. She rarely earned more than 7*s* or 8*s* a week, because she had other things to do, and did not want to give more than about four days a week to the work. The work was regular and she had not had three weeks' "holiday" in the last twelve months. Other hands who have worked for this factory even longer, in some cases more than twenty years, confirm the statement of the employer that outside hands are paid the same rate as indoor hands, and that good workers can find regular employment. Very few factories give out work; fancy goods are only given to well-known hands and to women who can be trusted; and in the brush trade, therefore, this combination of skill and honesty being requisite, many of the brush-drawers working at home are the most skilled, and independent enough to decline to take more work than they can comfortably do in a nine hours' day. Tooth brushes are made in the factory and also given out. They are paid at the rate of 5s and 4s the gross. A girl fifteen years of age told me that she worked with her mother at home ; her mother took out a gross of tooth brushes at 5s a gross every two days ; the girl herself working ten hours a day could always do five dozen, her mother doing two dozen in her leisure time ; this girl therefore worked at the rate of $2\frac{1}{2}d$ an hour. Her sister took out two gross a week and did it by herself, making 10s a week. The three together therefore earned 25s a week and were free to choose their own hours of working, and if they wanted a holiday a little more help from the mother enabled them to get it. The work was regular.

But all the brush-drawers who work at home are not so well off. There are a fairly large number of people who buy the wood-work and ivory prepared for brush-drawing, and employ a few hands besides working themselves at the trade ; they supply retail shops, sell at a low price, and pay a low rate. The small brush-maker may make a little more perhaps than he could make if he worked for an employer, but the hands who work for him are badly paid and do not have constant work ; nor is it easy for a brush-drawer who has never worked in a factory to get work from one, and refuse to work for the small maker. Tooth brushes for which one factory in the East End would give 4s the gross are paid for by one small maker at the rate of 3s the gross, or rather 3d the dozen, as the drawer rarely has so much as a gross given her at a time ; a fairly skilled worker can only make about $1\frac{1}{2}d$ an hour and has very little work to do.

In one factory in the first week of January, when hardly any of the hands had worked the whole week, and where several were married women who would not come to work before 9.30, the wages ranged from 8s to 15s. In another factory 7s was the lowest sum paid ; a brush-tester received

9s a week, and the wages of the piece-workers in full work ranged from 12s to 15s a week, sometimes reaching 17s. I had the opportunity of finding the average wage throughout the year of three piece-workers to whom I had spoken in the factory. One had earned on the average 12s 10d a week, the second 12s 7d, and the third 9s 8d.

In the largest factory in the East End a great variety of work is done, and the majority of the hands are girls and young women, and their wages range from 8s or 10s to 18s or 20s. The work is very regular. In the trade as a whole shorter hours prevail than are customary in other trades.

Matches.—Considerably over one thousand women and girls are employed in making matches in East London. The splints for the matches, which are cut in lengths equal to two matches, are cut by men. They are taken by the girls and placed in a machine which arranges them regularly in a spiral around a strap, which as it coils up holds the splints in their place. The coils are taken and the ends dipped in paraffin by boys, after which men dip the ends in what the girls call the " phos," and the coils are taken by boys to the drying rooms. When dry the coils are placed on a spindle in a machine worked by boys ; this machine unwinds the coil and deposits the matches in narrow wooden trays. These trays are taken by the girls (cutters down) to their benches, where they cut the matches in two and place them in the match boxes.

In the wax vesta department girls make the taper, passing the thread through the wax mixture several times. This mixture is contained in a trough which stands between two large drums on which the thread is wound. The taper when finished is wound on smaller drums which supply frame-filling machines. These machines are worked by steam ; they cut the taper into the proper length for the lights and arrange the pieces in the frames in rows, the girl in charge having only to watch the machine, take out the filled frames and supply empty ones. When these matches have been prepared by the men, the girls take them out of the frames and fill the boxes.

The coil fillers receive 1s the 100 coils; cutters down 2¾d the "duck," *i.e.* 3 gross of small boxes or 2½ gross of large boxes, the same number of matches being used in both cases. Taper makers are on day-work and are paid 10s to 12s a week. The girls who watch the taper cutting machines have a certain task allotted them, being paid 10s a week and receiving 6d for every 100 frames above this task. The wax box fillers receive 5s the 100 frames. Packers are paid 1s 9d the 100 gross of boxes wrapped up. Girls of thirteen years of age who have passed the fourth standard (girls of fourteen whether they have or not), are taken on at 4s a week. The skill, industry, regularity, and ages of the women and girls employed vary so considerably that it would be very difficult to give accurate statements of the rate per hour or day represented by each of these rates. But the following table of wages earned in four different weeks gives an idea of the amount actually earned per week. The week ending February 8th was chosen, because it was the week when I called. The factories were then busy, and the table gives the wages earned in full work, although not at high pressure. In comparing the tables with the accounts of wages in other industries it must be observed that only in the match industry and in the confectionery industry have I obtained statistics of wages paid in slack times; moreover, these match and confectionery tables of wages include the wages of children from the age of thirteen. The match industry is slack in the summer months. From June to August the extra demand for hands in the jam factories is to some extent supplied by the match girls, and some of them go to the hop-picking in September. The table of wages for September gives the wages obtained when several of the girls were hop-picking; and in the table for May 11th, 1888, we have statistics of the wages earned when all hands were in the factories, but work was slack.

Percentage of Women and Girls' Earnings.

Week ending	4s to 6s	6s to 8s	8s to 10s	10s to 12s	12s to 15s	Over 15s	Compara-tive No. of Workers.
Feb. 8, '89	14·06	19·92	28·60	25·18	11·62	0·62	100
Sept. 14, '88	11·48	17·97	27·16	30·00	12·03	1·36	90
Sept. 16, '87	17·02	20·44	29·03	23·87	8·32	1·32	91·2
May 11, 88	21·59	29·73	29·63	14·86	3·96	0·23	102

These wages do not represent the wages that can be earned, but the wages that are earned. Even in February several girls were absent at least one day in the week, Monday being the favourite day for the holiday. Delays may also be caused owing to the state of the atmosphere, which may prevent the matches from drying so quickly as usual.

The match girls have always shown a remarkable power of combination. Those in the East End are nearly all under one management, and therefore live near each other in Bow, Mile End, Stepney, Limehouse, and Poplar. They are distinguished by a strong *esprit de corps,* one girl's grievance being adopted as the grievance of every girl in the same room. They buy their clothes and feathers (especially the latter) by forming clubs; seven or eight of them will join together paying a shilling a week each, and drawing lots to decide who shall have the money each week. They are fond of each other's society, and generally with-draw themselves from that of others whom they consider too aristocratic to associate with on equal terms. They all work under the same conditions, and from the nature of the industry the work must all be done in the factory. The difficulties in the way of trade union which would be found in every other industry are therefore much less here. There have constantly been small strikes in the match factories as in a great many other factories in the East End; and the prolonged strike in July 1888 resulted in the formation of a union, the largest union composed entirely of women and girls in England. Nearly 800 women and girls belong to this union, of whom about 650 have kept up their weekly payments. Such trade unions are really productive of good both to the members and to the employers. So far from encouraging strikes, they diminish the number of ill-judged disputes arising from faults on the part of the women, as often as from injustice on the part of employers. If employers are in the right, a practised committee responsible for consequences will much more readily yield to the force of logic; and if the employers are in the wrong, sensible representations made to them by the committee of a strong union will be attended to and acted upon much more promptly than if put forward by girls on strike. Not only is friction diminished, but friendliness between employers and work-people may be promoted.

The excessive quantity of phosphorus, which was formerly used in the manufacture of matches, rendered the operatives liable to a terrible disease, necrosis. Experience has reduced the use of phosphorus to a minimum, and necrosis, when it occurs, is due either to want of ventilation in the factories or of cleanliness in the operatives. Both in the Fairfield Works and those of an employer on the outskirts of the East End, whose factory was visited, the ventilation seemed good. The danger makes the enforcement of strict rules regarding cleanliness and carefulness absolutely necessary. The superabundant energy displayed by the match girls when their work is over, although they have to stand all day long at it, is inexplicable and in striking contrast to the tired appearance of machinists.

Confectionery.—Women have very little to do with the actual making of jam, preserves, pickles, or even sweets, although in the latter department nearly everything is some-times done by them except the mixing of the ingredients. All the work which requires anything beyond manual dexterity and carefulness is done by men. The girls and women fill bottles, wash them, tie on covers, put on labels and wrappers, pour syrups into tins, pack raisins, table jellies, crystallized fruits, &c., paint tins, solder them by machinery, peel oranges, squeeze lemons, and fill packing cases. Those engaged in making sweetstuff sometimes assist in the mechanical mixing of the paste; they knead it and roll it, cut the shapes, run liquid preparation for fondants, drops, Easter egg decorations, &c., through funnels or dippers. Very young girls fill surprise packets, wrap sweets, pick out defective lozenges, sugar jujubes, and do other light work requiring no previous training. In the fruit season a very large number of women and girls are irregularly employed in fruit picking. In the jam factories the nature of the industry renders the occasional employment of large numbers absolutely necessary whenever a large quantity of fresh fruit or vegetables has to be prepared for preserving at once. We therefore find in these factories three classes of hands. Most employers endeavour to keep the best hands regularly employed. Even when it is not possible to give full work to these regular hands, efforts are generally made to divide the work amongst them so as to give them above a certain minimum wage. In all well-established factories will be found women of this first class who have been in regular employment for 8, 10, 13 years or more. Then there is a second class of hands who are taken on whenever the factory is busy, perhaps only for two or three days in the week, perhaps regularly for several weeks together if there is a press of work. The quantity of jam and preserves made in the East End factories seems to have been steadily increasing, and there has been a tendency for the best of this second class to be absorbed in the first. Lastly, there is the mob which stands and fights at the gates in the fruit-picking season, from which hands are chosen, sometimes for a day, sometimes for a few hours only, as occasion requires. Old and young, married and single, disreputable and respectable, this class is characterized by one common feature. All its members are either voluntarily or involuntarily irregularly employed. The first day perhaps

some of them will earn twopence, and eat fourpence, and
then want the doctor, according to the statement of one
employer ; but when they have settled down to their work
the majority earn from 1s 6d to 2s 6d a day. Most of the
factories are situated near the docks. The fruit pickers in
another part of East London are nearly all children who
work on day work, not by the piece.

The total number of women and girls employed by those
employers who gave me information about the jam and
confectionery industry, and allowed their factories to be
visited, ranges from 1,100 in slack times to 2,000 in the
fruit season ; about 500 of these were only taken on in the
fruit season. I have been allowed to examine wage-books
by myself, from which I have obtained particulars of the
wages of nearly six hundred girls employed partly in jam
making, most of them in confectionery, in the weeks previous
to those on which I visited the factories. And other
employers gave me information most readily, and referred
me to the different evening classes or clubs where the factory
girls might be found and questioned.

One factory employs no one under 18, and pays no
one less than 9s a week. The work is more regular
here, and although the girls are not superior to the
most regular hands in the other factories, the absence of
young girls, and of irregular and incapable ones, from
their ranks, separates the girls at this factory in reputation from those of the others. [The East End investigator
does not so easily find these girls who "keep themselves to
themselves." There are large numbers of them in different
factories, but they are generally described as " very respectable, not at all like factory girls," and are not to be met
with in the haunts of the typical factory girl.] The majority
of the girls earn 9s or 10s a week ; as many as possible are
put on piece-work, but none of the piece-workers earn less
than 10s ; the wage-book showed that several had 11s and
12s, and a few had 14s. There were several forewomen
earning 16s, 18s, and 20s a week on time-work.

Another factory pays no one less than 7*s*, employing young persons above 16. Most of the time-workers earned from 8*s* to 10*s*; piece-workers earned 11*s* at least; one exceptional worker earned 18*s*. There were several forewomen who were paid 14*s* and 13*s* a week (including holidays).

Another factory paid no one less than 6*s*, and girls under 16 were employed; the majority were on time-work and earned 8*s* to 9*s* a week. Packers and labellers on piece-work earned most here as in the other factories.

In another factory where sweets are made time-workers are paid according to age, girls of 16 receiving 6*s*, girls of 17 receiving 7*s*, girls of 18 receiving 8*s*; of the piece-workers' wages I know nothing.

In the factories where 4*s* and 5*s* are paid to beginners, girls over 13 are employed, and this is especially the case in confectionery factories where there is much light work that can easily be done by such children.

Except in the case of forewomen the wages quoted above are the wages paid to hands in *full* work. It will be noticed that, whatever the minimum, the maximum is about the same in all the factories, and that where children are employed, the percentage earnings below a certain amount will always be greater, although the actual rate of payment in proportion to work done may be just as high as in other factories. From the wage-books of one factory I have obtained the actual amount earned by the jam girls in a slack week.

Percentage of Women and Girls Earning—

	Under 4*s*	4*s* to 6*s*	6*s* to 8*s*	8*s* to 10*s*	10*s* to 12*s*	12*s* to 15*s*	Above 15*s*
Actual Wages	7·8	13·3	28·3	31·1	12·2	6·7	0·6
Time Wages...	—	5	41	35	17	2	—

Whenever it is possible girls are put on piece-work, but if work is slack many of them are on day-work at a fixed rate, which does not represent their earnings when busy. When their wages fall below this fixed rate it is owing to their working short time. The second line gives the wages which would be earned if all the hands worked full time, but none of them on piece-work.

In sweetstuff departments, lozenge cutters generally earn the highest wages. In one factory the forewoman said that the lozenge cutters earned 11*s* to 12*s* : only a small number were employed here. In another, working longer hours several earned above 16*s*, and all earned as much as 10*s* on piece-work. In one factory a special kind of sweet-stuff was being made; most of the girls were lozenge cutters, and the employer was manager and mixer in one. He had orders for the delivery of this sweetstuff which insured regular work. The girls were paid a fixed sum, for which they were expected to get through a certain amount of work; when that was done they were paid for anything over; nearly all the girls earned this "overtime" as they called it, without working more than the ordinary hours; a few told me that they could earn it if they liked, but they generally preferred to leave off work. Several had been there five years, and only one girl who had been there had ever left of her own accord, except to get married. The ages of the girls ranged from 13 to 23. They were most of them daughters of skilled artisans. The lowest sum paid on time-work was 4*s*, but even the child who was paid this told me that she made 6*d* overtime. The following table of percentages taken from the wage-book of this factory represents the rate of wages earned under unusually favourable conditions; other confectionery factories might have a larger percentage earning over 15*s*, but I do not know of one which would have so small a percentage below 8*s*.

Percentage of Women and Girls Earning—

4*s* to 6*s*	6*s* to 8*s*	8*s* to 10*s*	10*s* to 12*s*	12*s* to 15*s*	Above 15*s*
11·43	3	31·4	20	31·4	5·77

The last table of wages that can be given here gives the actual wages earned in two successive weeks in January in a factory with a very large number of departments, some of which were busy, but most of them slacker than usual; the majority of the girls are employed in making English, French, or American sweets, but they have to be transferred occasionally to other departments. On the third line are given the wages that would be earned if all were on time-work and worked full time.

Percentage of Women and Girls Earning—

	Under 4s	4s to 6s	6s to 8s	8s to 10s	10s to 12s	12s to 15s	Above 15s
First week	12·4	26·3	25·3	18·2	11·8	3·6	2·4
Second week	10·2	16·8	26·8	27·0	13·1	5·0	1·1
Time wages	—	12·3	45·4	28·0	10·9	3·0	0·4

In the summer a larger number would be employed, and the wages from that time to Christmas are higher than those given in these tables, as I know by actual comparison of the wages earned in different periods of the year.

Employment in this industry is so irregular for many of the girls, that I am inclined to believe that the average wages of the girls throughout the year is less than in any other factory industry. But in the arrangements made in the factories for the convenience of the workers in the matter of dining rooms, club rooms, and societies, and also in the remarkable readiness to give any information that may prove serviceable, there is convincing proof that in no other industry would employers be found more willing to further any schemes which would alleviate the evils resulting from this irregularity of employment.

Among other industries which deserve more than a passing notice should be mentioned the following :—

Caps.—This trade is in the hands of Jewish employers, and both Jewish and Gentile women are employed in it;

but the former are being gradually displaced from the large factories on account of their observance of their Sabbath. The largest factory employs 600 girls; the wages of the hand-workers range from 8s to 12s, and of the machinists from 11s to 18s, from which must be deducted the cost of thread and silk, which they must buy on the premises. Although the weekly earnings are fairly high, the cap makers are hard worked, and strike one as looking unusually tired and worn. The small masters can only compete with the large masters, who have good machinery, by working long hours and paying low wages, and their hands earn considerably less than the wages given above. The factory system in this trade is beating the small workshops out of the field.

Artificial Flowers.—Hoxton and De Beauvoir Town are the centres; some of the flower makers live in the East End however. The trade is a season trade, and is also extremely irregular in the season, owing to changes in fashion. Very skilled hands, mounters, can earn 18s a week, and rose makers at home can earn over 20s : good workers in the factory can earn from 10s to 16s, but the majority only earn from 8s to 10s, and do not have constant work.

Book Folding and Book Sewing.—The wages are lower than in the City; the low wages, with very little range between the highest and the lowest, are to some extent balanced by the regularity of the work in the Bible trade. The majority earn from 9s to 11s.

Ostrich Feather Curling cannot at present be regarded as an East End industry, as changes in fashion have thrown the feather curlers out of work or reduced them to work on half-time. City workgirls used to be able to earn from 9s to 18s, or even more ; in busy seasons they took work home. It was one of the few industries at which Jewesses worked. Although it was a season trade, they could earn good wages in busy times, and increase them by taking feathers home to curl; the Jewish girls are always encouraged to save, and the possible high wages in the season made up for the slackness of work at other times, a drawback which would otherwise have been sufficient to deter them from entering the trade. Now they are withdrawing from it when possible, and the orthodox economist may look here for an example of the hypothetical readiness of labourers to adapt themselves to changed industrial conditions.

Laundresses in laundries for soiled linen are fairly well paid. Women at the tub receive from 2*s* to 3*s* a day and have from three to five days' work in the week. Shirt and collar ironers earn from 8*s* to 15*s* a week according to capacity, and work from four to six days. Folders are generally on day-work and do sorting part of the time, earning about 2*s* a day.

Shirt and collar ironers who do clean work for shirt and collar warehouses are better paid. The work must be done well, and 4*s* to 5*s* a day can be earned.

HOME-WORK.

The women who take work home from warehouses, factories, or sub-contracting agents are, with comparatively few exceptions, married or widows, if we exclude from consideration that large class described as dressmakers or sempstresses. The home-workers are to be found in every grade of society among the wage-earning class; in the home of the middle-class clerk and in the room of the dock labourer; rarely, I think, in the tradesman class, where wives can add to the family income more effectually by assisting in the management of the shop. The home-worker may be working for the barest necessaries of life or to provide for the future, or for luxuries, or it may even be that she works at a trade which is easy to her in order to pay someone else to perform the more distasteful household duties. The young wife of the clerk with regular employment but small salary takes sealskin capes home from the warehouse where she worked when a girl, because a good housewife has time to spare when she has only three rooms to keep tidy and only two people to cook for, and is glad to add something to the savings which may be useful some day when the children are being educated or started in life. The wife of the carman with 18s a week may make butter scotch boxes in order that her children and her rooms and her dress may look as well as those of her sister who is married to a mechanic earning 32s a week. The wife of a drunkard in reduced circumstances will do plain sewing or shirtmaking that she may have a decent dress to wear when she goes to see her friends and may conceal from them the depths to which she has fallen. The wife of the dock labourer out of work will finish trousers to keep herself and her children from the workhouse. The widow, whose husband was mate of a ship and left her at his death unprovided for and helpless, will finish shirts at 5d or 4d or 3d a day, perhaps, to maintain her independence of character and self respect, although forced to accept the charity of friends or of societies or outdoor relief from the parish.

I have said that the home-workers are usually married women or widows. There are exceptions to this rule. In the lower middle class especially will be found many girls and single women who do not care to enter into competition openly with a class of labourers whom they consider beneath them, and hence prefer the privacy of home-work. This class is not of necessity pecuniarily better off than the artisan class below it, but the wholesome theory that the man should be the breadwinner of the household pervades it. It is keenly sensitive to social distinctions, is fairly educated, and its anxiety to keep up appearances demands an increasing expenditure on dress, furniture, and food, and perhaps even service, which is more than commensurate with its income. The daughters as they grow up make themselves useful at home either in house-work or by assisting in the shop, and are to a certain extent distinguished from the class below them by the fact that they need not go out to work. In this class there is a tendency among girls to exaggerate the income of their fathers and to imitate the habits and living of girls of the upper middle class. They are sometimes inclined to imagine that to work for a living is a thing to be ashamed of, and frequently hard-working girls will libel themselves by representing or allowing people to imagine that they have no occupation beyond their share of domestic duties. As an actual fact, if they are to dress as they think suitable to their superior position, they must work for money to find the wherewithal; their parents could not afford to keep two or three girls in board and lodging even, who were earning nothing. These girls will frequently endeavour to get work in a City warehouse; failing that, it may be in preference to it, will take a situation and assist another home-worker, or someone in a small way of business, at a low salary, finding compensation in the promise that they shall be treated as one of the family. Some will take home plain or fancy needlework, which any lady might be supposed to do for herself and which does not necessarily reveal to all around that they are working for money. The majority of the skilled artisan and shop-keeping class, however, are not ashamed of working, or of working for money, but are most anxious to make it clear that they are only earning pocket-money—pursuing a trade of their own free choice, not because they are obliged. Besides the girls who do take work home may be found single women who are skilled enough to be able to support themselves without going into a warehouse or factory if they dislike doing so; others who, having perhaps worked at the trade, take large quantities of work home and employ young assistants; and some who have been left in reduced circumstances, with no inheritance except a firmly ingrained belief that shabby gentility and starvation wages earned by stealth are less derogatory to ladyhood than good wages openly earned.

The motives which are at the root of home-work suggest the only classification which seems to me of any practical value in the treatment of this subject from an economic point of view. I propose to consider home-work, not according to class distinctions, for the position of the married woman is what her husband makes it, whereas her industrial condition may depend largely upon her position and occupation before marriage; not according to the rate of wages they may receive for their labour, for reasons which will appear later on; not according to their trades, which may at different stages and under different conditions engage all sorts and conditions of women; but according as the conditions essential for effective competition seem to me to be present. To have perfect competition there must be freedom of movement from place to place, and in proportion as that movement is obstructed there is danger of loss, to the wage-earning class at least, and at the outset, therefore, we must notice this economic disadvantage under which the married woman labours even more than women in general. Even men who have given up the practice of working for a living have not given up the theory that they are trying to do so. The habitual drunkard and loafer, who never does a day's honest work if by any trouble and ingenuity on his part he can save himself from it, nevertheless lives near the spot where he might get work if he chose to exert himself for it. If he calls himself a ship's carpenter, his wife may have to walk or take the tram from Poplar to Whitechapel for her work, and when after some waiting she has received her dozen shirts must certainly "tram it" back again from Whitechapel to Poplar. In giving the rate of payment in the different industries I have made no mention of this, but the cost and difficulty of locomotion is an important element in estimating the wages of home-workers. That a shirt maker who receives 5d for finishing a dozen shirts should have to spend 2d of it on tram fare is a fact which points to economic loss both on the side of employer and workwoman. Here then we find a total absence of one of the most important conditions

for effective competition, due not to faults in the industrial
system, but to an unalterable feature of the social organism.
The married women never can have the freedom of movement without which population cannot follow industry.

It has been shown that the principal articles which are to
some extent manufactured at home are boxes, brushes,
corsets, umbrellas, artificial flowers, ties, trimmings, furs,
trousers, vests, and shirts. Two of these trades, viz., the
brush and the box trades, are somewhat exceptional in that
they are nearly always learnt in the factory. It is true that
there are a small number of brush-makers who employ their
daughters and perhaps one or two girls in their little
workshops; and the few women who have learnt the trade
in this manner are generally limited to the same class of
employers if they wish to take work home. But in the
East End nearly all the brush drawers have at one time
worked in the factory or have been closely connected with
people who have done so, and it is only in exceptional
circumstances that more is given out than can be done by
one hand. When such a quantity is given out, it is
generally to a woman whose skill and honesty are well
known to the employers and whose daughters give evidence
of the same qualities. In the box-making industry as in
the brush-making there is no advantage to be obtained by
employers in the East End itself in giving outdoor hands
more work than they can do alone; and although a box-
maker with children old enough to assist her might be glad
and would be allowed to take home enough work for her
family to do, she could have no inducement to employ an
assistant, except perhaps a young girl to do odds and ends
and to take the work to the shop. For unless the girl
objected to working at a factory she could learn the trade
much more completely there than from a homeworker, who
receives only a particular class of work. And if she did
actually learn to make that class of box from the home-
worker, the box manufacturer would be quite as willing to

give the work direct to her as to give a double quantity to
her mistress. In these two trades (brush and box), then,
we find that the home-workers have generally been trained
to the work before marriage, that this training has generally
been obtained in a factory, that the women have therefore
been used to work and are not ashamed of it, that they
belong to the same class as the indoor hands, and can
therefore, to some extent, communicate with them and discuss
the different rates obtaining at different factories; and that
they obtain their work first-hand. The industrial conditions
are, therefore, favourable to the wage-earners, provided
home circumstances do not operate in an opposite direction.
For effective industrial competition, besides freedom of
movement, there must be power to choose between occupations, and the ability to give up a trade which ceases to be
remunerative, *i.e.*, to give an equivalent for the labour
expended. Have married women this power of choice, and
do they exercise it ? And does the married woman working
for extra money take a lower rate than the home-worker
who has to support herself ? My experience has all tended
to make me answer the latter question in the negative.
Over and over again I have met women in comfortable
circumstances who have told me either that they left off
taking in work because it did not pay for the trouble, or
that they only worked half the week because they had the
washing to do and the clothes to mend, and the time was
worth more than the money, or that someone paid so little
for his brushwork, or trimmings, or whatever it might be,
that they " just took the work back again undone and told
the governor that he might try to get some poor woman to
do it who had nothing else to fall back upon; they weren't
obliged to work for nothing, thank God." And, on the
other hand, the women whom I have found working at
really starvation wages—sack makers and carpet slipper
makers—were women who had either to support themselves
or to fall back upon charity or the workhouse. Many widows

who find it difficult to obtain work, owing to infirmity it may be, take shirts to finish at 3*d* or 2*d* per dozen, although they can only finish a dozen and a half a day. They nearly always complain that other married women take them at that price because they need only work for pocket-money. But I have never yet come across a married woman in the working classes with such an eagerness for pocket-money that she would work for it at the rate of ½*d* or 1*d* an hour. Whenever I have found women who said they worked at very low rates they have been working for their living and for that of their children; their husbands have always been men disabled or out of work.

But while many married women are independent enough to give up work which is not remunerative, the majority have little power to change from one branch of a trade to another, still less from one trade to another. Much of the irregularity in home-work is due to the fact that the home-worker is so frequently unable to do more than one branch of the work, and cannot, therefore, be kept constantly supplied. In many of the domestic industries this incapacity is the reason why many women have work given them for a few months in the year instead of a small number having constant employment.

In proportion as these conditions which obtain generally, prevail in the two trades which I have chosen as examples, the workwoman will receive as adequate a remuneration as the prices paid for the articles permit. Even where a woman with a husband out of work and children to keep is unable to go to the best paying manufacturer, and is obliged to take work from people who pay lower rates, the rate earned per hour never sinks so low as we find it in these industries where sub-contract exists. Nor have I met with any instance of women underselling each other at the same factory, although in a neighbourhood where the majority of the workmen are known to be poor, the employer sometimes pays a lower rate than can be obtained elsewhere.

On the other hand, such an employer has frequently to
return the work because it is badly done, has more difficulty
in getting it brought in punctually, and really gets less
for his money than the employer of higher-class labour at
higher pay.

The comparison of the box trade and the brush trade with
each other brings to light another important element in
determining wages.   There are very few factories which give
out work in the brush trade; there are several in the box
trade.   The brush-drawers are, therefore, much more dependent on the individual employer.   Meanness and avarice
on the part of the largest manufacturer in the district could
easily lower their wages.   Whereas in the box trade there
are several small factories employing out-door hands, and
several men who employ only out-door hands (besides the
cutters).   These factories are to be found in all parts of the
East End, and box-makers, if not pressed by actual want,
can turn to other factories if one employer pays less than
the rest.

We have, therefore, in asking the reason why home-
workers' wages are high or low, to consider :—

I.   The nature and state of the trade itself.

II.   The effect of the competition of employers for
contracts.

III.   The remoteness from the employer.

IV.   The relation between indoor and outdoor hands.

V.   (a)   The skill required in the trade.

(b)   The range of skill in the trade.

VI.   The private circumstances of the home-worker;
position, training, and occupation before marriage;
individual efficiency.

I.   *The nature and state of the trade itself.*—The regularity of employment is inevitably affected by changes or
irregularity in demand.   Boxes, brushes, and corsets are in
fairly constant demand, the latter having, however, to be made
after different designs, but being otherwise not much affected

by changes of fashion. Foreign competition is complained
of, especially in the brush trade; but it is impossible to
determine by the mere statements of employers whether we
are really being beaten out of the field by foreign labour.
An inquiry into the condition of the German brush-makers
and a comparison between the productive power of the
German girl and the English one would be instructive, but,
without a similar comparison between the rates of profit
obtained by the German employer and by the English one,
would be incomplete. In all the trades this German competition seems only dreaded in the commoner class of work,
e.g., plain boxes, common tooth-brushes, cotton sunshades,
unnatural flowers. Wherever we compete in the production
of these common goods, there is a tendency for prices to be
cut down, for bad work to be given in return, for a lower
class of labour to be employed, and irregularity of employment seems to be an inevitable result. The umbrella-
makers who are doing low-class work suffer severely from
this competition to supply the languid Hindoo and the
poverty-stricken Chinee with protection from the sun. In
every one of the domestic industries in the East End where
this low-class work is done it will be found either that
wages are low or work is irregular. I have said that even
the commonest umbrellas are paid at a fairly high rate per
hour, compared with other articles in the East End; but
against this must be set the weeks and half-weeks in the
year when there is no work given out at all. The prices of
trimmings have fallen considerably, and the slack times are
much longer than they used to be. The common and cheap
fur capes and caps and trimmings give badly paid employment to women for barely seven or eight months in the
year. The violets and primroses which resemble nothing
ever seen growing between earth and sky are often made
by girls or women who can make nothing else, and are
only asked to make them for a few weeks in the year. And
every reduction in the price of these low-class goods

must and does have the effect of diminishing the demand for good work and increasing the demand for slop work among our working classes.

But in most of the trades enumerated there will always, under the best conditions, be irregularity. In the present state of meteorological knowledge the demand for umbrellas and sunshades cannot be calculated to a nicety beforehand; the times at which men will order ties and the particular reasons they have for preferring one kind to another are facts shrouded in mystery; the fashions in feathers, flowers, furs and trimmings depend on the decision of a few leaders of fashion, who carefully refrain from giving notice of the coming changes except to a few leading modistes and manufacturers. The latter, after all, probably really initiate the changes, paying high premiums for the favour shown to them; but the East End manufacturer is not one of those, and must wait in ignorance of what the morrow will bring forth, and the direction in which labour must be employed. Wherever irregularity is inevitable it seems to me that the employment of married women at their homes has one good effect. On all sides, in every trade in the East End where work is given to outdoor hands as well as to the factory girls, evidence is given that the work in the factory is on the whole regular. The number of outdoor hands in employment increases and diminishes, but the indoor hands have regular and constant work. The bad effects of irregularity of employment amongst girls are incalculable, even if we quite neglect the question of wages. Wherever the home-workers are being supported by their husbands, as they ought to be, this irregularity is in itself a slight evil. Of course the married women and widows who have to support themselves and their families suffer to an extent that can hardly be exaggerated.

II. *The competition of employers for contracts* seems to be the cause of an irregularity of employment which is increased by the facility with which out-door labour can be obtained. We have to distinguish between the irregularity which is diminished by the employment of home-workers and that which is the result of the transfer of orders from the employer of indoor labour, to the contractor who offers to produce at a lower rate and does so by reducing expenses for rent, coal, gas, &c., to a minimum. The home worker does not always incur extra expenses for these things, but in all cases she does diminish the expenses of the contractor' The contractor on the other hand has much extra labour imposed upon him and time is wasted in examining and returning bad work. Where no trade union exists the contract system puts an end to the competition of employers for labour, which in economic theory is always supposed to raise wages. The consumer obtains the whole advantage. The employers compete to obtain the contract at the lowest price; the inefficient manufacturers, of whom there are a large number in the East End, rely on cutting down wages, and also it must be admitted, frequently add considerably to their own labour, obtaining low profits with increased effort on their own part. When a tender has been accepted and the rest have been rejected the competition of employers is really ended, and the successful employer is left to make his terms with labourers unhindered by competition. The effect of the contract system is to make an unconscious combination among employers to obtain labour below a certain maximum rate. There is practically the pressure of a masters' union upon labour which can only be prevented from crushing it by the counteracting pressure of a trade union. In some of the strong men's unions, that of the ironfounders for example, the union has to be consulted when contracts are made. Wherever women's labour is employed the contracts are made without any reference to them, and the employment of outdoor hands and the withdrawal of the work from the indoor hands makes it unnecessary to risk a dispute by lowering the wages of the girls in the factory. In the box trade it has been stated that the boxes made by home-workers are of a cheaper kind than those made in the factory, and that it would not pay to make them at the same price in the factory; but unless foreign competition is very great these cheap boxes would be required and would be paid for at a higher rate if the buyer could not get them at a lower one. Nor is it at all probable that the cheapness with which boot-boxes, soap-boxes, &c., might be made abroad would compensate for the cost of carriage. When all hands in the factory are fully employed, and there is unusual pressure of work, the employment of outdoor married labour is beneficial. But whenever the work is taken from the indoor hands and offered to married women the result is prejudicial to all interests except those of the immediate consumer. Employers of inferior ability are enabled to compete to the detriment of production eventually; for industry moves from a higher to a lower grade of labour, and in a short time the low prices, which result from low-paid labour instead of from improvement in organization and methods are matched by the bad work given in return. To keep up the prices of labour and so to eliminate the employer who makes his small profits by sweating farthingsworths off shillings, is really the interest both of workwomen and of employers who rely on their business ability and good management.

III. *The remoteness from the first contractor.*—Under this head should be considered the loss incurred by actual distance in space between the home-worker and the contractor; and also by the interposition of sub-contractors. The umbrella-makers all have to get their work from City warehouses and incur considerable expense and loss of time. The shirt-makers, especially the finishers, receive miserable prices through the intervention of sub-contractors. Sweating exists in the fur trade, but there is rarely more than one sub-contractor, and the low pay of the fur sewers is due to the competition among the chamber-masters and not to the amount of profit intercepted between the wholesale house and the worker. We may here also notice the greater difficulty of resistance on the part of home-workers or in-door hands who work for a City warehouse. The factory girls in the East End can call impromptu meetings in the street, and the home-workers who meet together at the factory when they fetch work have ample opportunity of discussing innovations or reductions. This is impossible in the City. In addition to this the employer in the East End who comes into personal contact with his labourers, has, if not a greater sympathy with them, at least a greater objection to disputes than the manager in the City who employs out-door hands of whose lives he knows nothing; or who leaves it to sub-contractors to deal with disputes and suffer the ensuing loss.

IV. *The relation between indoor and outdoor hands.*— Wherever communication between indoor and outdoor hands is prevented, whether by deliberate arrangements of employers or by class or natural separation, it is always much easier for the employers to play one set of hands against another. The brush and box home-workers, as has been pointed out, have worked in the factory them-selves and belong to the same class as the indoor hands. In several City warehouses the indoor hands belong to a higher social grade than the outdoor hands, and they come from all parts of London. It is almost impossible for the indoor and outdoor hands therefore to unite together to resist a reduction in the rate of payment, and the City firms force the indoor hands to accept it by declaring that the outdoor hands will take the work at the reduced rate, and effectually prevent resistance on the part of the outdoor hands by telling them that the indoor hands have accepted it. Sub-contractors are carefully hindered from finding out the rates given in the warehouse. The facility and readiness with which City firms take advantage of this hindrance to communication between workers is unequalled by anything in the East End.

V. *Skill.*—Women in the East End are rarely called upon
to exercise their brains, but there is a fairly wide range in
the opportunities for exercising manual dexterity. In the
home industries, which I have studied, umbrellas and sunshades might be placed at the head of the list as demanding
most skill, fur-sewing and match-box making at the bottom.
These two latter industries, in the branches done outside the
factory or workshop, require neither skill nor strength. As
I have said, a child can make match-boxes, and if it were
possible to place any reliance on the statements of the class
of women employed in match-box making it would seem
that there was little scope for improvement.

The wages, even for the lowest class of umbrella or
parasol, *i.e.* the rates per hour, are high compared with
wages in other industries. Skill is required to some extent
throughout, and the degree of skill required is greater
according to the class of umbrella. The cheapest parasols
are those sent to India, China, and Africa; the natives of
these climes are not very particular about the finish and
little details to which we attach some importance; and
perhaps they still labour under the delusion that low-priced
articles are necessarily cheap. Wherever bad work will
pass muster, the necessity of supervision being less, employers are always glad to be saved the trouble of hunting
up unskilled workers, and the sub-contractor will most
probably be found. But even common umbrella work
must be machined, and a machinist is always to a certain
extent a skilled labourer; the space required for umbrellas
and parasols prevents the employment of several assistants
in small workrooms; and finishing requires some skill too,
and in the better class parasol requires very careful and
good work. Even at the worst, therefore, the price of
umbrellas seems higher than the price of other work. But
other factors tend to complicate this question of payment.
The price of the umbrella or parasol rises with the skill
required, but it does not in this or other trades rise in the

same proportion. In many cases women employed on the better work could earn more if they were employed on the commoner work; the less skilled hands, if put on to this better work at the higher price, would earn considerably less than on their ordinary work. The City fur-sewers exemplify this fact as well as the umbrella makers. And employers themselves unthinkingly make the admission when they maintain that so far from making most profit by their low-paid hands, it is the women who earn high wages who are the most valuable. This is quite true; they are the most profitable servants, and moreover they produce for consumers who could well afford to pay more for what they consume if prices were forced up. The explanation of this diminishing acceleration in the rate of pay may perhaps be found in the variety of social grades among the workers and the absence of competition between them. The higher the skill, as a rule, the higher is the social grade. On the side of the employer there would always be a reluctance to give the commoner work to a good hand; he prefers to give it to people who do it as well as need be, and who could not do other work. On the side of the skilled workman there is a corresponding reluctance to do the commoner work; partly because there is an æsthetic pleasure in doing good work, and partly because, for example, a West End sunshade maker would not care to be classed with the makers of cotton sunshades living in the neighbourhood of Petticoat Lane. The girl who makes sealskin capes at a City warehouse does not wish to work for an East End chambermaster even though she could make more at the commoner work; just as a soap-box maker would not care to make match-boxes even though skilled enough to make more by it. If skilled women are working at the same trade as less skilled women they are always paid more, but not so much more as would be proportionate to the difference in skill. The competition in the lowest class is diminished, that in the highest is increased. The em-

ployer or the consumer, perhaps both, reap the benefit of
this social sensitiveness in women. But the contentment
of women themselves when they have obtained enough for
their standard of living is another reason why competition
is so ineffective among highly skilled workers.

VI. *The private circumstances of the worker; position,
training, and occupation before marriage; individual
efficiency.*—It is useless to generalize on this head. Accounts
of home-workers in extreme poverty would, however,
bring one fact into prominence, that among married
women such poverty and misery are caused by the industrial
position of the husband, or by mental and moral defects
on the side of either husband or wife inevitably weighing
the other down, or by sickness or accident. An increase
in wages, which would change the condition of the self-
supporting single woman from one of struggling poverty
to that of comparative comfort, would be of little avail to
the woman whose husband has failed, from whatever cause,
to support his family and himself. Here also we may
notice another cause of the irregularity of employment of
married women (for all home-work employment is irregular),
viz. the irregularity of married women themselves. Many
of them do not want to have full work, and of those who
do the account of long working hours stretching far into
the night is accompanied by the lament that so little is
given out. I have generally been able to ascertain the
time taken to do a certain quantity of work at a given rate
of payment, and also the ordinary weekly wages earned at
home, and, by a process of simple division, have found
that except in the cases where married women were working
absolutely for their livelihood and that of their children,
the number of hours worked in the week rarely approaches
the number of hours worked in the factory, if the statements of the women are to be accepted. On the whole,
the home-workers are the first to point out that as they
have their children to attend to and the meals to prepare,

and the washing and mending and cleaning to do, they cannot give very long hours to their work. But unskilled working women—shirt makers, match-box makers, trouser-makers—do undoubtedly work very long hours when they have others to support. Life to large numbers of married women in the East End is nothing more than procrastination of death. They bear children and bury them. Their minds have been starved and their senses dulled. "Abandon hope, all ye who enter here" might well be inscribed above the entrance to the Red Church. For these women but little can be done. The position of the married woman can only be affected through the better education of the child, the training of the girl, and through everything that tends to raise the man morally and industrially.

FACTORY WORK.

Of the industries carried on in the East End in factories only three of any importance numerically are managed entirely in the factories, viz., the cigar, confectionery, and match industries. Outdoor hands are employed in all the other trades, although not by all employers in these trades, and I have already touched on the question of the irregularity in the employment of indoor hands prevented or increased by this practice. On the whole, work in the factories is regular. More single women would be employed if work were not done at home, and domestic competition perhaps prevents wages from being so high as they would otherwise be. But it is obvious that any employer who uses machinery must be anxious to utilize his machinery and rooms to the utmost; and on the whole the irregularity in the employment of factory girls is due to the state of the trade, and not to any carelessness on the part of the employer, who would always like to give full work throughout the year if he could. The system of employing outdoor hands makes it unnecessary to unduly increase the number of indoor hands in very busy times, and when trade returns to its normal condition the home workers are left unemployed, but the factory girls earn about the same as before. In these trades, except in flower-making and fur-sewing, the indoor hands are generally single ; or if married they have nearly always been employed before marriage and have stayed on. The cigar trade has been fully discussed, and its exceptional character need not be considered here. But the irregularity which is unavoidable in confectionery, and to a less extent in match-making, has consequences which are of the utmost importance in their effect on the condition of women. Only half the number employed in the busiest season in confectionery are regularly employed throughout the year, although this ratio is only obtained by considering the factories collectively, and is only exactly true in one factory that I have visited. Most of these jam and sweet factories are established in the midst of the dock labouring community, and the irregular employment offered is generally accepted by the wives and daughters of the irregularly or casually employed dock labourers. As the permanent staff are to the preferred dock labourers, and the preferred dock labourers to the casuals, so is the regularly employed jam factory girl to the irregular hand, and the irregular hand to the fruit picker engaged in the fruit season. The better the management the smaller the proportion of irregular to regular hands. The more intelligent and trustworthy the girl the more easily can she be moved from one branch to another, and the less need is there to dismiss or take on extra hands. But irregularity there must be, and wherever there is irregular employment, married women will be found amongst the employed. No girl who respects herself will be content with irregular work if she can possibly obtain work elsewhere. Unfortunately, among the dock labouring class can be found many girls with a low standard of comfort and with nomadic tastes, whose wants are fairly

well supplied by three days' wages in the week, and whose
natural dislike to settle down to steady continuous work
is stimulated by the fact that such work is never offered
them. The married women employed in factories are
frequently the most industrious, but they generally exert a
most mischievous influence on their companions. Those
who go out to work have generally had a marital experience
which seems in most cases to have brutalized and degraded
them ; no respectable man would willingly let the mother
of his children go out to a factory, nor would the 10*s* a
week she could thus earn make up for the loss incurred by
her absence if he brought home even so little as 18*s*. The
effect of mixing these married women with young girls in
factories seems infinitely worse than that which may be
observed when girls and men work together, and if employers
only knew or cared to know the coarseness of many of these
women they would think twice before exposing respectable
girls to daily contact with them. As so many have only
irregular employment, and as these hands are generally of
a very low class, an impression is left on the mind of an
outsider that the majority in jam factories are badly paid
and rather disreputable. But the regular hands are a class
apart, both socially and industrially. From the table of
wages given on page 468 no idea can be obtained of the
average earned throughout the year by irregular hands,
although the rate may generally be assumed to be the
same as that of the lowest paid regular hands. Nor have I
any data by which I could arrive at any approximation to
their average wage. The irregularity in the match industry
is of a different order; jam manufacturers have a busy
season when they are obliged to take on large numbers of
hands, for whose welfare afterwards they feel in no way
responsible. In the match factory there is a slack season
when either the work must be shared, giving smaller
earnings to each, or the inferior hands must be dismissed.
During this slack season many of the girls leave of their

own accord, and sell flowers and water-cresses, pick fruit, and go hopping, but this does not fill up the whole time.

Which alternative should the employer choose? Should he divide the work among them all, or should he in slack times dismiss hands?

This problem, in some form or other, must be faced by employers in every trade. Is half a loaf better than no bread? During a temporary scarcity it is. In the factory the expense of machinery and buildings tends to prevent the employer from taking on more hands than are required in full work, and in slack times it seems best to divide the work among them all. But, unless the girls have saved in their best times, they naturally complain so much at their smaller earnings that it sometimes pays the employer better to dismiss the inferior hands and to give the rest the opportunity of earning their usual amount. And the girls never do save. If their standard of living included saving for slack times, they could force wages up to that point in the season. But so long as they only wish they could save, and always spend all their money, so long will full wages merely correspond to necessary wages; *i.e.*, they will only be enough for present wants.

The same question—whether half a loaf is better than no bread—presents itself to the employer in another form. Granted that three girls at 10*s* a week are worth the same as four girls at 7*s* 6*d* a week, is it not better to give employment to the four than the three? If the employer decides that he will employ no one who is not worth 9*s* a week, he really divides the work among a smaller number of fairly efficient girls. It may be true that no girl by herself can live respectably on less than 9*s* a week; but it is also true that there are many girls who would not be worth employing at that rate. In other words, there are girls who, as things are, are not worth decent maintenance wages. The employer who only employs girls who are worth this may preserve the even tenor of his way, and congratulate himself that he at least is free from the guilt of employing hands at starvation wages. But what about the large numbers who are thus left unemployed? This is the question asked by a large number of manufacturers, and their answer to those who demand that a minimum wage should be fixed is that in that case they will have to dismiss many of their hands. What would be done with the great mass of un-employed left to starve? I do not attempt to answer this question. But two facts should be noticed. Fix a minimum rate of wages, and an incentive is given to those, whose working power has hitherto been below par through indolence or lowness of standard, to raise themselves to the required level. Those who are left are the physically or mentally incapable, or the idle. Secondly, if these are left as the wholly unemployed, they can be dealt with much more easily than the half-paid or partly unemployed, who drag down population to their level. They are not left to starve. The parish rates and charitable contributions, which at present are spent in doing harm to the many, and in lowering wages, could be wholly devoted to the improvement of the condition of the few, either in pleasure-houses or workhouses, according to the circumstances of the case. The inefficient are always irregularly employed. Irregular employment causes irregular demand, and irregular demand causes irregularity of employment. Each force acts with increased momentum.

Factory Supervision.—Under this head should be noticed the treatment of girls by foremen, systems of fines or deductions, and rules to be observed in the factory. To such points as are dealt with by the factory inspectors no reference need here be made, except to mention the remark-able unanimity with which inspectors, employers, and work-people prove that with such wide areas to be covered by so few inspectors, the wonder is that the Factory Regulations should be respected as much as they are, not that they should be so frequently disregarded.

The factory girls make very little complaint about their

work or their wages; they, in many cases, have assured me
that the fines imposed are just and absolutely necessary,
because some of the girls would otherwise be so careless.
But they repeatedly complain about their treatment by foremen. " The masters are kind, but the foremen treat us like
animals." It is very difficult to decide in any particular
case whether the foreman is in the right or whether the girl
is telling the truth. But if in a factory the foremen are
habitually tyrannical and subject the girls to rough treatment, the employers must be regarded as represented by
the foremen, and many of them deserve the severest censure
for their indifference in this respect. Forewomen should
superintend girls whenever it is possible; and if suitable
women cannot be found for the post, the greatest care
should be shown in the selection of the foreman. A very
little reflection on the darker side of life in the East End
will show to what insult a girl may be exposed by her
employer's indifference to the moral character of the man
to whom he intrusts the management of young girls. The
system of payment adopted by some employers, who pay
their foreman by the piece and leave him to engage and
dismiss the girls in his department, confers on him a power
which the average foreman will be strongly tempted to
abuse, unless great watchfulness is shown by the employer.
It is not likely that these men should be more incorruptible
than other men who have power given them. Bribery of
officials is not an unknown thing to employers—they have
even occasionally, perhaps, stooped to employ such means
themselves; and it might occur to them that if they delegate
their functions to their foremen, the latter may be tempted
to increase their incomes, or indulge themselves at the
expense of the girls, who must find favour in their eyes
if they wish to be left unmolested in other ways. But
nothing, perhaps, reflects more discredit on employers than
their wilful blindness with regard to the drinking which goes
on in many factories, especially the day before Christmas

—in the factories, not merely outside; a practice which could hardly be carried on without the deliberate connivance of the foremen. I do not wish to convey the impression that the girls in the East End are always exposed to petty tyranny or laxity on the part of the foremen; but I do wish to remind employers of a danger which they must know exists. To these girls, who spend three-fourths of their waking hours at the factory, the question of supervision is of far more importance than that of wages. "Pleasant words are as an honeycomb, sweet to the soul and health to the bones."

Wages and the Standard of Living.—In the following table of wages no attempt has been made to give the proportion of wage earners whose weekly earnings are near the lowest level to those whose earnings are near the highest. The table only states the wages earned by women above eighteen in full work. The wages of forewomen are not given, and with the exception of the umbrella factories, the table refers to East End factories only. In confectionery factories and in the match factory, where unskilled work is done, children at once receive at least 4s a week on time-work. The minimum paid varies in the different factories, but I find that the minimum age varies with it. Where the minimum paid is 9s no one under eighteen is employed; where the minimum is 7s no one under sixteen; in the factories where 4s and 5s are given girls of thirteen who have passed the fourth standard or girls of fourteen are employed. In all the other trades except fur-sewing and rope-weaving girls are taken on as learners for some time on terms which vary with the employer.

The wages given in the second column represent the wages that are earned by a few of the most skilled workers, or by the most industrious; that is to say, they are attainable by good workers who work their hardest, or by clever workers who work without any special strain. They do not represent the maximum attained by the one woman in a

thousand, who is to be found in a factory occasionally
displaying almost miraculous quickness and dexterity.
The maximum in the collar factories is probably put too
low, but it is the highest I have heard of in the East End.
The maximum put down in artificial flower-making and in
rope-weaving, is time-wage, and it must be remembered
that 11s time wages are often preferred to 14s or 15s on
piece-work. The time-worker does not have to work at
such high pressure as the piece-worker.

Wages of Women in Factories in Full Work.

					Ordinary.	Highest.
Artificial Flowers	...	...	...	...	8s to 12s	18s
Bookbinding	...	...	...	...	9s to 11s	16s
Boxes ...	...	...	...	...	8s to 16s	20s
Brushes	...	...	...	...	8s to 15s	20s
Confectionery ...	...	...	...	...	8s to 14s	15s, 18s
Collars ...	...	...	...	...	11s to 15s	17s
Caps ...	...	...	...	...	8s to 16s	20s
Corsets	...	...	...	...	8s to 16s	20s
Fur-sewing	...	...	...	...	7s to 14s	18s
Do. in Winter	...	...	...	...	4s to 7s	
Matches	...	...	...	...	8s to 13s	17s
Rope	...	...	...	...	8s to 11s	11s
Umbrellas	...	...	...	...	10s to 18s	20s

The most striking feature in this table is the uniformity
of maximum wage, and the difference in the skill required,
and I believe it to be the fact that the match girls and the
jam girls, who are at the bottom of the social scale, do not
have to work so hard for their money as, for example, the cap
makers and bookbinders, who in the majority of cases belong
to a much higher social grade. And whereas the bookfolder or
book-sewer who earns 11s a week exercises greater skill, and
gives a closer attention to her work than the jam or match
girl who earns the same amount, that sum which would be
almost riches to the docklabourer's daughter, represents
grinding poverty to the daughter of the clerk or bookbinder,
with a much higher standard of decency, if she is by any
chance obliged to depend on herself. How is it, then, that
this uniformity prevails, and that efficiency brings with it
nothing but the privilege of working harder for the same

money? The competition of the home-workers may be one cause, but there is a more potent one than this. I have said that married women who really work for pocket-money do not lower wages to the extent that married women working for the necessaries of life lower them. But the effect of "pocket-money" competition among unmarried women is very different. The match girl and the jam girl and the rope girl, work for their living; they generally live at home, but they pay the full cost of their board and lodging. Their standard of living is so low that if they remained single and depended on themselves, they could, if they chose, live more comfortably than the "factory girl" ever dreams of living. They pay their parents 5s or 6s a week for board and lodging, and startling as the fact may be to many readers, that sum really covers the expense. The bookbinder, the cap maker, and the corset machinist pay less to their parents in proportion to their standard of living. If the girl's parents are in very comfortable circumstances, she frequently pays nothing towards the home expenses, and spends all she earns on dress and amusement. These skilled workers compete with each other, not for a livelihood, but to procure the dress and luxuries which are almost as necessary to them as food and lodging. The number of single women who work for their livelihood is so small relatively, that their standard has no effect on the rate of wages: they must either live on the sum which their richer sisters use for dress, or they must work harder than any of them.

As has been pointed out, competition is much obstructed between different social grades. The girl who has to work hard at cap-making to earn 17s a week, competing with girls on the same level of skill as herself, could probably earn as much with less labour in the jam or match factory, where regularity, intelligence, carefulness, are so rare as to be at a premium, but the loss in social status would be too great for her to think of competing. The

middle-class parent imagines that he is doing his daughter
a kindness when he pays the cost of her board and lodging
for her, and lets her work ten and a half hours a day for
what she is proud to call "only pocket-money." He is in
fact making a present to his daughter's employer which
may or may not be shared by the employer with the consumer. His daughters are not one whit better off. If they
were compelled to pay the full cost of living, or to put in
the savings bank its equivalent, their wages would have to
be raised to meet their standard. They would not have to
work harder, for in the more skilled industries the girls
are kept at work as hard as they possibly can be already.
They could not be replaced, for their skill is due largely to
inherited qualities and to their better standard of living.
At present the clerk with £120 a year lets his daughter
work for £30 a year, and live at an expense of £40 perhaps.
To maintain the same standard of living, if she had later on
to support herself, the cost to her would probably be about
£50. She is much worse off than she would have been if
she had earned her livelihood when under her father's roof;
then she would either have earned more or accustomed
herself to living on less. She would have no reason to dread
the future. The workgirl in the lower middle class, when
she begins to reflect on the future, does dread it. There is
hardly one thing which the Girton or Newnham girl requires
in the way of food, clothing, or lodging, which is not
equally desired by the City workwoman in this rank. Of
the two the Girton girl can resign herself the more easily
to shabby dresses and hats, has no fear of losing caste on
account of poverty, and can offer her friends weak tea and
a biscuit without any dread of being considered mean and
inhospitable. She has the happy conviction that her own
personal merit is all sufficing. The young lady who goes
to a warehouse or a superior factory is singularly modest in
this respect. She seems to imagine that her whole future
depends on those appearances which must be kept up.

When she is left to support herself, the importance she
attaches to outside things shows how much more keenly
she is actuated by ideal than by material wants. She starves
herself first, living on tea and bread-and-butter ; she stints
herself in bed clothing and underclothing next, and attributes
her colds and bronchitis to original weakness of constitution.
And in the reaction that follows, the sickening distaste for
the drudgery and the struggle, she too often sacrifices
maidenhood itself. The substance is thrown away for the
shadow. These girls do not sell themselves for bread ; that
they could easily earn. They sin for the externals which
they have learnt to regard as essentials. It is this class
who are regarded as the best paid for their work. Does
not the reader in his heart think that £30 a year is a very
good income for the daughter of a clerk with £120 ?
Would he think the same thing if he were told that
she could only earn 12*s* a week ? Twelve shillings
a week seems so much less than £30 a year, whereas in actual
fact it is more. I have no hesitation in asserting that if
these girls worked for their living instead of working only
for pocket-money, their wages would rise considerably ; early
marriages would be much less common and the greatest
temptation to immorality would be removed. It is among
these skilled workers that union is most needed and that the
economic question of wages is of the most importance.

There is one other fact which makes it the more desirable
that wages should be forced up to the level of the standard
of comfort of the worker, and that these girls should be
able to support themselves entirely. This is the fact which
becomes evident in the census statistics for East London, viz.,
that the surplus of women over men is greatest in the districts
inhabited by the more well-to-do classes. It will be observed
in these tables on page 303 that in Hackney there is a large
excess of unmarried women over unmarried men and that
in the rest of East London there is an excess of unmarried
men over unmarried women. The percentage of unmarried

women in Hackney is higher than in all London, and cannot be explained by the influx of servants to Hackney, nor balanced by the efflux from East London. Whatever the causes may be, the chances of marriage among women in the poorer middle classes are less than among the working girls in the East End. Every girl in the lowest classes in the East End can get married, and with hardly any exceptions every girl does marry. This is not true of the middle classes.

There are a great many steps between the warehouse workgirl and the girl who has been accepted as the type of the factory girl, but it is difficult for an outsider to have anything but a vague consciousness of the distinction. But at a certain stage the ground of distinction becomes obvious; there must be differences in the thoughts and habits of the family who live in a cottage and of the family who herd together in one, or at most two rooms. And the manner in which one set of girls in a factory keep themselves aloof from another, and in which one factory regards itself as superior or inferior to another, laughable as it seems at first, is not nearly so ridiculous as much of the class prejudice satirized by Thackeray and Du Maurier. In trying to give some idea of the life and condition of the factory girl, I must not be understood to refer to all girls in factories. By the "factory girl" is meant the lower grade of factory workers who may be found in comparatively small numbers in box, brush, and cap factories; who are in the majority in the jam factories, and who hold almost undisputed sway in the rope and match factories. Girls in factories often earn 11s and upwards; the "factory girl" generally earns from 7s to 11s—rarely more, for the very good reason, in many cases, that she does not want more. She can be recognized on ordinary days by the freedom of her walk, the numbers of her friends, and the shrillness of her laugh. On Saturday evenings and Sunday afternoons she will be found promenading up and down the Bow Road, arm in arm with two or three other girls, sometimes with a young man, but not nearly so frequently as might be imagined. On those occasions she is adorned and decked out, not so much for conquest as for her own personal delight and pleasure, and for the admiration of her fellow women. She wears a gorgeous plush hat with as many large ostrich feathers to match as her funds will run to—bright ruby or scarlet preferred. Like all the working women in the East End, she wears good tidy boots on all occasions, perhaps with high heels, but generally suitable for walking, although a little higher always than those adopted by the Rational Dress Society. She goes to penny gaffs if nothing better is offered her; she revels in the thrilling performances at the Paragon or the music halls; and only too often she can be seen drinking in the public-house with a young man with whom she may or may not have been previously acquainted.

This is the girl to whom everyone refers in the East End when they speak of "the factory girl;" and this is the girl whose condition I wish to depict, making it clear beforehand that I do not refer to the thousands of quiet, respectable, hard-working girls who are also to be found working in factories. Among the skilled workers wages are too low for the standard of living. Among these factory girls the standard of comfort is lower than their wages.

In looking through the wage-book of the Victoria Match Factory I was much struck by finding that out of the 32 who had earned less than 9*s* in the week 6 had been absent two days, 7 had been absent one day, and 6 had been absent half a day, and that the holiday was nearly always taken on Monday. This irregularity of attendance is found in all factories among what might be called the 8*s* to 10*s* girls. These wages give these girls as much as they care to work for, and after that they like holidays best. They are often the daughters of dock labourers or other irregular workmen, frequently of drunkards. They have been brought up in stifling rooms, with scanty food, in the midst of births and

deaths, year after year. They have been accustomed to ups
and downs; one week they have been on the verge of
starvation, another they have shared in a "blow-out." They
have been taught unselfishness by the most skilled of
teachers, self-indulgent parents. They have learnt to hate
monotony, to love drink, to use bad language as their mother
tongue, and to be true to a friend in distress. They care
nothing for appearances, and have no desire to mix with any
but their equals. They are generally one of seventeen,
of whom all may be surviving or a dozen dead. I have
not sufficient data for tracing any connection between
infant mortality and married women's labour. One
girl told me that she had fourteen brothers and sisters
all living; her father had been in regular work for
20 years, filling coal-sacks; he drank sometimes, but
not very much. Three months before I met her he had been
out of work on strike; her mother was confined a few days
after he went out; the girl herself was staying away from
the factory in order to nurse a sister through her confine-
ment; and for a fortnight no money was coming in from
any member of the family. Her father afterwards got work
as a navvy, but the few weeks' interval may well have been
the beginning of a downward movement. Another girl, the
daughter of a drunken dock labourer who got a job occasionally, was one of thirteen, of whom only three were
living; she was not eighteen, had worked in two factories,
been to service three times, had gone hop-picking and fruit-
picking and sold flowers and water-cresses in summer; she
had set up for herself in lodgings with other factory girls
and gone home again when the novelty had worn off.
Clever and bright, she had never passed the second standard
at school, and could neither read nor write. Another girl
was actually one of seventeen, of whom only three survived;
she liked reading story books, but had never passed the
second standard, because the babies were always ill, and
she had to stay at home to nurse them; she also was the

daughter of a dock labourer in irregular work. She had been to service once, and during that time had gone to church on Sunday evening, because she had to repeat the text and mention the hymns to her mistress afterwards. With unconscious irony she told me how delighted she was to find in the reading room in the People's Palace, on Sunday, books "that you can read on a weekday." Another girl, the daughter of a dock labourer in fairly regular work, was one of fourteen, of whom ten were living; three were married, and of the seven living at home only two were earning money; her mother did trouser finishing, and their united income amounted to about 35s a week on the average.

These and many other instances have inclined me to connect the rate of infant mortality with the irregularity of employment of the father. Amongst this class the mortality is enormous. The mothers discuss the number they have buried with a callousness amounting at times almost to pride in the vastness of their maternal experience. Next to births, the commonest events to the factory girl are funerals; and she enjoys few things so much as taking part in a funeral procession. On the whole, these girls, outside their homes, lead a healthy, active life. They do not over-exert themselves at the factory, following the example of the little girl who was neither very good nor very naughty, but just comfortable. They rise early and have plenty of open-air exercise, both on their way to and from the factory and in their evening walks. They are rough, boisterous, outspoken, warm-hearted, honest working girls. Their standard of morality is very low, so low that to many they may seem to have none at all: and yet the very tolerance of evil that is shown by the girls who so willingly subscribe for a companion who has "got into trouble" may be one reason why these girls have such a repugnance to the worst forms of immorality. Their great enemy is drink; the love of it is the

curse they have inherited, which later on, when they are
no longer factory girls, but dock labourers' wives, will drag
them down to the lowest level, and will be transmitted to
the few of their children who survive. They are nearly all
destined to be mothers, and they are almost entirely
ignorant of any domestic accomplishment.

"Something should be done" is the vague declaration
made by would-be social reformers. The something which
should be done is to some extent being done already
by quiet workers among the East End working girls,
who, coming in contact with them in their clubs, their
evening classes and social gatherings and in their homes,
know well that improvement in the condition of these
girls is identical with improvement in their moral character.
What is needed for working women in general is a
more practical education in the Board Schools; greater
facilities for the exercise of thrift, and definite instruction
in the advantages and best methods of saving. If the
women and girls will not go to the Post Office Savings
Bank, is it quite absurd to suggest that the Post Office
Savings Bank should go to the women and girls? And
lastly, and not least, trade union is wanted; not union
against employers, but union with them; a recognition
on the one side of the need and advantage of having
good organizers whose exceptional ability makes them
worth an exceptional reward; an acknowledgment and
acceptance on the other of the responsibility which lies
with everyone whose position, talents, or advantages have
made him his brother's keeper. The question of wages is
trivial compared with the question of regularity of employment and kind and just treatment.

Married state of the East End in comparison with London and England and Wales, 1881.

REGISTRATION DISTRICTS.	MALES (over 20).				FEMALES (over 20).			
	Unmarried	Married	Widowed	Total	Unmarried	Married	Widowed	Total
In numbers.								
Shoreditch ...	8038	23,060	2280	33,378	7142	23,146	5952	36,240
Bethnal Green ...	7044	22,765	1942	31,751	5916	22,794	5035	33,745
Whitechapel ...	8145	11,722	1235	21,102	4079	11,466	3067	18,612
St. George's East ...	3946	8449	881	13,276	2193	8505	2392	13,090
Stepney ...	4290	10,355	888	15,533	2726	10,582	2382	15,690
Mile End Old Town ...	6586	18,583	1613	26,782	6264	19,077	4983	30,324
Poplar ...	10,350	28,256	2448	41,054	6529	28,399	5534	40,462
Total East End ...	48,399	123,190	11,287	182,876	34,849	123,969	29,345	188,163
Hackney ...	11,857	29,868	2555	44,280	19,037	30,644	8282	57,963
London ...	291,828	640,884	56,820	989,532	354,403	647,927	173,098	1,175,428
England and Wales ...	1,837,433	4,371,038	434,696	6,643,167	1,911,075	4,405,546	998,828	7,315,449
In percentages.								
Shoreditch ...	24·10	69·07	6·83	100·00	19·75	63·85	16·40	100·00
Bethnal Green ...	22·17	71·71	6·12	100·00	17·55	67·50	14·95	100·00
Whitechapel ...	38·60	55·55	5·85	100·00	21·90	61·60	16·50	100·00
St. George's East ...	29·70	63·65	6·65	100·00	16·80	64·90	18·30	100·00
Stepney ...	27·62	66·65	5·73	100·00	17·40	67·40	15·20	100·00
Mile End Old Town ...	24·60	69·37	6·03	100·00	20·75	62·80	16·45	100·00
Poplar ...	25·22	68·81	5·97	100·00	16·15	70·25	13·60	100·00
Total East End ...	26·47	67·36	6·17	100·00	18·52	65·88	15·60	100·00
Hackney ...	26·80	67·45	5·75	100·00	32·80	52·90	14·30	100·00
London ...	29·49	64·77	5·74	100·00	30·15	55·12	14·73	100·00
England and Wales ...	27·66	65·79	6·55	100·00	26·12	60·22	13·66	100·00

CHAPTER IX.

SWEATING.

THE word "sweating" seems to have been originally used by journeymen tailors, among themselves, to describe contemptuously the action of those of their number who worked at home, out of hours. Aided, at first in the way of overtime only, by their wives and daughters, these men gradually found it convenient to do all their work at home, and thus introduced a complete system of home-work. Finally, employing others besides members of their own family, many of them became sweaters in the second meaning of the word: that is, those who make others sweat.

The word as a picturesque nickname soon spread to other trades. Among bootmakers, who early took the word from the tailors, it is still used to mean the journeyman, while the small master (the present "sweater" of the tailoring trade) is more appropriately called the "chamber" or "garret" master. Cabinet-makers followed later in using the word, the small master being called indiscriminately "sweater" and "garret master." In other trades it is the sub-contractor or middleman who is termed the sweater; and by the general public the word has been readily accepted as meaning any employer whose workpeople are badly paid, harshly used, or ill-provided with accommodation, or any sub-contractor or middleman who squeezes a profit out of the labour of the poor.

As used in the trades themselves, unless pointed by some opprobrious adjective, the word is scarcely a term of reproach, being applied to good and bad alike. To the public mind, however, it usually implies something definitely bad ; with the result that, as all alike bear it, all alike are branded by it. The functions of chamber-master, sub-contractor, and middleman, which are really distinct, become confused ; every sweater passes for a middleman, and sub-contract is supposed to be an essential feature of the "sweating system," as this medley of ideas is called. In fine, every hardship and every horror in the lives of the suffering workpeople of East London has been attributed to the iniquitous action of some peculiar industrial system. At last, public opinion insisted on inquiry ; a committee of the House of Lords took the question up, much evidence has been heard, thousands of pages of evidence bearing witness to the searching ability and un-exampled patience of the questioners have been printed, and we now await the report.

Failing the report, the confused nature of the popular ideas about sweating has been a serious drawback to any thorough comprehension of the value of the various kinds of evidence taken before this committee. Their Lordships have received information as to unpunctual payments, discounts off cheques, tips to foremen, bad language, and high-handed manners. Wealthy firms have been accused of taking advantage of the position of the poor seller of made-up goods who cannot afford to lie out of his money, and parts with his work at a loss rather than face immediate ruin ; while now and then some poor worker, in his simple answers, has unconsciously told a sad tale of gradually blighted hopes and narrowing existence, too surely the lot of the helpless who, in these pushing days, are passed in the race by more competent or fresher workers. All this has been deeply interesting, and in many cases deeply pathetic, and although it is unlikely that all the stories told have been literally true, yet, after we have made due allowance for passion, personal pique, and race antipathy, enough remains to fill us with pity and horror at the thought that such lives can be led, such hardships endured by our fellow men.

Meanwhile, in such manner as has been possible for a private inquirer, I, too, have sought the truth, and am able to assert without hesitation that there is no industrial system co-extensive with the evils complained of, although there is unfortunately no doubt at all that very serious evils exist. It is not one but many systems with which we have to deal, each having its special faults. First there is the form of sweating which is practised in the clothing trades, where wholesale manufacturers find it convenient to abdicate the position of employer, and instead of hiring workpeople themselves, make a contract with someone who does, the materials needed being nevertheless provided and prepared by the wholesale house. This may be described as *employment at second-hand*. It is not sub-contract, but is based upon a partition of the function of manufacturer between the wholesale house and the sweater, and without doubt facilitates a very acute form of competition. Again, when the wholesale house, in place of dealing directly with the workers, employs a go-between, who distributes and collects the work and perhaps performs some part of it, we have a practice, not indeed confined to industries which are said to be sweated, but definite enough. This is the sweating system as it applies more particularly to female home-workers. It is one only too well adapted to take advantage of the necessities of the very poor. Or if the wholesale house, instead of ordering what it wants beforehand, stands ready to buy from those who, having no other work to do, put their labour on to materials, trusting to sell labour and materials together, we have the sweating system as it applies to cabinet-making. This last plan, which has been called "sub-purchase," may be made a terribly efficient engine of oppression. Or, to take quite another field, if the chamber-master is able to obtain a constant supply of learners (usually poor foreigners) who, as "greeners," will work long hours in return for bare keep, and so reduce the cost of production, the result is to aggravate competition and depress regular wages. This is the sweating system as it applies to foreign immigration; perhaps its most intense form. Or finally, if systematic deductions are made from men's earnings by labour masters, who can thus pocket any difference that may exist between the authorized pay and the lowest competition value of the work, we have sweating as it applies to the Docks. There may be other systems of employment which fall under the general head of sweating, but these are the principal ones; and it does not concern me to make the list complete, as it is rather with the evils, however caused, that we have to do, than with industrial organizations, in which they are by no means always present.

If no system, however good, can secure the incompetent, or even the unfortunate, from oppression; happily, no system, however bad, can prevent the flow of natural kindness, or altogether check the development of wholesome industrial relations. And this leads me to a second definition of the word "sweating," which attaches itself not so much to a system as to the character of the employer under any system; and here the ground has been rendered somewhat confused by the popular conception of the sweating master. While not blaming the small man, who is admittedly nearly as helpless as, and but little better off than, those whom he employs, popular opinion has fixed upon the larger sweating master as a kind of monster of inhumanity; although it is proved beyond dispute that the conditions of employment under the larger masters are better than under the small men. But define the system how we may, the fact remains that within the limits of our definition we find considerate as well as harsh employers, and fully-paid as well as ill-paid workpeople, whilst outside of it, however, it may be defined, there is industrial oppression and wretched pay.

With five or six different systems, and more than one

way of looking at each, it is not surprising that there should have been five-and-twenty different and inconsistent definitions adduced in evidence before the Committee of the House of Lords. My own, given in May, 1888, "The advantage that may be taken of unskilled and unorganized labour under the contract system," is neither complete nor correct.

Bearing in mind these divergences of opinion, it may be well, before proceeding further, to attempt to clear up the confusion existing in the popular mind between sub-contractor, middleman, and chamber-master, or sweating master.

A *sub-contractor* is only to be found when work, already contracted for, is sublet. This is sometimes the case with a middleman, but it only occurs with chamber-masters under special circumstances. Sub-contract is most often to be found where several distinct processes of work are involved. The first price includes the whole of these, and the partition of it involves sub-contracts; a very harmless arrangement, entirely unconnected with grinding the poor The better paid work, involving the use of a machine, is very commonly the part sublet.

A *middleman* is one who interposes between producer and consumer, or between any other men who are linked together by commercial relations. A sub-contractor is necessarily a middleman, but a middleman is not necessarily a sub-contractor. A chamber, or sweating, master is usually neither one nor the other.

A *sweating master* is neither more nor less than a small manufacturer. He takes orders and executes them with the assistance of those he employs. This is *contract*, not *sub-contract*; and if he is to be accounted a middleman, so every one is who seeks to make a profit out of the employment of labour.

Connected with the distribution of home-work, there exist both middlemen and sub-contractors. They are employed mostly when the workers are scattered in their homes and separated from the wholesale house by the vast distances of London. Distribution of this sort is not, however, confined to London or to the so-called "sweated industries," but is found all over the country, especially in connection with village work. The distributor is no parasite, but earns his (or her) profit for finding the workers and being responsible for the due return and proper execution of the work.

When the work is partly done by the distributor, or on his or her premises, we have a hybrid system, involving home-work and small workshop as well as distributing agency. Such work as can easily be given out is eagerly taken up by those who cannot conveniently leave home, and the whole forms a very elastic system, adapting itself to the conditions of city life, to the habits of the people, and to the peculiarities of each industry. This may create some confusion in practice, but in principle the functions of chamber-master, distributor, and sub-contractor are distinct enough.

We are now able to put forward this general proposition :—That the production of certain results is an essential part of any practical definition of sweating, and hence we may abandon all talk of this or that system, and, beginning with the evils, work back to the causes.

We thus reach the third meaning which may be attached to the word sweating. Passing by, as incomplete or misleading, the prevalent conceptions of certain systems or their consequences, we may finally accept "sweating" as expressing in a general way all the evils which the workers in certain trades or under certain conditions suffer. Thus an examination of the sweating system resolves itself into an inquiry into the conditions under which occupations recognized as "sweated industries" are worked, and into the causes, whatever they may be, of the evils which are suffered. This is the conclusion to which I have been led, and the method which I have accepted. The facts remain the same, but the aspect under which they must be regarded

is greatly changed by ruling out the all-pervading but
imaginary system which has been supposed to be their
cause. Some of these evils may be due to one method and
some to another, but many, or perhaps most of them, are
not due in any way to the manner of employment. Their
roots lie deep in human nature. They are, alas! not the
less real because no trade or place has a monopoly of them,
and must be considered as part of the general troubles of
poverty. The accounts which have been given on preceding
pages in this book of Dock work, Tailoring, Bootmaking,
Cabinet-making and the Employments of Women, describe
all the sweated industries, and from these, as well as from the
schedules of Vol. I., it may be seen that the majority of the
workers are above the level at which there is any call for
Official inquiry or State interference. But in each, working
under exactly the same system of employment as their more
successful comrades, are large numbers of impoverished and
more or less suffering people. Each has its per-centage of
very poor as well as of poor, and each its fringe of abject
misery. In each we find poor struggling people leading
painful lives, small earnings irregularly received, every kind
of misfortune and every kind of incapacity. In all we are
conscious of the oppression of the weak. Such troubles
have not, on the whole, much to do with any system of
employment ; they are part of the general inequalities of life,
inequalities of capacity, prudence and temper, of perseverance, of strength, of health, and good luck, as well as of
birth or wealth. "Any trade does very well if you are
pretty good at it," said a boot finisher to me, and the reverse
is, unfortunately, no less true. But, allowing that many
of the troubles attributed to sweating are not industrial at
all, and admitting that those which are industrial are neither
essentially connected with any system of employment nor
to be attributed to inhumanity, still, the trades of East
London undoubtedly present a serious case of economic
disease, with painful and alarming symptoms.

This disease is closely connected with the multiplication of small masters (of which there is evidence) in all the sweated industries. Of the tendencies common to all industry—on the one hand, towards the increase of successful enterprises at the expense of unsuccessful ones; on the other, towards disintegration and fresh beginnings in a small way—it is the second which has prevailed. The quite small workshop, which is, in truth, no workshop at all, but an ordinary room of an ordinary house, lived in as well as worked in, stands at some advantage over the properly appointed workshop of a larger size. The capital needed for a start is very small. A few pounds will suffice, and the man becomes a master. It is a natural ambition, and one that appeals with peculiar force to the Jews. The evils which follow are patent. Men are content, at least for a while, to make less as masters than they would receive in wages as journeymen. The wholesale houses can take advantage of the competition which arises, and prices are reduced, to the immediate loss of the sweaters and the ultimate detriment of those whom they employ.

It is this state of things which really leads to the sweating evils of long hours, low pay, and unsanitary conditions. As to *long hours*, with small employers, it is the master who sets the time. He himself is ready to work any hours, why not those he employs? They must, and they do. Long hours are a natural concomitant of irregularity of employment, which, though not usually counted as one of the evils due to sweating, is closely interconnected with those evils. Irregularity of work is by far the most serious trial under which the people of London suffer, and results naturally from the industrial position of small workshops and home-work. The smaller the capital involved and the less the permanent fixed charge of working a business, the better suited is it for irregular employment. High organization makes for regularity : low organization lends itself to the opposite. A large factory cannot stop at all without

serious loss; a full-sized workshop will make great efforts
to keep going; but the man who employs only two or three
others in his own house can, if work fails, send them all
adrift to pick up a living as best they can. In regard to
low pay, it is connected with poor work that we find it.
What is called cheap work, but is in truth bad work, is
likely to be undertaken by small men commencing as masters.
These men themselves supply all the skill and use the
cheapest available assistance, such as the almost unpaid
labour of "greeners." Moreover, there is ample evidence
to show that the largest shops supply the most regular work.
The terms of employment in the larger and better shops,
though no doubt susceptible of improvement, can hardly be
accounted grievous.

Turning to the general question of wages and hours of
work, we find that, compared with any standard in England,
or still more on the Continent, London rates of wages are
high. This is one of the attractions of the metropolis.
Hours of labour must be taken in connection with employment by seasons. The best paid artisans in trades which
are extraordinarily active in certain seasons, adapting themselves to this condition, work hard when employment is
good and take their holidays when there is nothing to do.
Such men look to make full time one week with another,
and, with them, the push of work at certain seasons is
not accounted a grievance. If a grievance at all, it is
common to well and ill-paid alike. The ill-paid do not, as
a rule, work longer hours than the well-paid when the push
is greatest, but they have more enforced idleness.*

It should be said that the very long hours, carrying work

---

* In all shops alike, large or small, the wages paid are according to the
skill of the operator, and according therefore to the class of work undertaken.
There is a curious compensation in favour of " cheap work " by reason of the
pace at which it may be done. Speed is another kind of skill, and the two
kinds are not interchangeable. Put a first-class workman on to common
work and he is as helpless to earn " fair wages " at it as the rapid low-class
workman would be if good work were demanded, like the well-known fable
of the Fox and the Crane.

far into the night or beginning it very early in the morning, are in home industry frequently connected with the
intermixture of domestic concerns—the baby, the dinner,
the washing, if not neighbourly gossip, occupying time
which must be made up. It is a hardship to have to work
full time in such cases, but rather a hardship of life than of
industry, and to speak of the work as 16 or 18 hours a day
is incorrect. Long and late hours are also often due to
loss of time going to shop and waiting for work. There is
in the giving out of work much reckless want of consideration on the part of the employers. This is a very real
grievance, and one which is not beyond remedy, hardly
perhaps by legislation, but it may be reached either
by a quickened sense of responsibility on the part of the
employer or by a growth of independence and conscious
power on the part of the employed, which may enable them
to insist on more reasonable treatment.*

Passing now to consider the third evil of the sweating
system, *unsanitary conditions*, it is at once evident that the
smaller the workshop the less likely it is that sanitation
will be cared for. Inspection hardly reaches such places,
and the standard of requirement of both employer and
employed is very low; but with large workshops the case
is different. In this respect we have in fact a sliding scale
from the factory to the larger workshop, and thence downwards through the small workshop to the home. In

---

* East London does not get up early. It says with Burns, " Up in the
morning's na for me, up in the morning early." Any observer whose restless
spirit takes him into the streets between 6 and 8 A.M. finds every blind down.
The few stragglers then going to their work shut the door on sleeping
women and children, and seek their breakfast at some early coffee-stall.
Between 8 and 9 the tide of life begins to flow. In sympathy with this, the
evening hours are late. Work and cleaning up usually run till 8 or 9, and
pleasure till about 12, and these hours apply especially to the industries
we are discussing. The trades which still begin and end at 6 are unimportant
compared to the mass of work which does not begin till 8 or 9. Home workshops and home-work most readily fall in with these conditions, but the
same hours are also accepted by factories in many instances.

proportion as inspection becomes possible, the evil becomes manageable. Overcrowding, again, which exists in a more dangerous form in the home than in the workshop, assuming its worst shape when home and workshop are combined, is not present in any serious way in large workshops and vanishes altogether with factories.

All this being so—the bigger workshop being comparatively innocent of evil—it is remarkable that the larger type of sweating master should have been seized upon by the public imagination as the central figure of a monstrous system. It is difficult, not to say impossible, to prove a negative—to prove that the monster sweating master of the comic papers has no existence. I can only say that I have sought diligently and have not found. If a specimen exists, he has at any rate nothing to do with the troubles we are investigating. Among the larger employers there are hard men, but the necessary conditions of their business compel them to keep on regularly a staff of competent workpeople : who must have fair wages, and can and do protect themselves from oppression. The sweating master I *have* found, and who is connected with the troubles under investigation, works hard, makes often but little more, and at times somewhat less, than his most skilled and best paid hands. He is seldom on bad terms, and often on very kindly terms, with those who work under him. There is here no class division between employer and employed—both in fact belong to the same class, and talk freely together; social amenities of all kinds going on naturally and easily between master and man. Or if they quarrel it is with that happy equality of tongue which leaves no sentiment to rankle unexpressed ; mutual abuse and oaths clear the air, and friendly relations may be promptly renewed. In this state of things we find nothing that is monstrous, much that is very human. The proprietor of a model factory, who has employed a skilled engineer to arrange a model system of ventilation through-

out his spacious premises, certainly provides better security
for the health of his workpeople than the sweating master
in his crowded and stifling room, but he is less likely than
the poor sweating master to be sympathetic with the
individual who has a cold in his head and feels the draught,
and after all sympathy does more than the best of sanitary
appliances to sweeten human relations and make life worth
living. But all this may look like special pleading in
favour of an evil state of things. Why should not the
large employer be kind, too? Doubtless he may be, and
continually is; but it is not he, but the sweating master,
who has been the object of a strangely excited attack, an
attack prompted by indignation at the hardships suffered
by the poor, and seeking a victim on which to vent its
anger, but at times compounded largely of lower motives.
On this account I have thought it just to recall my own
experience of the much-abused sweating master.

I have said that the trades of East London present a
clear case of economic disease, and I have pointed to the
multiplication of small masters as the tap-root of this
disease. There are, however, other special causes of
mischief affecting East London which should be considered:
all of them are forms of competition. There is the competition of provincial England in manufacture, or in effect
that of the factory with the workshop; and there is the
competition of women's work, which is really a contest
between the workshop and the home. Then we have that
resulting from the influx into London of vigorous countrymen; and, finally, foreign competition of two sorts—(1)
that which by importation of goods makes use of cheap
labour abroad, and (2) that which owing to foreign
immigration can make use of equally cheap labour at
home. The former is in effect the competition of the
Germans; the latter that of the Jews.

The unfortunate East End worker, struggling to support
his family and keep the wolf from the door, has to

contend with all these forms of competition. He is met
and vanquished by the Jew fresh from Poland or Russia,
accustomed to a lower standard of life, and above all of
food, than would be possible to a native of these islands;
less skilled and perhaps less strong, but in his way more
fit—pliant, adaptable, patient, adroit. Or he has to contend
with cheap importations, and curses the blessings of free
trade; or he is pushed on one side by the physical strength
of the man whose life has hitherto been spent among
green fields. Or again, women are his rivals, working to
support fatherless children, or to eke out their husband's
or their children's earnings, or even to earn a little
pocket-money to be spent on pleasure or dress. And
beyond all these, outside London, but now, owing to the
perfection of railway and telegraphic communication, at
our very door, the vast strength of provincial England
enters the field.

In the provinces factories can be managed more successfully than in London, and work suitable for them
is apt to leave the metropolis; and it is to be noted that the
competition of the provincial factory is doubly pernicious
to London, as it can be better withstood by the socially
bad but economically advantageous small workshop
than by a metropolitan factory. It thus not only
depresses London labour, but depresses it in its best form,
and favours its worst features. For, while a trade leaves,
the people stay, and form the unemployed or partially
employed class, who with their striving women provide
the mass of cheap labour and the facilities for irregular
work in which small masters and small middlemen find
their opportunity. The small workshop and home-work
thus obtain a better chance, and a very vicious equilibrium
is reached, which the attractiveness of London, Circe
among cities compared to dull towns and duller country,
helps to maintain.

As a weapon of competition, the influx into London is

double-edged. He who comes brings usually fresh powers
of body or mind, and finding employment—or more often
coming up to employment already found—displaces some
Londoner, or at least takes the position some Londoner
would have held. This is the forward cut of the weapon,
but the backward cut is even worse, for the displaced
Londoner, and probably his wife too, can only join the
sad throng who go hunting for work and find it not, or if
they succeed, it is some other who goes to swell the host
of those who are irregularly employed or not employed at
all. This would be different if trade were not leaving
London : but I fear it is doing so. On the other hand,
the transfer of manufactures from London to the provinces
cannot be regretted; and one must rather hope that
population will gradually adjust itself to the facts, and
that compensation for the passing misery in London will
be found in the growth of healthy manufacturing com-
munities such as we now see planting themselves in the
Midland and Northern counties, and indeed in all parts of
England where conveniences of rail or river are found.

From these considerations it will be seen that the
strength of the small masters' position lies in the economic
merits of the evils they encourage or produce, and that
these evils stand forth as the bulwarks of London trade—a
point which must be borne in mind when remedies are
considered.

Again, as to foreign importations, it is of little use to
tell the East End worker who feels the grievance that all
trade is an exchange, and that some one else in England,
or in greater Britain, or in that greatest Britain which is
subject to British capital, will benefit as much and even
something more than he may lose. The argument does not
interest him, and it is not surprising that those directly
affected by this competition, whatever their political colour,
are against free trade.

Finally, as to the Jews; I can add nothing to what

appears in another chapter as to the peculiar character
of their competition, but I may particularly point out that
the *force* of this competition depends on a continual stream
of new-comers. Let this stop, and it at once changes its
character. For a time it tends to reduce wages and so
lower the standard of life, but, apart from a constant influx,
this is not its permanent effect. In the long run it is a competition of greater industry and greater skill. We may desire
to exclude further arrivals of poor refugees; to do so, if
practicable, would be very reasonable, and as popular with
the Jews themselves—those who *are* here—as with our own
people. But we can only do it on the ground of "England
for the English;" we cannot do it on the cry of no
admittance to paupers. From top to bottom, old-established
or new-comers, the Jews are a hard-working and very
capable set of people, who readily learn to keep themselves,
and usually get on in the world.

To summarize the position I have taken up: we have
seen first that an inquiry into the Sweating System must
be an inquiry into certain evils which, though having no
special connection with any particular system of employment or caused by any particular form of tyranny, are
none the less present and intense. These evils, so far as
they are industrial at all, I attribute mainly to the multiplication of small masters and their tendency still further
to increase, owing to the smallness of the capital needed
for commencing business in the so-called "sweated"
industries.

Secondly, we note that present in all these industries
are to be found overcrowding, irregular hours, low pay;
periods of terrible strain, overtaxing the powers and
exhausting the vital forces; periods of slack employment
or absolute want of work, discouraging and slowly un-
dermining the persistent energies and bread-winning
determination of the worker not possessed of heroic
elevation of character. These terrible evils are not, unless

I am entirely mistaken in my reading of the facts which have been under my notice, necessarily connected with any of the systems with which they have been coupled in the public imagination. They are not due to " employment at second-hand," as in tailoring and boot-making, for we find this system in company with regular work and high pay. They are not due to the intervention of the middle-man, for while the middleman throve they were less conspicuous than now; where he has been driven out they still remain, and where he has never stepped in the evils often appear in a very intense form. The same may be said with regard to sub-contract. Sub-contract may " go hand-in-hand with plenty," providing good pay and regular employment. Nor are the evils necessarily connected with the manufacture of goods on speculation, as in cabinet-making, which we have called " sub-purchase," though this system is doubtless most pernicious to those who have neither knowledge to forecast nor capital to await their market. In further proof of these assertions I need only refer again to the accounts given in preceding chapters of the several trades.

These, however, are the evils which, if they do not necessarily belong to the system of small masters and small middlemen prevalent in East London, at least co-exist with it very extensively, and are aggravated by the atmosphere of competition in which the trades so handled are compelled to fight for an existence.

Coming now to the consideration of remedial proposals, I may say at the outset that my expectations of rapid and certain remedy are not high. For that large proportion of the misfortunes of poor workers which they encounter, not because they are workers, but because they are poor, our hope, if we decline the solution of socialism, must rest on the prospect of a gradual raising of the standard of life, upon which efforts of many kinds and from many directions must be concentrated if success is to be achieved. For the

larger trade troubles which I have mapped out—the
troubles due to various forms of competition—some remedies
are suggested: protection of native manufacture; State-
aided emigration, which shall seize hold of the stalwart
countryman before he enters London; the exclusion of
"pauper" immigrants; the regulation of home industry, or
even its suppression. For my part, I cannot support any of
these. They appear to me either impracticable or not less
dangerous than the disease—on these points I see no safe
policy but "laissez faire." The road is long and steep, but it
is the only one that we can safely follow. As to the minor
though more searching trade troubles it may be different.
Cut-throat competition amongst the small masters themselves
and between large master and small could and should
be checked by combination. The lack of united action
between small masters and those they employ, plays into
the hands of the sole approach to a "monster" I have met
in my researches—namely, the wholesale house, which
strictly puts into practice the precepts of the economists,
cheapening that which it buys, irrespective of personal
feeling. It must, however, be said that business is not on
the whole worked in this manner. Wholesale firms may
not be more successful, but are certainly not less so, when
they take a more human, and, I think, more reasonable
view of industrial relations and recognize that the best
bargain is that in which the advantages are fairly shared.
Better organization and concerted action among the masters
would go far to raise prices, shorten the hours, and mitigate
the irregularity of work—and would go hand in hand with
organization of the journeymen if these too could be
banded in an efficient union. The interests of masters and
men are closely allied; but the unselfishness and good faith
needed to cement common action are sadly wanting. For
these minor or inner troubles of trade—irregularity of work,
long hours, and low pay—it is only as to long hours that any
legislation is suggested. An enforcement of an eight-hour

day is the proposed cure. This too I fear is impracticable or at least premature. Combination must pioneer the road. Finally we have those evils as to which the outside public has by past legislation already definitely asserted its right to interfere. These are hours of employment as regards women and children, overcrowding, and questions of health generally.* All these are questions of inspection, and their cure lies in more efficient supervision by the authorities.

It has been noticed that the larger the premises the less prominent the desire to evade the law, and the more effective the action of the Factory Inspector. This inequality I should desire to obviate if possible, and with this aim should advocate a double system of license—a license to be taken out by the owner of any premises used for manufacturing purposes as well as one to be obtained by all manufacturing employers. I should suggest also, that the two systems be linked together : a reference to the one license being in each instance endorsed on the other. The definitions of "manufacturing" and "employing" would be similarly linked, so that the letting for manufacturing would necessarily involve the letting to "an employer."

It is nothing of the nature of a tax that I propose; it is merely the acknowledgment that manufacturing industry involves the responsibility of two parties to each other and to the State. These two parties are the owner of the premises and the employer of labour. The object is simply to secure the execution of the law by making the responsibilities under it definite and intelligible, and by facilitating inspection. I imagine that on the licenses would

---

* The questions of sanitation and overcrowding become industrial in proportion as it is easier to inspect the places where the people work than where they live. The standard of requirement as to pure air is very low amongst the East London poor ; but it must be admitted that, in pursuit of pleasure, no class shrinks from a stifling atmosphere. Over-crowding of workshops is a very real and serious evil, but as a grievance it is not so genuine.

be clearly set forth (in simple language and not solely by
means of excerpts from Acts of Parliament) the responsibilities involved. These licenses would be obtainable on
application at any post-office and be renewed annually.
The owner's license must be obtained first, and produced
for endorsement when that for the employer (or occupant)
is taken up. Each would be then officially endorsed.
Counterfoils would be forwarded from the post-office
to the factory department of the Home Office, and
from these a complete directory of every employer
and his place of work could be framed and revised
annually. Except in cases where the wife alone helps, no
exceptions must be admitted. If the children assist they
are in so far employed, and the parent comes under
obligation to the law. The definition of manufacture
would not then, I think, offer serious difficulty. Manufacture would be said to be carried on where anyone employed
another in making anything on contract or for sale, and it
would be for the owner to see that his premises were not
so used without a license.

The responsibility under the law as to sanitation would
ultimately rest with the landlord, and as to overcrowding
or illegal hours, with the employer; but it might be well
that in each case the responsibility should primarily rest
with the other party—that is, that the landlord should be
required to prove that he had done his utmost to check
overcrowding or illegal hours of work, and occupant that
the bad sanitation was due to no fault of his. I should not
hesitate further to make the landlord ultimately responsible
for any fine imposed upon his tenant, the employer, which
could not otherwise be collected.

It is not, however, to the direct action of the law backed
by the imposition of fines to which I should trust so much
as to the moral effect of inspection, publicity, and the open
acknowledgment of responsibilities. The results already
attained by Government inspection have been unduly

slighted. We have heard that in this or that workshop the inspector was never seen, or of the hiding from him of the girls working at illegal hours. There will be such instances under any possible system, but it is only fair to say that the devoted services of the Factory Inspectors have not been wasted. They, however, need the support of some system of registration, so handled that their out-door work would be confined to visiting. They should not first be obliged to discover the places they have to inspect and their indoor work should be systematized and shared by clerks. Their action would also be made more efficient if all manufacturing employment were included under their inspection, and not merely that concerning women and children. Even if the hours of employment of men are left free, the rules as to overcrowding and sanitation and the provisions of the Truck Act apply to all factories and workshops alike, and should be regulated and enforced by the same system of inspection.

This is the only distinct suggestion which I can make towards the cure of the evils passing under the name of sweating. I regard these evils as being for the most part directly connected with the poverty of the sufferers and the irregularity of their employment, to be cured only by such thorough-going remedies as will strike at the causes of poverty itself. Sweating is but a symptom of this fell and capital disease, and it is only a quack doctor who prescribes for symptoms without attempting to trace them to their fountain head.

It is not in the power of foot-notes to acknowledge the contributions of my friends and co-workers to the materials I have had before me in treating this subject. To them, and especially to Miss Potter, Mr. Schloss, and Mr. Aves should belong any credit which may attach to the investigation into the sweating system of which this chapter is the final outcome.

INDEX.

INDEX.